Avoid Market Loss
with
Trust Deed Investing

Avoid Market Loss
with
Trust Deed Investing

The How-to Book on Investing
in Trust Deeds

Casimir J. Domaszewicz

Writers Club Press
New York   Lincoln   Shanghai

Avoid Market Loss with Trust Deed Investing
The How-to Book on Investing in Trust Deeds

Copyright © 2002 by Casimir J. Domaszewicz

Writers Club Press
an imprint of iUniverse, Inc.

iUniverse books may be ordered through booksellers or by contacting:

iUniverse
2021 Pine Lake Road, Suite 100
Lincoln, NE 68512
www.iuniverse.com
1-800-Authors (1-800-288-4677)

INVESTORS/LENDERS CAVEAT

The information presented should only be used as a guide. The variations in each Trust Deed investment can be significant. Each Trust Deed has a different value for each investor. The property, borrower, and method of handling each situation may change. This is not only due to the changing property value, but also to changing economical conditions and legal regulations. Investors are advised to consult an attorney versed in this field when making these type of investments. Some guidance on California law and regulations can be gleamed from the Internet Web site: http://www.leginfo.ca.gov/calaw.html.

ISBN-13: 978-0-595-23802-6 (pbk)
ISBN-13: 978-0-595-73624-9 (ebk)
ISBN-10: 0-595-23802-5 (pbk)
ISBN-10: 0-595-73624-6 (ebk)

Printed in the United States of America

Contents

FOREWORD

Casimir Domaszewicz (Cas) has written a very detailed guide for those investors wise enough to learn about trust deed investing using *Avoid Market Loss with Trust Deed Investing.* Cas has invested with my company over the past nine years, and I have come to respect his detailed questions and thorough analysis. With the unpredictability of corporate earnings, past accounting scandals with potentially more to come, and the Federal Reserve's conjured low interest rates, where is an investor to turn for a decent return with safety?

As a certified financial planner for the past nineteen years and a very experienced investor, I would answer, "First Trust Deeds." I am fully aware of the risks, rewards, and commission costs of most investments that are available today. I chose to invest a large percentage of my personal assets in first Trust Deeds. My clients and I act like a small bank. We lend our investment dollars in first trust deed position secured by real property with title insurance. Real estate values have risen dramatically in recent years, but I do not recommend buying non-owner occupied residential property at this time because of the unpredictability of values and management headaches. Why own when you can get a high yield with low risk and minimum headaches by holding a secured mortgage position on property.

With trust deed investing, the borrower pays all of the cost of the loan and commissions and the investor gets true, no load yields of 11 to 14 percent without fluctuations in principal value. These yields at a time of 2 to 3 percent inflation are a tremendous real rate of return on your money, and at the same time you have a hedge against deflation because you are only lending 65 to 70 percent of the property value. When properly done,

I consider first Trust Deeds to be the highest return at the lowest risk of any available investment.

The risks that do exist in this form of investment can be greatly mitigated by following the excellent guidance provided by Cas, using his experience and attention to detail. Great profits lie ahead for you if you master this material or find an honest and experienced loan broker to help you with *first trust deed investing!* Here's to the fortune I know you can make! It is not about good luck. It is all about knowledge, applying principles, and hard work! Follow the example of a wise teacher who has done extremely well, investing in Trust Deeds! Enjoy the wisdom of Cas Domaszewicz!

To your wealth,
Daniel Muhe, PhD, CFP President
Financial Freedom Services
Carlsbad, CA 92018
(760) 434-7850

INTRODUCTION

Avoiding Market Loss with Trust Deed Investing provides an alternate investment media to investors that are sacked by the present unstable stock market. It provides detailed information on how to put money to work in a relatively safe investment with a high return. The book has been written to inform new investors on how to invest their hard-earned money in Trust Deeds and provide seasoned investors a reference source on trust deed investing. After investing in Trust Deeds for a large number of years, I have found a large amount written on Trust Deeds but not in one consolidated format. I believe this book has addressed this annoyance and added additional information on trust deed investing.

By using the guides presented, double-digit returns with security can be achieved. Investors can do this by using Trust Deeds secured by a borrower's house, apartment building, or other real estate property. Additionally, the investor does not have to be a resident of the state where the real estate security is located.

In this book are the methods of evaluating Trust Deeds, avoiding dangerous loans, expected interest rates, problems to expect and how to minimize their impact, as well as other procedures that should be followed to ensure a safe return.

The major theme of this book covers making money with trust deed note investing in spite of foreclosures. The book is not about making money with foreclosure acquisitions. Although money can be made purchasing foreclosure property, there are precautions that should be taken to avoid loss. Some of the guidelines and methods used in trust deed investing can be applied to foreclosed property investing. The main principle that would be used is to achieve cost containment and fast action. This would apply when dealing with any real estate and real estate Trust Deeds.

This book has been written specifically for investing in Trust Deeds in California. It can be applied to other states that use Trust Deeds. Caution should be used due to the other states having variations from the California statues and *case laws*[1]. These differences can include legal regulations, foreclosure periods and foreclosure case law. The basic principles discussed can be applied to those states that use mortgages providing a power of sale is included in the documentation. Of major concern would be the redemption period after a foreclosure when lending in unfamiliar trust deed states and mortgage states. Although many states use Trust Deeds, Mortgages can also be used. When dealing with Trust Deeds from other states, a mortgage broker licensed in the state having jurisdiction over the trust deed activity must be involved.

Additional information about foreclosure law can be found on the Web site: http://www.foreclosurelaw.org/.

In popular usage and in this book, the terms below are sometimes used interchangeably:

- Mortgage…Trust Deed with Trust Deed Note,

- Mortgagee…Lender…Beneficiary,

- Mortgagor…Borrower…Trustor,

- Mortgage broker (commonly used)…Trust deed broker,

- Point…1% of a loan. Two points would equal 2% of the loan,

- Trust Deed Note…Promissory note,

- Debt service…Interest, interest with principal payments,

---

[1] *Case law* can take precedence over legislative law. This occurs when a trial judge interprets differences between the various laws, laws that are not clearly defined or previous case law. Using the civil codes, professional codes and legislated laws can sometimes lead to incorrect interpretations unless the case law is also researched.

- Trust Deed...Deed of trust (often used to identify the combination of a Trust Deed and Trust Deed Note),
- Encumbrance...lien,
- Escrow...Receiver...Neutral person...Fiduciary...Trust Fund...Trustee[2],
- First Trust Deed...Senior Trust Deed...First-tier lien,
- Second Trust Deed...Junior Trust Deed...Second-tier lien.

---

[2] There are different trustees that use the same name. Some of the trustees are:

- Trustee of a Trust Deed Note,
- Trustee for a bankruptcy,
- Trustee for a trust fund,
- Trustee for a living trust.

Section 1

WHAT IT IS ALL ABOUT

Figure 1. *Don't worry; I have this special book on how to turn Trust Deeds into real money.*

Let me tell you about two investors. The first was Jane. She had a substantial amount of money and used a financial advisor to invest in the stock market. Everything was going fine when the stock market spiraled upward. When the market turned down, her portfolio shrank as she did everything her advisor recommended. The portfolio continued to lose value until it was much less than its original principal value. She not only lost part of her principal and all of her gain, but also the time value of her money.

The second investor, Alice, decided to invest in Trust Deeds, prudently. She was perplexed when the stock market spiraled up and she was not on the boat. However, her dismay turned to glee when the stock market spiraled down and she had turned her $200,000 initial trust deed investments, into a $400,000 portfolio over a five-and-a-half-year period. This was achieved by using the trust deed's high interest payments and reinvesting these payments with the original investment in other Trust Deeds. This won't happen to everyone, but there is a good chance Alice could be you with prudent investing in Trust Deeds.

Obtaining a return on investment money can be accomplished using bank deposits, corporation bonds, REIT (real estate investment trust, sometimes referred to as a real estate trust), tenancy in common ownership (when up to thirty-five investors own real estate together for the income and property appreciation), limited partnerships (where there is a general partner that controls all activities including the amount of profit you can receive), limited liability corporation (LLC) (discussed later), tax-free bonds, insurance annuities, mutual funds, or mutual money market funds to name a few.

In any investment, the real return is always questionable after paying taxes and adjusting for inflation. Any investment, therefore, should have a rate of return that compensates for this erosion.

There are the speculative investments such as the stock market, junk bond funds, commodities funds, oil and gas drilling investments, viaticals (buying a future payoff on life insurance policies), ATM/CTM machines, pay phones, gemstones, gold, derivatives, or even Las Vegas. Each of these can provide a higher return but with great risk. These investments do not always have an underlying security. Oil and gas drilling investing has its own attributes and cautions. The projected returns and tax write-offs can look spectacular. Dry wells and syndications putting the investment together can drain most of the profits before any money is paid out to you as an investor. There is also the real danger of a Ponzi scheme that may be in place, so detection of fraud is months or years away.

Real estate trust deed investing, when loans are secured with real estate property, can be classified as a secured investment. These secured loans also have protection against bankruptcy filings by borrowers. The security is in the value of the real estate. In the stock market, the stock value is usually only a fraction of the book value of the business and is typically based on yield or potential yields.

A real estate Trust Deed Note and Trust Deed are a set of documents that allow the financing of real estate property or withdrawing of *equity* from real estate property. *Equity* is the remaining value in property after all liens and sale cost are subtracted from the market value (discussed later). Associated with the Trust Deed Note and Trust Deed is a trustee that holds title to the property. Trust Deed Notes and Trust Deeds are created to allow for the purchase of real estate when there is insufficient money available to pay for the total cost of the property. It is similar to an installment purchase, where the buyer makes payments over a period of time. After all payments have been made, the property is fully owned by the purchaser. The documentation used in real estate is called either a Mortgage or a Trust Deed with an associated promissory note. Trust Deeds are predominately used in California. When property has appreciated or the amount of down payment is large, equity is created in the property. This equity belongs to the property holder and can be used as collateral or security for a loan. The collateral can be converted into cash when the property holder assigns it to a trustee using a Trust Deed. The Trust Deed defines the property's legal description and the type of ownership. Although the holder or *owner* of property when there is a Trust Deed involved think they own the property, this is not true. During the loan period, the ownership is with a trustee of the Trust Deed. The Trust Deed Note is the agreement or contract that the borrower agrees to fulfill in exchange for the cash. The Trust Deed Note describes the terms that must be met during the loan period.

The use of a Trust Deed makes it easier and faster than a Mortgage for a lender to foreclose on a property if the borrower doesn't meet the agreed terms of the Trust Deed Note. The amount of recovery in this type of foreclosure, called a *statutory foreclosure*, is limited to the securing property.

The *statutory foreclosure* is a foreclosure that is provided for under the civil code. It can be processed outside the judicial court system.

The alternate foreclosure procedure would be a *judicial foreclosure* when the terms of the loan are not met, the property does not have adequate equity, and the borrower has other properties or funds that might be pursued. A judicial foreclosure is not allowed when the property purchased is classified as *purchased money*[1]. This purchase-money status means that a lender can only recover the amount owed (including advances) by foreclosing on the property assuming there is enough equity in the property. Advances would include such things as property insurance and payment to senior lenders that the junior lender had to pay to protect the loan. Obviously, if the property's equity is less than the amount owed, you the lender might lose some of your money. There are methods of handling this situation that will be discussed later.

A *judicial foreclosure* is accomplished by filing a suit in court to recover your investment if the borrower has not fulfilled the terms of the Trust Deed Note. If the suit is successful, a deficiency judgment would be received to allow a claim on both the borrower's other nonexempt valuables and the subject property. An exempt valuable would be tools of his trade and other essential items required to live and make a living. As can be imagined, a judicial foreclosure will take time and legal fees. The actual sale of property would be supervised by the court. There is a downside with a judicial foreclosure in California in that the borrower has the right to redeem the property. The laws vary for each state, so contacting an attorney when dealing with property in other states is advised.

---

[1] *Purchased money* occurs when money is loaned on real estate that is being purchased. There is a disadvantage to lenders that make purchase-money loans. These loans on owner-occupied one to four units cannot be foreclosed using a judicial foreclosure.

A Trust Deed and accompanying Trust Deed Note are also used when the property owner, (called the borrower or a trustor), borrows money on the equity of a property. Equity is equal to the value of the property minus the liens against the property. These liens can include Trust Deeds, judgment liens, taxes, labor and material liens (construction liens), and assessments (condominium). The priority of a lien is determined by the date and time that a lien is recorded with the associated property's County Recorder's Office. This priority is very important. It will establish who has the prior (senior) claim to the property. When there are several Trust Deeds against the property, they will be designated as a first, second, or their ranking as established by the recorded date and time. A first Trust Deed would be the senior Trust Deed. Other liens may have seniority if they were recorded prior to a new Trust Deed. Property taxes will always have a priority over other liens.

With present banking regulations, there is an opportunity for relatively safe investments to be made. This opportunity is created by the present restrictive banking regulations covering real estate loans. Banks and many mortgage companies will not make loans to borrowers with poor or significant dings on their credit history. Their restrictions also include certain income requirements. This will force a borrower into the secondary market for *hard-money*[2] and purchase-money loans. The borrower can only participate in this secondary market when there is adequate real estate equity. There are other restrictions placed on borrowers and lenders when a hard-money loan is being issued.

Alternately a deed-in-lieu of foreclosure sometime called equity purchase (discussed later) might be considered. This would save some of the

---

[2] A *Hard-money* loan is money that is loaned on real estate *after* a property has been purchased and escrow has closed. A refinanced loan is also considered a hard-money loan. Hard-money loans also would include purchase of property where the loan is not a standard conforming loan due to poor credit of the borrower or questionable security.

normal foreclosure cost. This has the problem that all senior and junior liens become your problem. In order to determine if there are other liens and to protect against other unknowns, title insurance coverage should be obtained.

It is important to be aware of the status of a Trust Deed that is being considered. If the Trust Deed was in existence because of its being purchase money (discussed later), purchasing the loan from the original lender does not change the legal status of the Trust Deed.

In trust deed investing, major consideration must be given not only to the rate of return but also the return of the investment. This will require having Trust Deeds on property that have adequate equity. This is especially important in a declining real estate market. If the borrower isn't making payments, this may be acceptable if the cash flow isn't immediately needed. However, if the nonpayment eats too much into the property's remaining equity, the safety of the Trust Deed can be in jeopardy. This loss of safety can be caused not only by a declining real estate market but also by foreclosure cost, cost to fight a borrower's bankruptcy, and a variety of other unplanned events.

Direct investing in Trust Deeds is not for everyone. The emotional trauma of collecting from a delinquent borrower or foreclosing on a family may be unacceptable and require ventures in other investment vehicles. Investing in a real estate investment trust fund (REIT) rather than an individual Trust Deed where there is a manager to handle the distasteful tasks, might be more palatable. REITs come in a variety of flavors. Some invest in building projects, rehabbing property (rehab), a pool of Trust Deeds, and commercial property that produces income. There are many variations with different rates of return that complicate your decision process. The REIT funds, however, normally provide a lower rate of return. There is potential danger in using a REIT. The managers of the REIT might not be as careful with the investment as you might be. This would be due to the investment not being their money and their need to put the investor's money into something as quickly as possible to have an apparent high return. When a loan is placed, the REIT managers can immediately generate a commission for themselves. There are REITs that offer very high rates of return. These however can be very unsafe. There are REITs that exceed the *pig line*. The *pig line* expression is used to describe when the REIT takes more than a fair share of the profits. It should be noted that some REITs invest in new building projects for strip malls or other building projects. This in itself can be dangerous due to an unproven location. One of the problems is the cost to have your investment returned. Many charge a fee of several percent to do this.

Properties located in an older area that has been developed for some time has special dangers. If the property is to be refurbished, knowledge must be obtained on city or federal plans for redevelopment of the area. In this case your project could be demolished after renovation. The renovation of a site that has had business after business fail is an indication of future failure. The site, for some known or unknown reason, has something wrong with it. There may be inadequate parking, difficult access, or competing locations that have everything right. Knowing about the subject site is very important not only for REIT but other investments loans as well.

An indicator of the viability of a REIT is the status of the project. This would be if the property is owned, an option to purchase is being used, if planning department and controlling council have approved the project, if permits for the work to be conducted have been obtained, and what other phases of the project have been completed. The actual progress of the preliminary stages of a project is an indicator that there is a real project. If the general partner is doing everything on-the-cuff, this might be a bad indicator. This would indicate the general partner doesn't have his own real money in the project. Project expenses that can be put on-the-cuff are building plans, engineering, advertising, environmental reports, and other costs. The people that are doing the on-the-cuff work are usually offered a larger than normal percentage of the project. Paper is cheap. A brochure and cost numbers can be generated inexpensively to give the illusion of a viable project. A total project analysis must be preformed. This would include determining the amount of work that has been done with building inspector's sign off, and the amount of work remaining to complete the project along with money cost and profits.

You will not always get what you pay for if due diligence (discussed later) is not conducted. Due diligence is something that many investors ignore because of the extensive research (time) that is required.

If a higher rate of return above a REIT return is desired, owning an individual Trust Deed can be rewarding when selected carefully.

Investing in Trust Deeds does require some knowledge of real estate principles and economic trends such as housing needs and recession.

The direct investment in Trust Deeds can have similar emotional trauma as investing in rental property. Some investors are not able to handle being a landlord with tenant problems, eviction, property damage because of vandalism, and cleaning up of tenants' dirt and mess.

There is an advantage of making money from trust deed nonearned income. (Funds received from investment interest are nonearned income. Earned income would be funds received from wages, salary, professional fees, and amount received for work actually performed.) There is no social security tax (FICA) or state disability insurance tax on the nonearned income. The downside is that investment expense must be deducted using the Federal Income Tax Schedule A with an associated deduction threshold before the expenses have an effect on the taxable income. The exception would be if an acquired property was owned and then sold after one year of ownership. Those expenses associated with the property might be claimed as part of the long-term capital gain transaction. Tax laws continue to change, so contacting your tax accountant is important.

The amount of return from any real estate investment should compensate not only for the risk, but also the effort and associated expense.

The funds used for hard-money lending can be looked upon as an income generator. The more that is available—the more income that can be generated. The money used for loans can be funds that are available before or after paying of taxes. Before tax is better, in that there is a larger income generating capability. In effect, money can be used that has not been paid to the government in the form of taxes. These funds are typically individual retirement accounts (IRAs).

Hard-money lending also can be looked upon as equivalent to a business. Business has a cash value based upon its money-generating capability. Hard-money lending is a money generator. It, however, has certain disadvantages. The main disadvantage is being susceptible to inflation. Businesses tend to increase in value with inflation over the long term, thereby providing some protection. Hard-money lending is similar to a standard business in that there are people working to pay the trust deed owner. A business will have employees and customers, in effect, working for the business.

Business has the advantage that the plant and equipment can be depreciated. Hard-money lending doesn't have this advantage. However, the business's advantage can be questionable because of the recapture of the depreciated property and capital gain tax on the sale of the business. The lack of inflation indexing in the tax code on capital gain is another disadvantage of a standard business. There may be an apparent gain, but the government is really triple taxing, and in certain cases quadruple taxing. There is the obvious state income tax, federal income tax with social security taxes, sales tax on the money that hasn't been taken by previous taxes, and the hidden tax because of the reduced value of the dollar caused by inflation.

In hard-money lending, additional funds can be borrowed on your other property that has high equity. A line of credit (discussed later), when offered at a low rate, can provide additional income as a result of an interest spread. This would be achieved due to the spread between the rate of interest you would be paying and the rate received on a new hard-money Trust Deed. There is however, a dangerous downside. If the cash flow wasn't always available to make your payments on the borrowed money, you would be forced to sell a Trust Deed, possibly at a discount, to be able to meet your commitments. The other downside is the interest from the hard-money loan would be taxed as nonearned ordinary income. (The amount that can be deducted on your income tax is limited to the interest paid up to a $100,000 line of credit on a new loan. There is some relief if the amount used to payoff an existing loan is *grandfathered*[3], if the loans were made prior to October 13, 1987, or if it is from a refinance of an existing loan. This is complicated by an additional limit if the loan exceeds $1,000,000 or exceeds the market value. These caps are reduced by 50 percent if you are married and filing separately, see IRS Publication 936. The advantage of a new loan is reduced if there aren't other deductions that equal or exceed your standard deduction. Due to the complexity of the tax law, contacting your tax accountant about deductibility is advised.)

Hard money loaned to borrowers, because of the apparent risk, will have a higher rate of return than most conventional loans. Conventional lenders won't make hard-money loans unless there is adequate security with compensation for the risk. For the borrowers, they don't have any choice but to pay the high rates when they need money. This is the only game in town for them. Even if this sounds callous, a hard-money lender provides a service to the borrower. Borrowers need someone willing to help them out of a bind when conventional lenders won't step up to the plate by providing funds that are necessary because of the loss of a job, operating a business, buying a car, sickness, or for "play time money" they think they need.

With new legislation against predatory lending, some borrowers will not be able to obtain hard-money loans, or will only be able to obtain a loan if their equity is very large in comparison to the loans and they have income to support the payments. This will cause the loss of their property in the

---

[3] *Grandfathered* is a term that allows a condition to continue even if there are new legal requirements or changes. It also applies to property use in accordance with the original zoning or special permits.

future in a foreclosure or to sharp buyers that won't pay market price for their distressed sale. Borrowers that have been refused loans will be put on a watch list so the property can be acquired at a below market price. The predatory lending, although necessary due to some lending practices, will cause the loss of equity to some borrowers because of foreclosure.

The real rate of return isn't always as large as it would appear. After the potential costs of foreclosure, normal wear and tear on the property, wasting of property by the owner in foreclosure, bankruptcy costs, and the time to deal with these problems, the final rate of return is substantially reduced. There are other costs that are not too extensive, but real. This would involve your time to inspect property, evaluate records, purchase of Trust Deeds, servicing Trust Deeds, and research to keep aware of changes in the market and laws. Even with these costs, there will be more than an adequate rate of return when attention is given to details.

Although there are many hard-money lenders, not all are totally successful. Their failure can partly be attributed to believing what borrowers and trust deed mortgage brokers tell them, believing appraisals, not paying attention to details, or just poor timing of their investments. The other cause of failure is being too greedy. There is also the lack of due diligence or checking *all* aspects of the investment. Some hard-money lenders will look for and make loans that have too high of a rate of return. They are blind to, or ignore the reason for the high rate of return. The usual reason for the high return is because of the poor security for the loan. The old cliché, *high return means high risk*, also applies to real estate trust deed investments.

Your success as a trust deed investor will depend on your prudent analytical ability. Placing too much trust in mortgage brokers and trust deed sellers can cause your failure as a trust deed investor. When investing in Trust Deeds, finding mortgage brokers and trust deed sellers can be difficult. It can be done, but all must be looked at with a jaundiced eye.

Section 2

SOURCES OF CASH

Figure 2. *Brother, can you spare $20,000 so I can invest in a Trust Deed?*

The money that is required for trust deed investments can come from saving accounts, money market funds, stocks, mutual funds, or IRA funds. A 401k fund that has been converted to an IRA fund can also be used.

The appealing benefit of an IRA fund is that it is pretax money. In effect, part of the money is the government's money. This money will produce a return of ordinary, nonsalary income. This income can then be reinvested or spent. However, if any of the money is taken out of your IRA, only the remaining portion after taxes will be available for reinvestment. The government's portion, when funds are removed from the IRA account, must be sent to the Internal Revenue Service (IRS) along with any early withdraw penalties. Obviously nonwithdrawn IRA money will increase faster than an after-tax fund. At some time the IRA funds will have to be withdrawn.

Other sources of money for investing in Trust Deeds are:

- equity in property, a car, a boat, a truck, a business, or anything that one would consider valuable that can be used to obtain a low interest loan,
- an increase in wages,
- disposing of other investments that have a low return,
- borrowing on personal retirement funds,
- borrowing on marginal accounts,
- interest-free loans from relatives,
- sale of surplus property or trade for a Trust Deed,
- inheritance,
- cashing in your life insurance or borrowing money against it,
- borrow on[1] or sell your real estate,
- selling your antiques and heirlooms,
- line of credit.

Obtaining a *line of credit* is of special interest. A *line of credit* establishes an amount of money that can be withdrawn on the equity of your real estate holding up to a set amount. When using your residence or other property, a line of credit can usually be obtained at a low interest rate. These loans are usually first position and have a low loan-to-value (LTV)

---

[1] Borrowing on your real estate at a low interest rate and lending the loan at a high rate can yield a net gain. There is however the issue of deductibility of the interest on the loan of your real estate due to the IRS 1040 standard deduction. The interest that you pay will not start to reduce your taxes until it exceeds the standard deduction. There are limitations on the amount that can be borrowed and still be deductible. Contacting your tax consultant is advised if you are not aware of these limitations.

(discussed later), usually below 65 percent. To obtain a line of credit, your credit must be excellent. When a line of credit is obtained only that portion that is borrowed and received will be charged interest.

The *rule of 72* will provide a guide on how a fund can grow. The *rule of 72* states that if you divide 72 by the rate of return, the result is the number of years it will take to double an investment. For example, if the interest return is 14.4%, the period to double the fund is five years. Continuing the example, if $50,000 is properly invested at 14.4%, in 20 years the fund will have grown to $800,000 (in a tax-deferred IRA account).

When a Trust Deed at a lower interest rate with more security is considered, the reduction can be looked upon as loan insurance. The difference between the lower and a potentially higher interest rate is the premium you would pay in providing a safer investment. This might be a sound strategy for you until the intricacies of trust deed investing are learned and to provide a low discomfort level. Remember, if a well-secured loan is for a long period, it may become a not-too-secure loan. This would be due to the potential reduction in real estate value that can occur over a long loan period. There is also the undesirability of a long-term loan if the loan needs to be sold.

Remember that when you are investing, you are dealing with real money. This is not a game of Monopoly. Money with high taxes cannot be easily replaced. It is money that may have taken years to save. This money may represent going without, not going to that prestigious restaurant, not going to the theater, not going to that wonderful high-priced vacation resort, not buying the latest electronic gadget, not buying the latest record, not buying the latest furniture, not replacing the slightly soiled carpet (but cleaning it), and not buying the latest clothes. In accumulating wealth, it's not so much what is spent but what is wasted. When the question, "Where did the money go?" has to be asked, there usually is not enough care taken in your many small purchases. These are the ones that most often make the money disappear. People usually will do a significant degree of price shopping with large purchases to save money. In the accumulation of wealth, credit and borrowing should be avoided. Lenders don't lend because they like you. They lend because they are making money from your efforts.

If a poor investment is made, you can only blame yourself. If someone cheats you out of the money, you have only yourself to blame. Most of the time if the required homework is done, the loss would not have happened.

When hard-money investors start out, very often they may not have enough cash to buy a complete Trust Deed. There are mortgage brokers that will fragment or fractionalize a Trust Deed. The Trust Deed is divided so a number of investors with small nest eggs can buy a large Trust Deed. There are disadvantages with fractionalized Trust Deeds that will be discussed later. A trusted friend might be asked to join in an investment. This can however, lead to the loss of a friend. When dealing with money, humans can act in strange ways.

If you borrow money to purchase a Trust Deed, and it requires your making payments of interest on a Trust Deed, you can potentially be in a precarious position. This can happen if the borrower for the Trust Deed that you purchased isn't making payments. This can cause you to lose more than you can gain. You should anticipate the downside in your investments and retain funds to make your interest payments or have a strategy to generate funds for negative events.

In generating wealth with investments using Trust Deeds, it is important to evaluate the Trust Deed using all the details. These details include information about the borrowers, the property, the mortgage brokers' history, information provided by the mortgage broker, and your research. This is especially true if you are leveraging using equity in other property that you own. If a trust deed investment goes bad, your total estate can be lost.

Remember, the safety of the invested amount will be based upon the diligence that you use in Trust Deed selection.

There is another safety issue after you have accumulated funds to invest or have a payoff of a loan that are deposited in a CD, savings or checking account. If deposited in a Federal Deposit Insurance Corporation (FDIC) insured bank, the funds will be insured up to $100,000. Amounts in excess of the $100,000 are not covered if the bank fails and could be lost permanently. Putting the funds into several banks or in one bank with different ownerships will work but can be annoying. There is an alternate approach. There are more than 900 banks nationwide that belong to a Certificate of Deposit Account Registry Service. This service is known as CEDARS. Amounts over the limit of $100,000 up to $20,000,000 are broken into insured amounts and distributed between member banks in the form of CDs that have varying maturity periods. Financial statements would be received from the bank where the initial deposit is made. There is a charge for this service in either a reduced rate of return or a service fee. Some banks will absorb the service cost to increase their deposits. The one disadvantage is the length of the CD term. If a new loan needs to be funded, the money may not be available immediately without an early withdrawal penalty. Comparison shopping can be done on Web site: www.cdars.com.

DIVERSIFICATION OF INVESTMENT

Diversification is the method of spreading your money into several investments or projects to prevent a loss of all of your assets. If one of the investments goes bad, the loss will be limited to only a portion of your investment portfolio. There is a downside to diversification of Trust Deeds. It will take more time and effort to find acceptable Trust Deeds. Unfamiliar communities may have to be used. This will take a significant amount of investigation to decide the soundness of the investment.

Diversifying the trust deed property locations is important to guard against business closings, military base closures, blight, or negative changes in an area. The locations can be out of area, out of county, or out of state. Other diversifications should also be practiced, namely, diversification among several borrowers. Even if a borrower has diversified properties and locations, there is the danger that the borrower could go belly up and pull all the properties down. This is especially true if the borrower is operating under a corporation or partnership where all the projects are under one umbrella.

Although Trust Deeds have a good return, it is important not to put all your eggs in one basket. A percentage of your funds should be placed in a money market checking account and a portion placed in a higher percentage return such as a certificate of deposit that has a reasonable short maturity for ready access. A percentage also should be in stocks and bonds. In this way, if the economy changes because of inflation or deflation, not all the funds will be in one income generator. The ready deposits will also provide immediate funds if required in the filing of a foreclosure, fighting a bankruptcy, obtaining property insurance, making payment on senior trust deed loans, and maintaining general living expenses.

There is an inherent problem in multi-investing. Not all the investments will necessarily have a high rate of return. However, it will protect your wealth so you will not have to start over again if there is a significant loss.

Section 3

SOURCE OF TRUST DEEDS

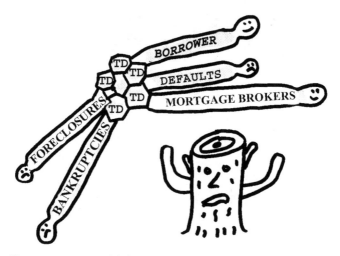

Figure 3. *I was told there may be snakes under these rocks.*

The first step in Trust Deed lending on real estate is to locate a borrower with property that has what I call lendability. This is property that has adequate equity to protect your investment.

This usually is accomplished by contacting a mortgage broker on an existing Trust Deed or a proposed Trust Deed that may meet your trust deed criteria. If the trust deed loan is acceptable to you, an escrow should be opened and escrow instructions generated if this has not been previously accomplished.

An escrow should be used to provide protection from most of the crooks. Many trust deed brokers handle their own escrow. This shouldn't be a concern as long as the broker has been around for a while and has a proven record of honesty. Of primary concern in your final decision in investing is the review of all transaction documents. Documents should agree with what has been offered by the mortgage broker. The documents would include:

- escrow instructions,
- appraisal,
- credit reports,
- loan application of the borrowers,
- Title Report,
- property insurance binder or policy,
- lender disclosures,
- Trust Deed Note,
- Trust Deed.

Take the time to read all the documents. If there are any questions, have them answered in detail to your satisfaction. The actual funding of the loan should only be done through an escrow.

Lending on personal property has its problems and is not recommended for the beginner. One of the problems in loaning on personal property is the ease of its being transported and hidden.

In the trust deed investment evaluation process, it is highly recommended to have a trusted friend who is familiar with real estate and financing to help evaluate your decisions. This sounding board will help put objectivity in your thought process and hopefully avoid brash judgment.

To be successful in trust deed investing means knowing property value and having knowledge of trust deed transactions.

Unfortunately trust deed investing is akin to finding a house or a mate, not all the desirable characteristics in your shopping list will be found. Compromises will have to be made in your decision. Your selection hopefully will provide a worthwhile investment.

NEWSPAPERS

Local newspapers have several classifications for investments and loans. These will usually be found under *Trust Deed for Sale* or a *Money Wanted* category. The terminology may be slightly different for each newspaper. With a little diligence, the appropriate advertisement can be found. The ads should provide some of the information that is needed, such as the loan amount, interest rate, duration of the loan, and possibly the LTV. If the ad is by a mortgage broker and not of interest, the phone number should still be retained for a later follow-up call. The advertiser may have other loans that are being worked on or being processed that might be of interest.

If the ad is by a borrower, there are multiples of regulations that must be followed—something that most investors are not geared to handle. Referring the ad to your favorite mortgage broker should place you in first place if the loan is doable.

INTERNET

The Internet has added a new dimension to lending. This covers Web sites and Spam. Unfortunately these two advertising methods have allowed solicitation behind a mask where borrowers and lenders need to be on guard. The one issue of great importance for lenders is the location of the mortgage broker and the security. Before lending on a property extensive due diligence must be conducted, something most private investors would have difficulty in conducting.

PLACING ADVERTISEMENTS

Trust Deeds can be located by placing advertisements in local newspapers. A large number of responses will have to be screened to find Trust Deeds with a reasonable return and with an acceptable LTV. There is the added problem of filtering out the crooks, lookers, and property with a high owner-estimated market value. Although a mortgage broker will take a large commission by way of points, he usually earned it. Only if a larger number of Trust Deeds are needed will a major effort such as placing newspaper advertisements be required.

The ad can indicate your desire to purchase an existing Trust Deed or that you lend money on real estate. Remember that if you are lending money as a private party on a new loan, your interest rate cannot exceed the 10 percent usury limit[1] unless a mortgage broker is used to generate the loan. Due to multiple regulations, a mortgage broker should be used to handle all the details. The cost of using a mortgage broker can be minimal. The mortgage broker can be selected by shopping and negotiating a fixed broker processing fee. This advertising effort often doesn't develop into a profitable loan. The potential borrower is trying to save the broker's commission, obtain a lower interest rate, or his valuation of the property is too high to allow for a reasonably safe investment. If the Trust Deed is in existence there could be problems with the loan such as the borrower not making payments, a small amount or no equity remaining in the property, problems with the property or defects with the Trust Deed documentation.

MORTGAGE BROKER

Calling mortgage brokers should provide the greatest source of Trust Deeds. By periodically calling the mortgage brokers that are listed in the telephone yellow pages and the list generated from newspapers, a good source of Trust Deeds will be found. It will become apparent very soon

---

[1] The 10 percent usury interest is not fixed and can vary not only under certain conditions but is also different for each state. In California, the legal rate of interest is 10 percent for personal, family, or household purposes. The general usury limit for home improvement or home purchase is 5 percent plus the Federal Reserve Bank of San Francisco's rate. The 10 percent rate will be used in this book to simplify the discussion. The usury limits for each state can be found by searching the Internet.

which mortgage brokers have good Trust Deeds and which mortgage brokers are selling their junk. It is important to learn early in your investment efforts if the mortgage broker is selling junk so your time is not wasted. If the Trust Deed has been heavily shopped (offered to many investors), there is a high probability that the Trust Deed is not desirable. Usually by looking at the appraisal date, credit report date, loan application date, and asking the mortgage broker if the loan has been shopped will indicate the Trust Deed's status.

Locating an acceptable mortgage broker can be a daunting task, one that can have a financial impact. Obtaining a referral from other investors can speed your selection process and minimize any potential investment loss.

There are two types of brokers that might be used to facilitate a loan. Most of your loans will probably be handled by a broker that is licensed by the Department of Real Estate (DRE).

If the loan is a very large one, it will most likely be under the regulations of the California Department of Corporation and the broker will have configured the loan in a limited liability corporation (LLC).

The reason for mortgage brokers to use the California Department of Corporation is to be able to fractionalize the loan and locate enough funds when the number of lenders will exceed ten. Using LLC will also provide some protection if the loan goes bad, a type of firewall for the mortgage broker but not for you, the lender.

There is an advantage in using only Department of Real Estate licensees. If for some reason there is a loss caused by the broker or his licensee, and you are unsuccessful in the return of the lost funds, the Department of Real Estate has a special fund, called a real estate recovery account, to reimburse some if not all of the lost funds caused by its licensee. This unfortunately requires a number of hoops that must be gone through. To recover any damages or lost funds, a final civil judgment, arbitration award, or a criminal restitution order must be obtained against the licensee. Then a reasonable search of the licensee's assets and reasonable effort to collect the damages must be performed. There are time windows that also apply. The California statutory limits are a maximum of $20,000 per transaction, with a possible total aggregate maximum of $100,000 per licensee.

A check can also be made to determine the California Association of Realtors (CAR) status for a real estate agent. Members that work directly with buyers and sellers normally would belong to this association. Mortgage brokers normally don't belong to CAR. The Internet address is: http://members.car.org.

The second type of broker is covered by the California Department of Corporations. There are two controlling statutes. One of them is enabled by the Financial Services Division; FSD. This division also issues licenses. Financial Services Division, license status can be obtained from: http://www.corp.ca.gov/fsd/financial.htm.

The other controlling statute is covered by the California Residential Mortgage Lenders Act–CRMCA. These brokers can lend on residential real estate. The exact authority is determined by the regulating section of the *California Code.* California Mortgage Lenders Act (CRMCA), license status on agents can be obtained from the Web site: http://www.corp.ca.gov/pub/mb.htm.

Don't always believe mortgage brokers. Some of them will say anything or conceal something about a loan to place a loan. Remember, mortgage brokers are dependant upon finding and selling loans to make their money. The more loans that they can place, the more money they can make. The sins of mortgage brokers usually are ones of omission and not commission.

It is important to find out the type of license the mortgage broker has, and that it is current. A copy of the broker's license should be obtained for your file. If the mortgage broker is a real estate agent, a copy of their license and the real estate broker that they are working for should be obtained. If the mortgage broker shows any hesitation in providing a copy, you can suspect the honesty of the broker. The reasons that the broker would not provide a copy of the license is if they do not have a license, the license is under suspension, they are only a real estate sales person not working for a broker or they are using a broker's license that was borrowed. Ask for a list of satisfied clients from the mortgage broker. If the mortgage broker is unwilling to provide a list, you should probably walk away from this person.

A check with the California Department of Real Estate (DRE, (213) 897-3399) is *mandatory* to determine the DRE mortgage broker's license status. The DRE will be able to tell you if the mortgage broker is properly licensed, for how long, and if there have been any complaints or disciplinary actions. This information can also be obtained on the Internet at: http://www.dre.ca.gov.

A call to the local Better Business Bureau should be made to check if the mortgage broker has had any complaints lodged. If there is any question about an escrow company, a call should be made to the Department of Corporation to determine the escrow company's status. The Department of Corporations is the usual controlling agency for most escrows. The telephone number in the Los Angeles area is (213) 736-2741.

Mortgage companies will sometimes have their own escrow. They cannot use a Department of Real Estate controlled escrow unless they are a party to the transaction. If the escrow is under the real estate broker's license, the Department of Real Estate will be the monitoring agency.

If the mortgage broker is using the *California Department of Corporation's License, (personal or a real estate lender)*, a call to the Department of Corporation or checking the Web site license listings should be made to determine the broker's escrow status. The Web site is http://www.corp.ca.gov/fsd/esb/.

Some trust deed mortgage brokers are not as ethical or detailed as we would like them to be. Too many are driven by the high competition as in many businesses and start to take shortcuts in their dealings. It is therefore prudent to be as thorough as possible to compensate for their shortcomings.

In the selection of mortgage brokers, consideration should be given to their mode of operation. In general the types of mortgage brokers that you will encounter are: brokers that primarily fund for their own or relatives' accounts and the typical residential property or commercial property mortgage brokers. The latter mortgage brokers specialize in different area of investment. There are the residential first and second trust deed types, the rehab loan type, and the larger and smaller construction project types. Although there is some crossing over in the types of loans that they become involved with, their specialty stays the same unless the market conditions change. In this case they are forced to seek other types of borrowers.

The for-their-own-account mortgage brokers are in the business of finding loans primarily for their own and their relatives' accounts. They will cherry pick and then sell to others the Trust Deeds that are not exceptional. They may still have some Trust Deeds that can be a prudent investment. These, however, may be sparse. If after checking with all the other mortgage brokers without results, dealing with these cherry pickers may still produce a reasonable quality Trust Deed. They may have missed one of the good ones. If the Trust Deed presented is unacceptable on the surface, changing the terms can change a marginal Trust Deed into a desirable Trust Deed. The changes could include:

- increasing the interest rate,
- changing to a variable interest rate,
- reducing the amount of the loan,
- placing part or all of the loan into an *impound account*[2],
- changing the loan period,

[2] An *impound account* is used to accumulate funds or hold funds until needed. Impound accounts are used to pay for taxes and insurance, building materials, portions of construction, or street improvements. An escrow company, a mortgage broker, or lender typically holds these funds. Money is paid out when needed or when a phase of a project has been completed.

- requesting additional security,
- cross-collateralizing (discussed later),
- including a coborrower or cosigner.

Other terms that can be added to the Trust Deed Note are prepayment penalty, jump rates (discussed later), and full or partial prepaid interest. There are, however, restrictions to these additional terms if the property is a personal residence of four or less units. These restrictions are discussed later.

The problem that may occur after changing the Trust Deed terms is the cherry picker may then keep the Trust Deed. After changing the Trust Deed to a desirable one, the mortgage broker may tell you that the loan went to another mortgage broker, the borrower doesn't want the loan, or the loan went to another hard-money lender that had first choice. If this occurs, this would be a mortgage broker to consider crossing off your Trust Deed source list.

The typical mortgage broker comes in different shades of honesty. Although they will all portray themselves as honest and working for you, remember they are working for themselves. This translates into your being ever vigilant of their potential sins of commission and omission and their providing accurate and complete information.

One of your most important efforts in obtaining a loan from a mortgage broker is to keep calling back. Frequently, even though brokers didn't have a loan last week, they may have one this week. Don't be too intrusive in your callback. But remember the old saying, "The squeaky wheel gets the grease."

BROKER INVESTMENT FUNDS

A mortgage broker investment fund (sometimes called a REIT) can provide an opportunity for a small investor. There are, however, some disadvantages and dangers in these investment funds. The disadvantage to an investor is that the rate of return may be lower than an investment in an individual Trust Deed, or the quality of the Trust Deed won't be exceptional. One of the reasons for a poor quality Trust Deed is the mortgage broker will need to place large funds in something and earn a commission to keep his business flourishing. The broker will manage the investment fund and most times charge a fee. This still can be an acceptable approach especially if the details of purchasing and servicing of Trust Deeds are unfamiliar. There is a downside to these funds. The funds have restrictions on removing your money and most times will charge a significant exit fee. There is a positive side in the broker's diversification of investments in many properties—that of reducing the danger of a major money loss.

There is a slight variation that can be found with some mortgage broker investments. This is when the Trust Deed offered is mandated to be serviced by the mortgage broker. These Trust Deeds can be fractionalized or individual, but still owned by you, the lender. There is the associated cost that would be your responsibility, such as cost to fight bankruptcy, cost to file foreclosure, unpaid senior liens, unpaid insurance, and any legal costs such as with fraud and insurance disputes (both title and property insurance). Although the mortgage broker could order actions for these costs, you would still have to pay up. The important distinction comes about by the amount of servicing fee that the broker charges for each interest payment. This can be anywhere from one-half to several percentage points of the interest received. As an example, for a loan of $100,000 at 14 percent—the monthly payments might be 2 percent ($166) paid to the broker and 12 percent ($1000) paid to the investor. The percentage really paid to the broker would be 14.3 percent. This would be in addition to the points the broker receives from the borrower for funding the loan. The broker's servicing fee in this case is excessive compared to the amount other mortgage brokers charge, such as $5 to $15, for a similar service. Guidance from the lower cost mortgage brokers such as filing foreclosure, fighting bankruptcy, and the hiring of an attorney usually would still be volunteered.

There is something to be said in the defense for the high servicing charges of these special mortgage brokers. They in general will use an underwriter (term used in the industry), to examine properties to avoid an extensive number of problems, thereby minimizing their efforts in monitoring and servicing properties. This thereby provides some due diligence on your investment. This is not to say that the lower cost servicing fee brokers don't do some due diligence.

The dangers of investing in an investment fund are numerous. First, the broker could be totally dishonest and sell the same Trust Deed to several investors. They might have you sign a power of attorney or forge your name on a power of attorney, reconvey the Trust Deed and generate a new Trust Deed. They would then sell the new fraudulent Trust Deed. With your power of attorney they could subordinate your position and fund a loan that is senior to your loan. When they have possession of the Trust Deed and Trust Deed Note, anything is possible.

The second danger in investing in a fund with a dishonest broker (only slightly a crook) is the result of a number of deceptive or unethical practices that might be used. The most common would occur when Trust Deeds are funded or purchased and the security is poor or the loan nonperforming.

The third danger is the broker, in order to continue to show performance, will use a pyramid or Ponzi scheme. This is when the last investor's money is used to pay for the earlier investor's payments. This technique will only keep the investors happy for a short time.

Any and all of these will have the historic consequence of your losing money.

The evaluation that should be done on broker investment funds is as follows:

- A detailed evaluation of the prospectus on the fund. The details of the prospectus should be made in solid statements with the absence of fuzzy or puffed-up proclamations.

- A call to the Better Business Bureau, Department of Corporations, and the Department of Real Estate to find out if there have been complaints against the fund or fund's originators. This check should be positive with no complaints.

- A list of the Trust Deeds in the fund with their position, LTV, and payment performance should be made available for review. If the list cannot be shown to you, this is a very negative indicator. As part of the evaluation, some of the Trust Deeds should be verified at the County Recorders Office to insure the fund has ownership of claimed Trust Deeds.

- A statement or list of the number of Trust Deeds presently in foreclosure, the number of past foreclosures, and the number of properties that are now owned by the fund should be obtained. If this list is not available, this is a strong indication the fund is operating in a questionable fashion.

If any of the indicators above are negative, it is advised to look for a different fund.

Another potential problem is if the amount of money in the fund is very large. The broker may invest in poor Trust Deeds in order to place all the investors' funds. These poor Trust Deeds can become nonperforming investments with little or no return. This style of investing is sometimes done by the broker to prevent having too much cash in a trust account with a low interest rate. They will be pressured to invest in something. This can be a fatal mistake in trust deed investing. Beware if investment funds offer a return that is higher than the present market return. The offered return can be a projected and not the actual return.

The trust deed fund may have Trust Deeds that are of poorer quality. This could include:

- high LTV loans,
- unrealistic high appraisal values,

- borrowers with very poor credit,
- properties that are in foreclosure,
- properties that recently have been taken out of a foreclosure,
- borrowers that are in bankruptcy,
- borrowers that have received bankruptcy counseling,
- borrowers that have had a past bankruptcy.

The Trust Deed could be on business property where the appraisal included the value of the business, which would consist of fixtures, inventory, and goodwill (discussed later). In a foreclosure the fixtures, inventory, and goodwill can evaporate quickly. Fixtures would include equipment and items required to operate a business.

There is another form of a broker investment vehicle that should be highlighted. That is a Trust Deed with multiple investors. In this investment vehicle, each investor owns a percentage of the Trust Deed and Trust Deed Note. This on the surface is an acceptable method of investing. There are however dangers and problems that can occur. Usually the mortgage broker will want an intercreditor agreement with the lender on how all aspects of the Trust Deed are to be handled. This is necessary so that:

- as mortgage payments are received they will be proportionally divided with respect to the lenders' interest and distributed,
- if a foreclosure is required or a reconveyance is to be issued—this can be done by the mortgage broker,
- agreement on issues and signatures will not have to be obtained from all of the investors. This on the surface is probably acceptable providing the mortgage broker is honest or is bonded to perform these housekeeping duties.

The intercreditor agreement might state that the investors can object to changes, but in practical terms this is not done or cannot be done prior to the event happening. This is due to the time required, one of the investors not having a majority of ownership, or the contact information on each investor unavailable for changing the direction decided by the other lenders. Some of the investors use IRA accounts where it becomes difficult or impossible to adequately make a timely contact.

What often happens is the mortgage broker talks to a majority of the investors and convinces them that the change is okay. This leaves some investors with legitimate concerns, unable to change the momentum of the mortgage broker's railroading of the change.

Some mortgage brokers will require an effective power of attorney in the management of the Trust Deed. The power might include the authorization to extend the loan, change the terms of the loan, or subordinate the loan. Each of these provisions has special meanings that can affect your wealth.

The modification of the Trust Deed has the potential of reducing the Trust Deed's value. The reduction in the Trust Deed value for any reason should require points, an interest increase, or both as consideration for the modification. There will be times when, due to the market conditions and the loan having performed, accepting the change without compensation will make sense.

The extension of a loan has value where points could be received from the borrower. The hard-money investors should receive some of these points. Often the mortgage broker will not share these points, usually claiming he has many investors that will take the loan without sharing the points. If the amount of the loan is small, this is probably the case, due to there being many lenders with small nest eggs.

The loss of security due to a loan extension is of great concern for the investor. The loss of security could be due to the potential property value decrease during a long-term loan as compared to a potentially smaller decrease during a short-term loan. The long-term value reduction would occur due to the greater probability of an economic downturn. (Real estate does not always go up in value. In fact improved property always depreciates. This is one of the reasons that the IRS allows and even demands that property be depreciated as a tax write-off.)

The other intercreditor agreement term is the subordination of the Trust Deed. This allows a new loan to be placed on the security (real estate) that is senior to the investor's loan. Here again there is value generated. Points should be charged and should be shared with all of the investors. If the subordination is done, points not paid, and the security compromised, it is time to take your ball (money) and go home.

Of great importance is that each of the investors has their name on the Trust Deed, Trust Deed Note, title insurance, and property insurance as one of the owners of the loan.

One of the manipulations of a Trust Deed by a dishonest mortgage broker is as follows: A Trust Deed at a high interest rate is generated. The Trust Deed would then be divided into two Trust Deeds, a senior loan at a low interest rate and the junior loan at the original interest rate. The mortgage broker would find investors to take the senior loan at the lower interest rate and find investors for the junior loan at the original rate. The borrower would still pay the high rate on the total loan. The mortgage broker could then pocket the difference between the amount that the borrower pays and the amount he has to pay the investors. The borrower would still be paying the higher interest rate and probably not even know that this has happened. The investor in the junior position potentially could lose all of their investment if the property significantly decreases in value and must be foreclosed on and sold. It can be argued that the investors are in a like position as before. This is not true. The *junior Trust Deed's*[3] security could be wiped out completely where as before, only a portion would be wiped out. The junior trust deed lender would not be receiving their fair value due to the increased vulnerability.

---

[3] A *junior Trust Deed* is any Trust Deed that is subordinate to another Trust Deed. It can be in a second, third, or higher position.

There is also the disproportionate amount of added cost to the junior trust deed holder in the situation noted above if there is a foreclosure, without receiving a higher dollar return. These foreclosure costs might include the senior loan trust deed payments.

The present DRE regulations in fractionalized loans are to only allow a Trust Deed to be divided among ten owners. To bypass this regulation, some mortgage brokers will configure the loan into a first, second, or even more loans and have ten investors for each loan. On the surface this may be legitimate, however the junior trust deed holders are in a less secure position. Another technique that mortgage brokers use is to have the transaction controlled by the Department of Corporations. They are lenient and have provided exemptions to the ten-lender rule, providing regulations and disclosures are followed.

Many fractionalized loans are set up as a limited liability corporation (LLC). This means the mortgage broker has limited liability in the event of money loss. Adding to the problem, the physical Trust Deed and, more importantly, the Trust Deed Note may be held by the LLC, thereby putting you in a weaker position for controlling your destiny.

There is another advantage that the mortgage broker has in handling the trust deed investment. If the property must be reclaimed through foreclosure and sold, the real estate broker's selling commission is retained by the mortgage broker and taken off the top of the sales proceeds before the investor receives back any of his funds.

After pointing out the advantages that the mortgage broker can obtain by combining investors, it must be remembered they have worked hard in finding the loan, investigating the feasibility of the loan, configuring the loan's terms with safeguards, and administrating the loan. With this effort there must be a reward. There should however be proper disclosures by the mortgage broker on his financial rewards.

PAST/PRESENT BORROWERS

Old borrowers, land developers, property rehabilitation contractors, and small tract developers should be contacted periodically. If they borrowed in the past, they may do so in the future. Present borrowers may want to refinance the loan when the *balloon payment* is due. A *balloon payment* is usually the last payment on a loan and is larger than the normal periodic payments. A refinance of the loan should be rewritten using a mortgage broker, so rates above a usury interest rate of 10 percent can be charged. (See previous discussion on limits.) (If the loan is extended and provided for in the Trust Deed Note, a rewrite probably will not be needed.) Points can usually be obtained for an new extension that requires a rewrite of the Trust Deed Note and can be between1 and 5 percent. If the market rate is 10 percent or lower (and acceptable) an escrow company might be used to set up the extension.

If a mortgage broker does not originate the loan, this can be a good deal not only for the borrower but also the lender. A mortgage broker should be used to process the loan. The mortgage broker's relatively small fixed fee can be charged to the borrower. Using this method of financing, the borrower won't have to pay the high points that a mortgage broker would normally charge. From the lender's standpoint, the borrower's track record is known. Because there are no points, a higher interest rate loan might be charged. Points could still be collected and could again be 1 to 5 percent. The points charged can be applied to the loan, so an amount more than the original face value of the Trust Deed Note would be financed. Escrow and title insurance should still be used so the documents are properly processed, the loan position established, and the loan insured.

LAWYERS

Another source of Trust Deeds is the client of lawyers that may need cash to continue with a lawsuit or post a bond. A hard-money lender can provide the necessary funds in an expeditious manner.

TAX ACCOUNTANTS

At tax time, there will be times that an accountant's client will not have cash to pay his taxes. Here again funds can be provided in a prompt manner.

EXISTING TRUST DEEDS

When a Trust Deed Note reaches the end of the loan period, there is usually a balloon payment that becomes due. This is always the case when the loan is not amortized. A new loan or refinancing of the existing loan will therefore be required. This can be a source of a replacement Trust Deed for your portfolio.

A source could be from a seller of property who has taken a Trust Deed as part of the down payment on the sale of property. The *seller carryback*[4] is sometimes necessary due to the buyer not having enough of a down payment to obtain standard financing, a lower interest rate is desired by a buyer, the seller wants an installment sale for tax purposes or the seller wants an income stream from his previously owned equity. Some sellers may still want to cash out (be paid off) after the sale. They therefore, will be willing to sell the Trust Deed to a hard-money lender. This Trust Deed very often will be sold at a discount to increase the yield to make the Trust Deed salable in the existing market conditions. There is a potential problem with carryback Trust Deeds generated by a property seller. Most often the carryback Trust Deed will have a high LTV (small equity) due to the purchase down payment being small. If the buyer has been properly qualified, the Trust Deed might be as safe as a traditional hard-money loan. It is still prudent to do a complete evaluation before buying the Trust Deed.

When the source of the Trust Deed is a hard-money lender selling part of his portfolio, there could be several hidden problems. These problems

---

[4] A *seller carryback* is a Trust Deed with accompanying Trust Deed Note generated during a property sale where the seller is the lender.

may have induced the lender to sell the Trust Deed Note. The problems could include a borrower that is about to default on the loan, has applied for bankruptcy counseling, filed a bankruptcy, or is inconsistent in making monthly payments on time. The property may have structural problems. There could be a change in the neighborhood due to a highway coming through, a blighted neighborhood due to drug sales, a rapid change in the economic composition of the neighborhood, a special property assessment, a senior loan that is foreclosing, priority liens that are coming due, or other negative situations. The seller has the advantage due to his knowing more about the Trust Deed than the buyer. When dealing with someone that wants to sell his Trust Deed, remember to count your fingers after shaking his hand.

DECISION TIME

The faster (with accuracy) that an investor can respond in the decision process, the better chances an excellent performing trust deed portfolio can be collected. There are a large number of competing investors looking for good Trust Deeds. If a decision cannot be made within a few hours about a Trust Deed that has been presented to you, some other investor may take it, if it is a good Trust Deed. When a lender can make decisions in a reasonable time, the mortgage brokers will be inclined to call that lender first. Therefore, when funds are available for investment, an energetic search with property analysis will be required to prevail over the other investors. It is important to have your funds available to invest. If you burn a mortgage broker by telling him you will fund and do not have funds available, that will guarantee that you will not be called in the future.

It may even be necessary to sleep with one foot on the floor in order to get to that good Trust Deed first.

You do not want to make the mistake of telling a mortgage broker that you will take the Trust Deed and then renege. This would turn off the mortgage broker in offering you other Trust Deeds. If you are not sure about a Trust Deed, let the broker know that you will be doing additional evaluations and will advise him within a reasonable period of time. This evaluation should be done within one day if the property is within easy driving distance. If the evaluation cannot be done within the time, call the broker and let him know the situation and what your plan is for making a decision.

In evaluating Trust Deeds, do not be shy in rejecting a Trust Deed if it does not feel right. When a Trust Deed is rejected and the same one continues to be advertised for sale, this is an indication that no one wanted it. This will not only confirm your judgment but help in your decision process in the future.

Some of the Trust Deeds that are offered will be shopworn. They have been offered to many lenders. It is a good policy to ask the broker if the loan has been offered to others or the loan is one that has not been shopped. Some brokers will contact other brokers for a list of Trust Deeds that have not been sold. If this is the case for the loan that has been offered, there is a high probability that this loan should be avoided. One of the ways to determine if the loan is shopworn is to check the credit report of the borrower. If there are multiple inquires by lenders, there is a good chance the loan has been shopped.

There will be Trust Deeds offered that will have a LTV that is tight or suspicious. This may be a case where the owner is trying to sell the property. What this means is after the loan is funded, the borrower will take the money and run, leaving a property that is probably not easily sold and with very little or no real equity. This incorrect LTV is often due to the appraisal being based on the square footage without proper adjustment to the quality of construction, age of the construction, lack of permits, a poor neighborhood, or a substandard building site.

Remember, a high rate of return on a Trust Deed is of little value if the borrower isn't making or can't make payments and the security is inadequate. When trust deed loans exceed the property value, this can translate into a loss of your money.

Section 4

TYPES OF PROPERTY

Figure 4. *But where's the rest of the house?*

TYPES OF PROPERTY

There are many types of properties and subgroups that might be offered as security for Trust Deeds.

There is personal property that has additional classifications. This would be property that is necessary for earning a living such as *tools of the trade* and other personal property. *Tools of the trade* would include items such as saws, hammers, power tools, and a square for a carpenter. Other personal property would include clothing, shaving gear, consumables, bed, car, and other life necessities. Luxury items would not be classified as items needed for living. Luxury items could be an extra car or a boat used for sport. However a boat that is used for commercial fishing would be a tool of the trade. As can be imagined, real property as with personal property can have different uses and definitions. Each situation must be looked at individually. A mobile home could be personal property or real property. If the mobile home is permanently attached to the land, it becomes real property. (There are other peculiarities of mobile home that are discussed below.) Many personal property items can still be used as security for a loan.

Real property is usually defined as single-family residences, apartments, land, condos, and industrial or commercial property. Apartments and commercial property are often referred to as income property. The terms industrial and commercial are often used interchangeably. Commercial property may also have a condo configuration similar to residential property. This would be the case if a building is divided into separately owned condo units. The owners would then operate their respective office or industrial space.

Income property can also include a business. Within the definition of business property is a category called *goodwill*. *Goodwill* is a unique classification that is associated with a business and has its own value. It is the public's perception of a business and the value that can be assigned to future business. The business may or may not have real property associated with it. Often a business has a lease that is a separate classification.

It is recommended that any property that is being considered should have an appraisal by a Member of the Appraisal Institute (MAI) or a Residential Associate Appraiser (SRA) admitted to its membership with an appropriate specialty elective. Often an appraisal will be presented that is not even signed by a licensed appraiser. This does not have very much value other than to make you suspicious of the deal. Licenses for appraisers are required by the State of California. The appraiser's license status can be checked on the Web site: http://www.orea.ca.gov/html/lic_appraisers.shtml.

SINGLE FAMILY RESIDENCE

Single family residences (SFR) are recommended for initial trust deed investments. Often the amount is relatively small and only one or two borrowers are involved. This will usually keep the complexity of the Trust Deed and borrower evaluation at a minimum. If the property is a duplex or apartment there is the added complexity of the rents, security deposit, and collection of rent's clause in the Trust Deed Note that would have to be addressed. A collection of rent's clause would also appear in the documents for a SFR. This clause would be desirable in the event the SFR is used as a rental or converted to a rental property from an owner-occupied status.

Land, commercial property, and income units often will not have enough comparable sales to easily determine market value. An evaluation of value would have to be done, using an income approach or land residual (discussed later) approach.

If property is acquired through a foreclosure, the market time (time to sell) for these non-SFR properties typically is long. The carrying cost would include interest payments on senior liens, taxes, security, property maintenance and a higher sales commission. These costs would be higher than a SFR property and deplete equity very fast.

If the appraised value of a SFR in dollars per square foot value was much different from the area's dollar value per square foot, the additional value would be for a portion associated with land value or other amenities. For example, a SFR on fourteen acres, or a house with a grove can be property that requires additional evaluation. Value added because of extra features of the house can distort the safe investment LTV criteria. This value might be for a pool and upgraded fixtures. Other distortions can be caused by a housing shortage in the area. A housing shortage could increase the square foot value to more than $400 per square foot. Loan equity can disappear very fast if the economy slows down, or if buying trends change.

A house on a substantial amount of land with a higher appraised value is not always easy to sell. The combination of a house and extensive land should therefore have a lower investment LTV than a house on a small lot to ensure a fast sale if acquired in foreclosure. A house with an ocean or country view (that can't be lost due to obstructive construction) can have good salability. There should, however, be comparable sales for this amenity to justify the additional appraisal value.

Property with a large percentage of land could still be good value if the land can be split off or subdivided without too much trouble or cost. An investment in a house with an avocado grove or fruit trees can be a deceptive investment. The grove can die off due to frost, fire, drought, irrigation system turned off, or disease. The value of the grove can be reduced significantly because of an increase in water cost, pest control, or competing foreign imports. Property with an orchard should have a smaller LTV to adjust for the potential loss. With a smaller LTV, the borrower will be less inclined to default. He has a lot to lose.

A property that is too close to a planned business, planned apartments, planned shopping center or a planned highway construction, or land that can lose its view by a neighbor's construction should have a smaller LTV. If there were a foreclosure, a high equity is needed to allow for the reduced price to achieve a fast sale.

Upward value adjustment might be made on property if there is a better land use. This would be due to the property being zoned for a higher use such as commercial, multiunit or special use. This will require a significant investigation to learn the true situation.

Properties that have an easement can impact the property value. This would be caused by part of the land being unusable due to the need to allow for power, water, sewer, telephone; or vehicle or pedestrian access.

If there are future plans for redevelopment of an area or a highway going through a property, it will impact the value. This is not necessarily due to an appraisal being incorrect, but the number of buyers being reduced or even eliminated due to the less desirability of the property.

Even though you may sell at or above the appraised value, it could take time, in the event that you end up with the property. Adding to this would be that during the time of ownership you wouldn't receive a return of interest on your investment. If the property were income property such as a single-family residence, renting, leasing or retaining tenants would be difficult. Tenants wouldn't rent, or leave at their convenience, due to the possibility of later being notified to move.

Properties that are in the right of way of a project will be acquired by the authorized agency using a simple purchase, or condemnation with eminent domain action if you resist the sale. Checking with local planning departments and the State Division of Highways can help determine future plans for the property. Future planning, however, can change, with a potential resulting reduction in value. There may be cases where future events on adjacent property can increase a property's value. This increase, however, is very difficult to determine or even predict. Although an appraisal may take some of these problems into consideration, an appraiser may not be aware of the situation and provide an incorrect appraisal. When there is a cloud such as this on a property, the intrinsic value may be there but the uncertainty can stigmatize the property and reduce if not totally eliminate buyers and therefore significantly reduce value. The uncertainty might not justify an investment in this type of property. If there are several loans to consider, one requiring extensive investigation with its uncertainty, or a simple one that has a sound appraisal—selecting the simpler loan even if the return is lower, might be a better choice.

CONDOS

There is a special type of real estate defined as a condominium. This type of property has a number of different configurations. A condominium, commonly called a *condo,* is a subdivision in air. The condo owner has ownership of the airspace. An association owns the common areas such as improvements, buildings, parking, parks, and pools on the property. The condo owner has the right to use the common area. Condos have different variations with the homeowner having additional maintenance responsibilities on the building. This could include doors, roofs, termite control, and building exterior.

There are other variations of condos with their own definitions such as:

- planned unit developments (PUD), with the owner owning the housing improvement and an association controlling common facilities, such as parking, pool, or a park.

- stock co-ops, with the owner having the right to occupy one unit of a building complex. There are other variations and restrictions that can have financial implications.

From an investment standpoint, the availability of standard lenders for these properties can be limited. This is the reason hard-money lenders are often asked to finance their purchase or provide an additional loan. The exact type of ownership in a unit is important. Some of the condos require the approval of the other owners in order to purchase the property. This occurs if it is a stock-type ownership. This can be a potential problem if you become an owner by foreclosure and need to dispose of the property.

The number of rentals in a condo complex can become part of the risk factors in a loan. When there are too many renters, the property becomes less desirable due to renters not having "pride-of-ownership" and their not always taking good care of the property. Standard financing requires 50 percent or higher owner-occupied status. If owner-occupied status is less, then higher interest and higher points are imposed on a loan. It should be remembered that when lending on a condo, refinancing cannot always be easily done, and disposing of the property after a foreclosure could be more difficult. Lending on these properties might in reality be the purchasing of the property due to possible foreclosure. Lending on this type of property should be done carefully.

Investing in condos or planned unit developments (PUD) has special considerations. The homeowner's association's (HOA) management can bleed off assets or have an under funded maintenance fund. If the complex is rundown with deferred maintenance, this is an indication that this could be happening. The deferred maintenance can include roof repair or replacement, tenting of the building due to termites with associated repairs and the cost of housing condo occupants, repainting, plumbing, or even repairing a cracked slab. If the unit that is being considered has termites, the association may not be responsible or may not take responsibility. This would require paying for the other owners' housing during a tenting procedure. Some of the other condo owners, every so often, refuse to vacate their unit for a tenting procedure. This can be a major problem.

If the association is responsible for repairs, this reduces the cost aspect provided there is adequate money in the maintenance fund. In the case where there is major deferred maintenance of the complex, a property assessment is sure to become a reality.

If the unit is a PUD where the unit owner is responsible for all repairs, this could become a major cost to the homeowner if there is substantial deferred maintenance.

When the condo is on leased land, the terms of the lease can impact the value. This could be due to the length of the remaining lease and a cost escalation clause in the lease when the term is extended. There is always the potential problem that the lease will not be extended.

There is an additional downside to trust deed investing in condos. This is due to some of the public's perception that condos are not a highly desirable property. This perception, in part, is attributed to the association fee cost not being deductible from income tax when used as a personal residence and the condo sometimes being considered a glorified apartment. This attitude changes when there is a shortage of housing.

A poor architectural design, even with large square footage, will reduce market value. Condo units that have large square footage and a high number of bedrooms have a special problem. They will load up with more children (bless their little hearts) than the complex was designed for initially. This will usually cause the complex to deteriorate at a fast rate with the resulting reduction in market value.

It would be prudent to review the condo association's minutes for the past year to learn if there are serious conditions that would reduce the property value. The covenant, conditions, and restrictions (CC&R) should also be reviewed to determine if there are restrictions that might reduce the property value.

MOBILE HOMES

Loan security on mobile homes can be impacted by the property's designation. There are two basic categories of mobile homes. There are units that are permanently attached to the land and units that are not attached. In the case of permanently attached property, taxes are paid directly to the County Tax Assessor. Those units that are defined as not attached *may* be licensed similar to a vehicle license. However, not all unattached mobile homes are licensed. The taxation method becomes one of the important issues. This is due to taxation method not always being based on how the unit is placed on the land but the date the unit was activated. These taxation regulations are complex and advice should be obtained from a knowledgeable mobile home broker to determine the dates when and how mobile homes are impacted. In general mobile homes are taxed by the Department of Housing and Community Development if licensed. If not licensed, taxes will be paid to the County Tax Assessor. It should be noted that units attached to the land typically have higher taxes.

The valuation of the mobile home is based on location, amenities of the mobile park, space rent, types of taxes, age, fee-simple ownership of space (lot), and unit size (width of unit, i.e., single, double, or triple) of the mobile home. The age alone has a special meaning. There are mobile home parks that require all mobile homes to be of a recent manufacture. If a mobile home doesn't meet the age requirement, it would have to be replaced with a new unit.

Mobile homes in general have a fast rate of depreciation. This is due in part to the mobile home construction, obsolescence of the unit, and changes in the mobile home park. If the mobile home park has changed to families with children, the units in the park can and often are reduced in value.

Loans on mobile homes should be done with great care. This is because of the fast depreciation of the unit as well as higher sales commission. In most parks, the park manager must approve new owners with restrictions on who can live in the park, such as seniors or a family.

Added to this problem is the potential that the mobile park can be sold to a developer for the construction of a shopping center or housing project. Moving a mobile home is expensive if a new location can be found. The new location may be a prohibitive distance with most likely a higher space rent if an older unit is acceptable. Although there are laws that provide some compensation for such a relocation, in most cases, it won't cover the actual cost.

A mobile home placed on an individually owned lot can be expensive due to the addition of the lot purchase cost. Even with owning the lot, there will be homeowner's fees that would consist of trash, sewer, cable, park maintenance, and management. There will also be the property tax on the lot. These costs can exceed the lease cost of a mobile home without ownership of the lot.

In a foreclosure, personal property such as porches, skirts, and appliances can disappear as well as the total unit. Even though there are restrictions for moving a mobile home, these may not stop a mobile homeowner from moving the unit. Ownership documentation should be reviewed with care to verify the borrower's ownership. The park manager should be contacted to determine the status of the rent payment and any other conditions that might affect the value, such as the park's requirement for unit upgrade, change in ownership, and future plans of the park. Some parks have escalation clauses that require an increase in space rent when there is an ownership change. Local laws provide some protection but there are often methods of bypassing these restrictions.

VACANT LAND

The investment in vacant land should be approached with caution. Vacant real estate normally does not generate income and may require a zoning change to be viable. Land can be an alligator—it eats money. These expenses could include taxes, payment on senior liens, brush removal, liability insurance, and protective fencing. The other potential danger is the possibility of down zoning by government agencies, thereby reducing the property value. Some land can generate income from the renting of the property for storage, a nursery for plants, sale of the topsoil, an advertising sign, Christmas tree sales, or Halloween pumpkin sales. When evaluating the value of land, this potential income can be considered minus the management cost.

Land or lots eventually will require building permits, school bonds, special assessment tax, offsite bonds, special studies such as environmental impact reports (including impact on traffic, trees, rare weeds, protected species, fish and game migration, and nesting sites), Coastal Commission approval permits, or archaeological digs when it is developed. This will decrease the apparent value of the property. (See building sequence paragraph below for additional details.)

In the case of raw land, there are the cost and time of subdividing the land into lots and obtaining a final approval. Even if the land has a final approval, there can be restrictions and bond requirements prior to any construction. If bonds (or money put into a municipal trust fund) have been furnished for the improvement, there is still the question if the amount is adequate to cover the required improvements. This can be further complicated by inflation that will reduce how much the bond will cover. Even after all of the approvals have been obtained, a building inspector can impose requirements that may require removing some of the construction and rebuilding to meet the municipality's requirements.

The land that is under consideration for a loan should be verified as to its exact location and the amount of land. A recent survey should have been done with survey markers in place. The legal description, although helpful, does not identify the location unless you are a survey engineer and are familiar with legal descriptions. Asking a real estate broker will usually not help. Most real estate brokers don't know how to translate a legal description to the real location.

Property that is on or next to potential mudslide zone, earthquake fault lines, on or near a flood plain, or near fire hazards will also reduce the property value. This is especially true if insurance cannot easily be obtained. City, county, state, and federal restrictions or regulations may also reduce the property value. If the property has a special use or a variation permit, the loss of the conditional use can reduce the property value. This loss would occur when a property has a use permit under a grandfather clause. This grandfathered use could change due to nonuse or the governing municipality changing the status and withdrawing the permit. One of the other cases that could come up is that a use permit might expire due to a project not being completed within a specified period.

A property that has been destroyed by fire can be a problem. The property improvements would have to meet present building codes. If the property had a septic system that must be replaced, the land must be large enough and meet percolation requirements to be buildable.

The value of the vacant land can be less than what it appears on the surface. There are other costs that take away from the land value. Improvement costs such as road construction, curbs, gutters, sidewalks, water lines, sewer lines, and power lines have the potential to devalue a property. There can be submerged or planned power lines with easements that prevent the use of a portion of the land. If the borrower states that an easement has been obtained to gain access to the land, it is best to verify that an easement has been obtained by reviewing a copy of the grant. The terms of the easement must also be reviewed to make sure there are no restrictions that would prevent the borrower's intended use. In the case where there isn't a sewer line connection available, a septic system with a drainage field would need to be installed. This would be at a significant cost, assuming the land is large enough, the septic system isn't near a portable water source, and meets the *peculation* requirement of the governing municipality. *Peculation* is the rate of water drainage into the surrounding ground and must meet a drainage rate as specified by the governing municipality. If the land does not peculate, a mound type septic drainage field would be required or a storage tank that requires periodic draining if permitted. In the case where a sewer line is available the connection must meet a specified downslope. If this isn't possible, a pumping system would have to be installed.

If the property was used as a service station or manufacturing site, there could be submerged storage tanks or contaminated soil. This condition not only will have to be removed at some point, but the extent of contamination can increase. The cost to correct the problem and the cost of the time required to do this will decrease the property value. If a storage tank was not tested for leakages recently or not changed to the latest required technology, a leak may have developed reducing the apparent property value. In order to sell property that was used as a commercial site, an environmental report is most often required by buyers. This cost usually must be borne by the seller.

There is another ingredient that can come into play. This is the change in value due to the land being defined as a wetland, finding of an endangered species, a location that is defined as a preserve, or ridgeline restrictions. The ridgeline restriction prevents building a structure that will exceed the ridgeline as viewed from a specified location. These can partially devalue the land due to its not being buildable or usable. To learn the status of the land would require extensive research with government offices. There will be those cases that a potential change isn't presently planned or the government agency will give incorrect information.

Interestingly, the land could be purchased as an offset by a builder and used as a green belt, allowing the builder to construct more improvements on another piece of land.

The other expense associated with vacant land would be the cost to dispose of the property. This could take anywhere from one to five years. The sales commission on land is also greater than improved property. Sale time can be reduced if the sales price is significantly reduced, assuming the vacant land is in a desirable location. This time aspect could convert into an expensive cost due to the lack of income from your nonperforming trust deed loan. If the hard-money loan is a junior loan and you own the property by way of a foreclosure, the expense can be greater due to the need to pay the senior lender to avoid his foreclosure.

When a loan is considered on vacant property, there are several other dangers that must be considered.

With vacant property, there is the danger that a scam artist will use the property as security for a Trust Deed. One of the reasons that he might select vacant property is that there is no one around to challenge the transaction. Counterfeit and forged documents can easily be prepared using present copying technology. The ownership can partially be verified by contacting the landowner of record. The owner's address can be located at the property tax counter of the County Recorder's Office.

The loan application should also contain details about the owner's background so there is enough information that can be verified to insure the applicant is who he claims to be. Although this paragraph addresses vacant land, the potential problem also applies to vacant improved property. This danger can be mitigated with proper title insurance.

The second danger is not having adequate liability insurance on the property. A vacant property that is under construction, in most cases, cannot be insured with a standard insurance company. Not all insurance companies will take on the additional risk. The specific dangers are unlawful entry with injury to the trespasser and vandalism.

When there is renovation or new construction taking place, a course-of-construction insurance policy can be obtained to provide liability protection and insure the work site. The cost will be at a much higher than a standard insurance policy.

Building Sequence

The process of building is complex. This is an understatement due to the permutations that can occur.

In the simplest terms, the sequence of building on a property is as follows:

- obtain a building permit and pay fees,
- obtain inspections during the various phases of construction,
- final inspection and obtain a certificate of occupancy.

In reality the details will vary depending upon the level of development the property has reached.

A lot could be the easiest to deal with but not necessarily so. There would still be many restrictions including: lot size, set backs from the street and property lines, in addition to some of the restrictions and requirements that apply to a large subdivision. In the case where utilities aren't available, soil percolation for septic system, location of water well relative to septic system, power line installation (inground or aboveground), requirements or restrictions on grading for drainage, building height, and location of butane or propane tanks must be dealt with.

Subdividing a parcel into four or less separate lots is the next level of difficulty. This process is controlled by the state's Subdivision Map Act.

The next level of difficulty would be subdividing property into five or more separate lots for the purpose of developing. (Sometimes a property owner will avoid the Subdivision Map Act restriction by dividing a parcel into four lots and then selling some of those lots to a strawman (temporary replacement buyer or borrower). The strawman would again divide his parcel into four more lots providing more than the four-lot restriction.)

The subdivision of property into five or more lots is regulated by the state Subdivision Map Act and the city and county regulations. Adhering to zoning regulations or obtaining a zoning change or a variance to existing zoning may also be required. Adding to the mix are the additional State and Federal restrictions, and requirements that would include but not be limited to:

- environment restrictions,
- Coastal Commission permits,
- wetlands restrictions,
- archaeological digs,
- bonds for offsite improvements,
- environmental impact reports,
- public hearings,
- conditions of approval to protect sensitive habitats, scenic areas, or other resources,
- compliance with the general plan, zoning requirements, and flood plain issues.

These processes may be the easiest compared to what can follow.

The next phase would be the submission of building plans to a planning department and other requirements to obtain utility service such as gas, electricity, water, and fire protection requirements. Planning departments are notorious for wanting changes and oftentimes require going back to the original plans, much like a dog chasing its tail. Following this would be the actual construction with inspections, traffic control, dust and pollution abatement, grading permits, rainwater control, and when necessary, a building demolition permit. The actual building would require the inspection of the:

- foundation,
- framing,
- roof,
- plumbing,
- electrical,
- lathe (wrapping of structure),
- insulation,
- drywall,
- heating and air conditioning systems,
- texture and paint,
- gas and water lines (for leaks),
- final fixture installation.

If the project reaches this stage with all of the requirement having been met, a certificate of occupancy can be obtained. This is the copy on the inspection report that is attached to the structure where the various inspections are noted.

In the case of subdivisions of five or more units, lots, condos, PUDS, leases, or timeshare projects, the Department of Real Estate must issue their preliminary subdivision public report (Pink Report, valid for one year) before reservations with refundable deposits can be taken. After the DRE gives their conditional subdivision public report (Yellow Report, valid for six or thirty months), sales (not closings) can take place. Only after the final subdivision public report (White Report, valid for five years) can final sales and closure occur. There are exceptions to the DRE public report requirements. The details can be viewed on the Web site www.dre.ca.gov.

Using due diligence to establish if the loan is sound can be a daunting task. The integrity of the mortgage broker therefore becomes most important in that they must use their expertise of construction phases and due diligence prior to offering the property to a lender. The only defense for the lender is to spot check any area of concern. Most important is checking the property status with the controlling agency (City or County Planning Commission) to establish the status of the property and the special requirements and restrictions that apply. Finding the agency's assigned project manager can be accomplished by asking at the front counter of the Planning Commission Agency's office. The project manager can provide details about the project's status. Although the file can be reviewed, this can be time consuming and difficult if you are not knowledgeable about requirements and restrictions that might be imposed on the project. The Planning Commission's location can usually be found in the telephone directory.

A borrower may indicate a property has been subdivided. This in itself doesn't necessarily tell the total story, due to the various stages that a project might have reached. Compounding the problem is the determination of the property's fair market value, something that even an MAI appraisal would have difficulty accurately determining. Adding to the mix is when the occupancy approval status will be reached and the property's market value at that time.

COMMERCIAL AND MULTI-RESIDENTIAL PROPERTY

An investment property such as a plant nursery, a grove, a strip mall, or multiuse residential real estate that is also used for business can have a high appraisal value. This appraised value would be based upon its income-generating capability. The appraisal does not always represent the intrinsic value after the tenants and business are stripped away. On income property, the vacancies and rents can be illusionary in many ways. Unfortunately there are property owners that can puff the property value. This can be done by overstating the rent income, the number of legal units and the actual occupancy. An investigation may be required to learn if the renters are real, friends, or in-laws that have overstated the amount of rent that is being paid. There is also the potential that the actual rent paid is discounted to retain tenants. A mailbox count may sometimes help in determining the true occupancy. Deceptive owners could insert phony names in the mail slots to imply that the unit is rented. Interviewing tenants also may help in determining if the claimed rent schedule is not overstated. A rent survey would be required to find if the rent claimed is similar to the area *economic rent. Economic rent* is the amount of rent money that similar properties in the area are receiving. Complicating the landscape are those communities that have imposed rent control, where rent increases can only occur under strict regulations. This can happen when there are more residential renters than available residential units in the community.

Security deposits are part of the property assets. When the property is in a foreclosure or the owner files a bankruptcy, don't make any plans to receive the deposits from the owner for return to the tenants. Deposits can disappear very fast. The tenants will still want their money as a cash refund or some rent reduction compensation. Additionally a business now occupying the property may move due to the uncertainty, leaving only vacancies and unpaid rent.

The value of a nursery or grove can be lost by an increase in the cost of water, a killing frost, the owner's neglect in not watering plants, or by just removing the plants from the property. If there is a moving sale advertisement that says "Bring your shovel," you can almost make book that there will be an unhappy investor in the future.

Other properties might have a business associated with the property use. For instance, if the property is a horse ranch, many of the facilities could be considered tools of the trade. Even if the sheds, corrals, training structure and feeders are bolted and cemented to the ground, in the event of a foreclosure, they could disappear.

Part of the value of property can be changed by the date of a lease. When the lease exists prior to the hard-money loan and has been recorded or acknowledged by the hard-money lender, it will continue to exist after a foreclosure. When the lease is generated after a hard-money loan, its status will depend on the actions of the hard-money lender. If the hard-money lender acknowledges the lease, the lease can continue even after a foreclosure.

The details of the lease will also affect the property value depending upon the terms. If the lease terms are very favorable to the tenant, this can reduce the property value. One of the significant terms of a lease would be if there were a triple net clause (NNN). This clause refers to the tenant paying for the taxes, insurance, utilities, and maintenance of the property. A lease with a NNN clause is therefore more valuable to the owner due to the rental income not having to pay for these items. There will be some leases that provide for only a portion of the triple net cost. If the owner is paying the utilities and the cost of electricity, gas, or water increases, the value of the property will be reduced unless there is a clause in the lease that the rent would increase in this event. A review of the lease is required to determine its status. Leases are not only covered by case law but more significantly by California Civil Code. When a property that is being considered has a lease, a lawyer with experience in leases might be contacted to help evaluate your exposure.

To assist in determining the LTV of residential rental income property, the appraisal should include comparable sales in similar areas to determine a reasonable true market value. This is often difficult to obtain due too few available recent similar sales when the property is high priced. Often an income method appraisal will have to be relied on. There are two methods of determining income property value: indicated gross rent value and capitalization rate value. Capitalization rate is often referred to as a CAP rate.

Indicated gross rent value is equal to the gross rent income times a gross rent multiplier. The gross rent multiplier is either a monthly or a yearly number. The number can be 100 for a monthly rent multiplier or 10 for a yearly rent multiplier. If the property has a gross monthly income of

$2,000, the indicated property value would be $200,000. The number of 100 monthly or 10 yearly will vary and can be determined from comparable income property. This value can be misleading due to not knowing:

- the number of rental units that are illegal,
- the number of vacancies that are reported with rent income,
- the amount of deferred maintenance,
- the actual maintenance and operating cost.

Capitalization rate is equal to the net operating income divided by the property value times 100. This can be calculated using a monthly or yearly income. As with the gross rent multiplier indicated value above, the desired capitalization rate can be determined using comparable income property. The capitalization rate is more realistic due to taking operating costs into consideration. There is still the question of the number of legal units, real rent, and deferred maintenance.

The final property value can be gleaned from the gross rent multiplier or preferably the capitalization rate. Oftentimes the property value can be increased by adding improvements and then increasing the rents. Waiting for normal appreciation over time can be unpredictable due to not having a crystal ball.

LEASEHOLD

A leasehold interest has many aspects. The primary security is the lease itself and not the land. Ownership of land sometimes is with a municipality. This type of interest can have many turns and unpredictable events due to approvals and restrictions that may be imposed by the governing body. When an individual or trust owns the land, law and case law most times can be relied upon.

The terms of the leasehold and other factors that should be considered are:

- length of the land lease,

- renewability of the land lease after its expiration and potential new lease terms,

- disposition of improvements at the end of the lease,

- conditions that are imposed on use of the land such as maintenance, changes, and additions,

- use of improvements such as condo project, hotel, restaurant, boat facilities, parking facilities, or entertainment facilities,

- the amount of income that is being generated, length of lease agreements with tenants, type of business that occupies the property, and success of the tenant's business,

- payment of rent and priority of these payments, i.e., who gets paid first,

- escalation terms on the rent that must be paid and how often changes can be made. This can be tied to various cost of living indexes.

When a loan is being considered on a leasehold, the terms of the lease are extremely important. Any term that increases the income production and preserves its relative value in a varying economy will increase the security value.

A personal guarantee from the owner of the leasehold is important if they have other assets. Their past performance with regard to bankruptcy and foreclosure is extremely important. There is no guarantee that past performance will provide protection but is an indicator of future behavior.

The real security in a leasehold, although the land lease has value, is the income-producing capability of the property. It is not only this income, but also the leasehold owner's past performance that enters into the mix. A personal guarantee for the loan by the borrower is desirable. The value can be questionable if a bankruptcy is later filed or the borrower cannot be located to file a suit.

CONSTRUCTION LOANS

Construction loans require special attention. There is often the need to control the loaned funds through an escrow account. These funds should not be released until a defined portion of the work is completed. This would include foundation, framing, dry walling, stucco, plumbing, electrical, flooring, painting, appliance installation, landscaping, and cabinet installation. There should be provisions that the payment for the labor and the materials used on the construction site goes to the correct supplier or contractor, and when appropriate, a construction lien release issued.

When this type of loan is being considered, the property must be free from any construction work for a minimum of ninety days. This is to insure that any previous work does not become a prior mechanic or material lien. The prior construction lien could take precedence over a new loan. If there were a recorded construction lien, this would be in effect unless there has been a release. If there is any question, a title insurance mechanic lien endorsement should be obtained.

A complete set of approved working prints or plans should be obtained. If there are any special *use conditions*[1] imposed by the local government on the project, the details should be obtained as part of the agreement to lend. This will ease the problem of the lender to complete the project in the event the property is acquired through foreclosure. Although project prints may be available at the City or County Planning Department, they may not be a complete set of working prints.

If the contractor has been selected to do the construction, a determination should be made that he has a valid state contractor's license. Due to the practice of some contractors borrowing a contractor's license, verification should be made that the actual work will be performed by the

---

[1] *Use conditions* are additional requirements imposed by municipalities to proceed with a project.

licensed contractor and subcontractors. This will help insure that the work will be performed in a workmanlike fashion.

The contractor should be licensed for the type of work to be performed. A licensed contractor is more likely to perform adequately to avoid loss of his license. If more than three types of licenses will be required, a licensed general building contractor should be used. There are approximately forty-three types of specialty contractor licenses, so it would be easy to confuse the uninformed. The contractor should be bonded, or an adequate cash deposit for the project should be placed in an escrow account. Although it should not affect your lien position, the contractor should have workers' compensation insurance. The property must also have the appropriate fire or course-of-construction insurance to protect your interest.

The method of verifying a contractor's state license status is to contact the Contractor's State License Board at (800) 321-2752 or (800) 432-7979 in California. By requesting a copy of the contractor's license, your evaluating time can be shortened. If there is any resistance in complying with the request, this is not a loan for you.

The license status can also be checked on the California Contractors' State Licensing Board Web site at www.cslb.ca.gov.

Checking recent projects of the contractor and impacted principals can also be done to determine if the work was satisfactory and completed in a timely manner.

The loan amount should not exceed the property's present value. The borrower must have something of value in the project. This could be the land, improvement, or significant money for the project to cover part of the construction and debt service. If this is not the case, the borrower is only obtaining your money to make money. It is a method of being hired to do a job. This being hired to do a job is common in refurbishment projects. Typically the contractor tries to purchase a property without using any of his money. In these cases you are a speculator, not an investor. Often it is possible to obtain a loan guarantee from the mortgage broker to purchase the property from you, or reimburse you for any loss. The logic of the mortgage broker giving such a guarantee is his not being afraid of owning the property (project).

When dealing with a contractor, there are special concerns. This not only includes the contractor's past performance in completing a project, but the economy (how fast will the project sell) and number of projects the builder is working on. In the last case, there is always the danger the contractor will move material and labor to one of his other projects. Only by doing a minute-by-minute monitoring of the project, something that can't economically be done, can you be certain the contractor isn't doing you.

One of the other deceptions that a contractor might do is form a corporation or company with a name such as Builder's Material, Inc. The contractor will purchase all of his material from this corporation. The corporation will purchase its material from a legitimate builder supply house, mark the price up, sell it to the contractor, and pocket the difference. Only by checking all invoices and knowing material cost can this deception be averted. There are other deceptions that the contractor can use. He can ask for a discount from a legitimate building supply house, with the discount being paid into his personal account. Building supply houses might do this in order to win a contract over competing supply houses. These deceptions can become a problem if the contractor defaults on your loan, with you ending up with the property less the siphoned money. If the contractor is doing work under a corporation or company name, there will be a responsible managing employee (RME). If the contractor is working as a partnership or sole proprietor, there will be a responsible managing officer (RMO).

An indication of the diversion of funding can be suspected when a project is significantly behind schedule.

MOVE-ON CONSTRUCTION LOANS

A move-on construction loan is often required when a building is to be moved. The move can be a few feet to many miles.

When a house, apartment or other type of building is to be moved to a new site, your loan examination is compounded over a construction loan. All of the concerns of a construction loan are present. There are the potential problems of liens, permits, construction liens, title insurance, property insurance, and other potential damage to the building being moved, other property, workmen, and bystanders.

The liens can be on the new site, the improvement that is being moved, and any legal actions, past or present. Permits will be required for the construction aspect such as lifting up the building, moving over roads, highways, other properties, and lifting power lines. City or county permits for placing the building on the new site must be obtained. The building must meet the building codes and aesthetic requirements of the new neighborhood.

If the building is to be moved over property not owned, the government agency that has jurisdiction and private owners must give permission for the building to trespass. Any utility such as a power company must give permission to allow their power lines to be moved or touched. Associated with these permits will be bonds or insurance to cover any potential damage.

A construction loan must be covered by obtaining additional title insurance due to potential intervening construction liens.

When a building is being moved, there are enormous risks due to the many unknowns. A company that has years of experience and success with the type of building being moved should only be considered.

A detailed plan for the project, when a move-on loan is being considered, will help mitigate the dangers. However, you can still be exposed to unknown problems. Insurance and bonding are a must when contemplating this type of loan.

Finally, unless your mortgage broker has knowledge about this type of loan, you are better advised to let someone else gain the experience.

PROPERTY USAGE

A SFR property should ideally be single use in determining market value. If the SFR property is on a commercially zoned lot or a lot that can have its zoning changed, the appraisal might be higher than what can be realized in a quick sale. Appraisals on single use property are usually straightforward. Properties such as a horse ranch, an orchard, a motel, or a boarding house can often be considered multiuse. The value of the property can very often include the real estate plus the business. The reason for being concerned about lending on a business is that the business can go bad very fast, reducing the value. There is also the potential problem that when lending on property that contains a business, part of the loan could be construed as a loan on the business, an unsecured loan. If the borrower files a bankruptcy, the portion attributed to the business could be treated as an unsecured loan. This would present a real problem because of potential loan *cram down* by a bankruptcy judge. A *cram down* is when the judge divides any debtor's assets between creditors. In the event of a foreclosure, the borrower could move the business with inventory and business equipment to a different location, thereby destroying the business portion of the loaned property.

If for some reason a loan is being considered on a property that includes a business, special precautions should be taken. The property equity should take into account the cost of hiring special management to operate the business. It is recommended to lend only on property with a business that is understood due to the possibility of owning it in the future.

The appraisal on other businesses indicated above, might include some of the fixtures. In the case of an orchard, the trees have a given value. This value can evaporate very fast if there is a foreclosure, a heavy frost, or if the owner decides to do heavy trimming.

PERSONAL PROPERTY

The property that is used for security normally should be real estate. If personal property is used in the appraisal, there are the problems of:

- the personal property can disappear, or
- the personal property can be used up or depreciated at a fast rate.

If the personal property is included with the real estate, it may inflate the appraisal. There is the additional danger that the personal property will be given to the owner or other creditors if a bankruptcy is filed, or the personal property may disappear during a foreclosure.

The items that can be considered as personal property are stoves, refrigerators, dishwashers, trash compactors, garage door openers, solar heating systems, portable barns, semiportable barns, horse exercise equipment, feed bins, watering troughs, drapes, carpets, machinery, trade equipment, well water pumps, storage tanks, and irrigation equipment.

When personal property is to become part of the security, a special provision must be included in the Trust Deed. This provision is intended to encumber the personal property. This is done with a fixture-filing clause. An attorney should be used to properly generate the encumbrances.

Section 5

LOAN SECURITY

The security of a loan can be broken up into several elements. These elements consist of property value, borrower characteristics, loan terms, and Trust Deed Note ownership.

Property value is discussed in "Type of Property," "Market Value," "Trust Deed Investment Criteria," and "Loan-to-Value," Sections 4, 6, 7, and 10, respectively. The borrower characteristics are discussed in "Borrower Profile," Section 8. The loan terms are discussed in "Loans" and "Trust Deed Purchase, Sale and Resale," Sections 9 and 13. Trust Deed Note ownership is discussed in this chapter and in "Ownership Title," Section 12.

Figure 5. *Can I take off the ball and chain at night?*

There is another area of concern, when lending on property—the dynamics of the economy.

Equity in property or security of a Trust Deed can at times be delusory due to the real estate security's change in value. This can be due to obsolescence, rezoning, change in taxation, deflation, economic hard times, government designation as a wetland or protected area, property waste in foreclosure, new assessment area, redevelopment area with all structures removed, or an area becoming blighted. These are often unknowns in determining value in a changing economy.

When single-family residences are selling well, properties with a poor location will also sell reasonably well. These properties would be ones located very close to a busy street, below street level, remotely located, located on a long dirt road, in a fire zone, or with hodgepodge construction. Condos will sell well in good times, but they will be difficult to sell in a slow economy. When there is a slowing or a slow economy, industrial properties can have a difficult time selling or may require a very long marketing time.

The economy of today is very different from just a few years ago. It is changing and will continue to change. Not paying attention to the ever-changing times and modifying the form and method of investment can be costly. In order to be successful, all the economic events and borrowers' craftiness that will be encountered must be foreseen. Without a comprehensive analysis, bad judgment will follow.

In contemplating an investment in a Trust Deed, a determination must be made. Can more be lost than gained? Loss can be caused by fire where the fire insurance was not adequate, loss of interest not paid, loss because of a lawsuit by the borrower, loss because of the reduction in property equity due to deflation, depreciation or obsolescence, expenses incurred, waste of the property by the borrower during a foreclosure, and expense of a bankruptcy.

This loss would be the total amount of your loan plus the interest that could be obtained from a secure government-guaranteed bank deposit.

The loss of your loan can be caused by the sale of the property by a senior lender where there is not an overbid at their foreclosure sale to cover your trust deed value.

The loss or partial loss of your loan can be caused by economic conditions, especially when you are in a junior position and the equity covering your loaned amount is wiped out by property value deflation and other costs.

A total loss or a partial loss can be caused by fraud when there is inadequate title insurance. This loss could be increased by legal fees in an attempt to recoup your loss.

A partial loss of your loan could be caused by your need for cash and the voluntary forced sale of your Trust Deed to a third party at a discount. This might occur when a Trust Deed must be sold fast to obtain money for an emergency and the property equity is questionable. As an alternate, if money is needed for a short term, the trust deed interest stream can be sold separately from the Trust Deed Note. This is similar to hypothecation and not unlike pawning something of value. This can be complicated, and reclaiming the Trust Deed Note income stream back can be a long drawn out process if you are not dealing with an ethical person.

When a property is in foreclosure, the value of a Trust Deed Note is reduced. If there is a bankruptcy involved, the value could be further reduced. This is best illustrated by the question, "Which of these three $100,000 Trust Deeds would you purchase first for the same price?"A Trust Deed in foreclosure, one in bankruptcy or one that the borrower is making on-time payments. If you selected one in bankruptcy, I have a bridge that I would like to sell to you. When the protective equity is reduced for any reason such as late payments, legal action by others against the trust deed security, the trust deed value is reduced. Buyers will only pay what the Trust Deed is worth. This defined value of a Trust Deed Note in the open market is called market value.

When the number of buyers for a Trust Deed is significantly reduced, the resulting market price will be reduced. This is caused by the economics of supply and demand. It will always come into play with problem Trust Deeds.

When there is a foreclosure, the investment will not be paying out any interest during the foreclosure period. However if properly stated in the Trust Deed Note and permitted by law, jump rate interest can be charged. This interest can be collected if the note payments are brought up to date or added to the credit bid in a foreclosure sale. (See Chapter 15 for definition of credit bid.)

An evaluation of a real estate investment should be made to decide the real return. The evaluation would take into account present and future inflation, time value of money and your tax bracket. Only a complete analysis will show the real return in terms of the purchasing power of the trust deed income.

As part of the evaluation, an *internal rate of return*[1] calculation should be made on an investment. This is important when there is an investment return with a variable cash flow. A variable cash flow can too often disguise the real return. Knowing the internal rate of return on an investment can provide information so an investment with a higher rate of return can be selected. Investors may select a lower return Trust Deed because they do not know how to do the calculation. If points are received, if there is pre-paid interest, or a Trust Deed is discounted—the rate of return is increased. If a personal computer is not available with business software, a business calculator is the second best thing to find the internal rate of return on an investment.

There will be times when a Trust Deed does not have reasonable security or the interest rate is inadequate. Reconfiguration of the Trust Deed Note will often correct this problem. Restructuring the loan by increasing the number of points paid up front or adding other property as security can furnish a satisfactory return with an acceptably secure loan, instead of having a marginally unsafe loan.

---

[1] *Internal rate of return* is the annualized return on an investment when there are variable payments. A mathematical iteration process is required to provide this rate of return or profit on an investment. As an illustration, when a conventional loan interest rate is expressed as annualized rate, this rate is higher than the monthly interest rate quoted. This is due to the monthly payments providing the bank with a higher return using an internal rate of return. The bank has the monthly payments that can earn interest, whereas if only one total payment were made at the end of the loan period, they could earn interest on the interest only after it is received. The bank's return would therefore be less.

Often the borrower will give a personal guarantee for the loan. This can make sense if the borrower has other assets. The other assets can be stocks, bonds, bank accounts, inheritance, trusts, real estate, or other forms of collateral. In the case of real estate, pledging a property does not necessarily provide usable equity for a guarantee if the property is already fully encumbered. There is also the potential that the personal guarantee has been previously assigned to others so you are in the last position. Only by doing a title search (discussed later), looking for other lien guarantee's interest in the equity, and recording your guarantee lien can you assure yourself of a true guarantee. Another danger is the borrower could sell the asset, leaving you with a worthless guarantee if a lien is not recorded. It would be difficult for the borrower to find a buyer that would purchase the property with a recorded lien unless the price is right. Your lien would still provide you protection even when a property is sold. These guarantee liens typically are junior Trust Deeds and remain with the property with the change of ownership.

Inflation can also impact the purchasing power (value) of the amount of money loaned. This impact can only be adjusted by receiving a higher interest rate to compensate for the loss of purchasing power of the money loaned and the interest money received.

In the event there is an existing or an anticipated high inflation rate, a higher interest rate should be charged. A variable interest rate that is indexed to a government rate might also be considered. Unfortunately the government's reported inflation rate does not contain all the factors of inflation. Excluded from the government's inflation numbers (Consumer Price Index, CPI) are state taxes, local taxes, insurance premiums, and college tuition. This will cause the reported numbers to be understated. The higher inflation rate is claimed by several economists. The real determination of inflation for you is the cost of products and services that you normally purchase. There is some foretelling to the eventual CPI that can be gleaned from the Producer Price Index (PPI). The PPI is the index of manufacturers' cost. There have been studies that show that in order to preserve the purchasing power of your savings, a return of 4 to 20 percent or higher is required depending on inflation and your tax bracket.

The standard perception is that money is loaned on equity of real estate for the interest payment or some form of compensation. On the surface, this is true.

There is a different concept that should be applied in hard-money lending. When the person that owns or controls property borrows money, he receives something in return for his equity, loaned money. When a loan is made, the owner's equity is reduced by the loan amount plus the amount of the interest to be paid over the life of the loan. The interest can and usually is replaced by the borrower with other earned income. This payment of interest from other earned income gives the impression that there is no reduction in equity value due to the interest payments.

Using this idea, when lending money against property, care must be taken that there is enough equity above the loan amount. This cushion is to take into account the interest that is to be received on the loan. Fortunately in most cases, if the borrower does not make payments, a foreclosure can usually be completed before the interest, and foreclosure expense becomes too large. This is one of the reasons, when payments are not made promptly, to proceed with a foreclosure without delay. Typically, no longer than two months of delinquent payments. If there are other violations of the Trust Deed Note, the time to foreclose might be reduced to a shorter time period. Some of these violations are nonpayment of taxes or property insurance. A violation that requires an immediate foreclosure would be waste of the property.

Economic conditions that affect your loan value cannot be controlled most of the time. You can control its effect by not lending in an area having massive layoffs. Knowing that the economy is slow or will slow down, you should invest only on property with more than an adequate LTV.

Depreciation of a building and its improvements is a given. This depreciation consists of functional depreciation, waste, and wear and tear. Functional depreciation is caused by changes in the economy or the public's use of the improvement. An example would be a shopping mall where a newer shopping mall has opened or the parking lot's location is not to the public's liking. The functional depreciation might be corrected but at a significant cost. There is a waste part of depreciation that can be caused by the borrower. This can only be controlled to a limited extent. Some of this control is discussed later in this book. Wear and tear usually can be corrected by refurbishment. The cost is not as significant as the cost to correct functional depreciation. Usually paint and plaster will do the trick for wear and tear. Functional changes will require parking facility changes, internal structure changes, or even a new building facade.

Lending on rental SFR has some advantage. Renters do not have the emotional attachment as property owners and are not as prone to inflict damage to a property in a foreclosure. There is also the usual poorer condition of a rental. The property does not have pride-of-ownership appearance. What you see is what you potentially could own. It is interesting to note that standard lenders charge higher interest rates, require a smaller LTV, or dictate a variable rate loan on rentals. This is their choice, but I lean toward rentals for trust deed loans for the reasons given above. There is the other advantage of rentals. This is the avoidance of Section 32, the high interest rate restriction laws that will be discussed later.

CROSS-COLLATERALIZED LOANS

A cross-collateralized loan is sometimes called a *blanket mortgage*. The *blanket mortgage* will include *all* securing properties. There is a special problem with cross-collateralized property. When a statutory foreclosure is filed, it would require the foreclosure on all of the properties to recover the loaned amount. There would, of course, after acquiring the property, be the associated selling cost of each of the properties. If only one of the secured properties is foreclosed on, a subsequent foreclosure could not be filed on the other properties under the blanket Trust Deed. This is the *single action* rule established by case law. The *single action* rule states that when legal action is taken to obtain only one of the securing properties, subsequent legal actions cannot be taken. This concept of single action would also apply in a judicial foreclosure.

When setting the credit bid for a foreclosure sale, the lender must be certain to set the credit bid for all of the properties (and not just one property). If the credit bid is defined for one property and it satisfies the loan, only one property could be foreclosed.

When there are several properties, there is a statutory requirement on the property to be disposed of first. An attorney should be contacted to provide guidance.

Usually there is no reason to cross-collateralize a loan if the borrower has a property with an adequate LTV. However, there may be times that it is desirable to accept other properties as security for a loan. With several properties securing the loan, the borrower would be more motivated to perform on the loan. As can be easily seen, cross-collateralizing a loan will complicate the foreclosure procedure. (It should be noted that diversification of investment money, discussed earlier, does not mean using two or more properties as collateral.)

Part of the problem with cross-collateralizing a loan is the complexity of selling several properties with the associated sale cost. Just because the total amount of collateral is large, the amount remaining after a foreclosure and sale of several properties can be small due to the total cost to sell. Remember that time to sell is one of the larger elements of the cost. Property taxes will also have to be paid (unless late payment penalties are tolerable). Income tax deduction could become complicated because of the different year that the expenses are incurred and the year that the cost can be deducted. If there are senior loans, these may have to be kept current to prevent their foreclosing and shutting you out.

With multiple properties, the headaches can become burdensome. If the loan must be made using several properties, adjustment might be made to the amount of interest that is charged. Alternately the amount of the loan might be reduced so only one property is encumbered or individual Trust Deeds on each property imposed.

The property owner (borrower), when several properties must be used for a loan, has put himself in a very adventurous position. His house of cards could start to topple.

FRACTIONALIZED TRUST DEED

There are a number of mortgage brokers that will put several investors into one trust deed investment. This usually is because the loan is too large and there isn't one investor available with adequate cash. Don't be deceived that because another investor is willing to lend money, it must be a good investment. You can easily fall into the trap of believing there is loan security because there are others that are willing to invest in the property. You must select the investment property very carefully on your own. There is no additional security when there are others around and the boat is sinking. Being part of a fractionalized (fragmented) trust deed loan however can be a satisfying method of investing.

The Business and Professional Code 10229(g) establishes the LTV[2] of the fractionalized Trust Deed. They are:

- 80% for single-family residence, owner-occupied,
- 75% for single-family residence, non-owner occupied,
- 65% for commercial and income producing properties,
- 65% for single-family residential zoned lots or parcels with offsite improvements as required by municipal jurisdiction,
- 50% for land that is zoned (as required) for commercial or residential development, and
- 35% of other real property.

---

[2] There can be a potential problem with the LTV if the appraisal is established by a broker or appraiser who is not a Member of the Appraisal Institute (MAI). Having the MAI designation provides some confidence that the appraiser has expertise to provide an accurate LTV.

One of the protections you should insist upon in a fractionalized Trust Deed is not to allow the Trust Deed Note to be subordinated. The Trust Deed that includes your name should also be recorded.

With a fractionalized loan, there is the problem of disposing of the property if acquired in a foreclosure. There are fewer property buyers that are able to buy higher priced properties. This may make for a long ownership period with the associated carrying cost. Obtaining agreement on refinancing, subordination to a new loan, and other decisions can become a quagmire.

There are brokers that sell fractionalized Trust Deeds as a normal part of their mortgage business. The number of investors in a fractionalized Trust Deed is limited to ten when the broker is controlled by the Department of Real Estate. One of the games a broker might do on large loans is to put an additional ten more lenders in a junior position. If the fractionalized investment that you are considering is a junior loan, it is important to review senior Trust Deed Note documents to determine if the senior loan has already been fractionalized. When there is adequate equity, this could still be an acceptable loan, providing the rate of return compensates for any additional vulnerability.

The mortgage broker or a loan servicing company will charge for disbursement of interest and principal payments from a loan. A $5 to $15 fee per check is reasonable depending on the amount of work they perform. Occasionally this servicing fee can be a fixed amount and also a small percentage of the payment. This could make the service fee very large and out of proportion to the work required if the interest payments and final payoff are large.

Occasionally a Trust Deed and agreement could constitute a security transaction. If it is a security transaction, the broker must obtain a separate securities license. The number of people in a security arrangement is limited to thirty-five investors. This would, under a security agreement, prevent investors from making any decisions on the handling of the Trust Deeds.

There are other investment configurations that will be discussed later.

There are dangers in this form of investing. When interest on loans is being paid (performing loans), there isn't too much danger, except if the brokerage company is dishonest or the real estate values are declining. To help in keeping the brokerage company honest, payments from the borrower should be paid directly into an escrow trust account and then disbursed directly to the investors. Even if the payments aren't received, when there is adequate equity, the interest will eventually be received. This makes the loan effectively performing.

The danger can become real when loans do not perform. Money will possibly have to be added by you. This money could be used to:

- file a foreclosure,
- pay attorney fees to get the property out of bankruptcy,
- pay attorney fees for the collection of rent,
- court filing,
- pay for fire insurance on the property (if the property is not covered),
- make payments on senior encumbrances to prevent senior lenders foreclosing,
- possible refinancing cost on senior loan encumbrances,
- early payoff fees on any senior loans,
- pay for security of the property,
- management fees that the mortgage broker probably has put into the contract,
- cost to prepare the property for sale in the event the group ends up owning the property—if the property is newly constructed, a 10-year warranty insurance policy may have to be purchased at a premium of 3 percent.

If a foreclosure is necessary, there will be a foreclosure credit bid amount. This will consist of the trust deed principal, accrued interest, late fees, foreclosure cost, and other incidental costs. The computation is similar to a beneficiary demand (discussed later) calculation, except for the additional foreclosure company's cost. There may be additional foreclosure costs that will have to be paid up front to the foreclosure company. Some foreclosure companies require payments during the foreclosure period to cover their out of pocket expenses such as title insurance, advertising cost, fees, and other incidental costs. In the event the group owns the property after an auction, the foreclosure company will demand total payment of its costs. In a fractionalized Trust Deed, each investor's cost will be based upon his percentage ownership of the Trust Deed.

In the event the credit bid becomes the highest bid at the foreclosure sale, the balance of the foreclosure company's costs must be paid in order to obtain title to the property. The method that the foreclosure companies use to ensure that they are paid is to delay completing the trustee's Deed and recording until they receive their payment.

It should be remembered that in a foreclosure, many borrowers would have siphoned a percentage of the equity out of the property before possession can be obtained. This lost equity would be caused by nonpayment of interest, lost security deposits, lost rent, stolen building material, vandalism, deferred maintenance, taxes, and insurance.

Bidders at foreclosure sales are looking for a bargain so they can make a profit. They will usually bid less than the market value, unless there is additional value to a specific bidder. Some reasons for this are that the bidder may need the property to enlarge a business, to add a parking area, or to gain access to other properties. This would be an opportunity for you, the lender, to dispose of the property. This might happen at a discounted price, but it may still be acceptable just to get rid of the headache. In order to accomplish this at a foreclosure sale, the credit bid should be set at a price to promote the sale to the bidders at the auction. Remember that any agreement that affects the bidding prior to or during the auction is not permissible (Civil Code 2924h). To do so would be *chilling the sale. Chilling the sale* would be any action that inhibits, restrains, or induces potential buyers not to bid normally at the auction.

In the event bidders at the sale do not bid above your credit bid, your credit bid will be the final sale price. There is no reason that would prevent you from offering the property to an unsuccessful bidder at a price lower than the credit bid after the sale has been completed. This has the advantage that tenant eviction, fix up, and sales commission cost can be avoided.

In the case of a fractionalized Trust Deed, a foreclosure may not be easy unless the majority of the lenders of the fractionalized Trust Deed agree on the credit bid. The actions that can happen may depend on the relationship of these co-beneficiaries. The foreclosure trustee in fact may not even start a foreclosure until a majority of the lenders are in agreement or one of the co-beneficiaries proceeds on his own. There is a provision in case law, (*Perkins v. Chad Development Corp. [1979] 95 CA3d 645*), that allows a partial owner of a fractionalized Trust Deed to foreclose individually. This partial owner would be obligated to the other owners for their interest in the Trust Deed. This can be done after the foreclosure or disposal of the property. Co-beneficiaries who held interest in the Trust Deed are entitled to an accounting of all profits. [California Corporations Code §15021 and Civil Code 2924].

There are other requirements that the mortgage broker must abide by. Civil Code 2941.9 describes them in detail. The most important of these requirements described by the civil code is also required by the Business and Professions Code Section 10232.5. It states that the authorizing agreement shall be recorded in the Office of the County Recorder of the county where the property is located and shall be included in a recorded document such as the deed of trust or the assignment of interests. The title insurance policy should also include the names of the fractionalized owners.

The status of co-beneficiaries becomes additionally murky, when there is a judicial foreclosure, deed-in-lieu of foreclosure, and substitution of trustee. If this is the case, an attorney should be contacted to clarify the situation.

When investing in a fractionalized Trust Deed, the mortgage broker that is putting the deal together should be highly recommended and have a proven record of honest and total disclosures.

It is highly recommended to control your destiny by being the sole owner of the Trust Deed or have a majority interest. In this way, you can be the primary decision maker based on your interests. For married couples, there is a potential for disagreement on how a foreclosure is to be handled. A marriage should be strong to endure the frustrations that can occur in a foreclosure and the work necessary for preparing a house for resale. Cleaning up someone else's filth isn't fun.

MORTGAGE-BROKER-COMMISSION TRUST DEED

There is another trust deed investing scenario that can occur. This is when the mortgage broker takes his loan commission in the form of a Trust Deed. This in-lieu-of-commission Trust Deed usually is due to the transaction not having enough property equity or cash to make the deal work. He probably looks at it as a venture where he has nothing to lose but some of his time. This Trust Deed should be a separate junior Trust Deed. There will be times where the mortgage broker will sneak it into your Trust Deed. He is trying to ride your coattail. If a foreclosure is required, he only has to sit back and wait for his money.

If the mortgage broker refuses to write the Trust Deed as two separate Trust Deeds, it is important that an agreement be generated and signed. The agreement should state that the mortgage broker position is junior to your position, and that you will receive your interest, penalties, costs, and principal first before he can receive any of his money. This agreement also should include an option to purchase their Trust Deed as well as the mortgage broker having to pay, up front, their portion of any cost associated with foreclosure and bankruptcy.

Mortgage brokers will use the argument that they will be taking a junior Trust Deed to point out that your senior Trust Deed is better secured. This is only the case if they are putting their own real money into the loan as an investment and there is still adequate equity above their junior position.

After the disposition of the property, if the mortgage broker refuses to abide by the agreement after written notification, an indication to him that a call to the Department of Real Estate is planned should get all the cooperation that will be required.

A mortgage broker's real participation as an investor can be an indication that the loan is a good one. In these cases, the mortgage broker's junior Trust Deed does truly provide additional protection. In the event there is a default, the broker would be the first to be hurt and therefore will take immediate action to protect his Trust Deed. His actions, thereby, will protect your senior position.

Mortgage brokers that invest their own funds can still be deceptive. Frequently a mortgage broker will fund a loan and later sell his investment to another hard-money lender. There is very little that you can do in this case. The past performance of a mortgage broker is the only evidence of the ethical behavior of the mortgage broker. Not all unethical mortgage brokers' bad behavior is reported to the Department of Real Estate, so recommendations from others are important.

There is an innovative method that a few mortgage brokers use to induce a trust deed lender to purchase a Trust Deed. Instead of talking about a LTV, they will talk about the amount of equity security. This amount may appear large, but property with a high market value requires a large equity for adequate protection. For example, on a property with a $400,000 market value, the mortgage broker will talk about a security of $60,000. This however, is only a 85% LTV. This $60,000 can be quickly eaten up by payments on senior loans, insurance, foreclosure costs, and drop in market value. There could also be lawyer fees if the borrower goes into bankruptcy. Property security is best evaluated as a percentage of the property market value using LTV.

HYPOTHECATED LOANS

Money can be borrowed against a Trust Deed Note by hypothecation. This is done when the lender (owner) of a Trust Deed Note wants to borrow money on all or a portion of his Trust Deed Note ownership. This is similar but not the same as selling the income stream from the Trust Deed Note.

The rationale for the Trust Deed Note owner to do this is to avoid a loss that would result when a long-term Trust Deed or a low interest rate loan is sold at a discounted market price. The discount for low interest or long-term loans is usually very large. By hypothecating the loan, the loss from selling the discounted note can be avoided. There will still be the short-term loss of the income stream, but this will not be as large as selling the note at a large loss. Additionally the note may want to be retained because of its desirability or other reasons.

The story begins on a bright warm, spring day when there was a gentle breeze and the birds were chirping. All was well with the world.

An acquaintance of mine, I'll call him Bob, purchased a Trust Deed Note from Jim using a method called hypothecating. This type of loan is used in hard-money circles where money is loaned on a Trust Deed. The new lender owns the Trust Deed for a period of time and any interest that is earned (but not necessarily paid). The Trust Deed is then returned to the original owner after an agreed period of time after the payment of loaned money plus any unpaid interest. This is similar to a pawnshop loan where a valuable is left with the pawnbroker in exchange for money.

The terms of the loan were very favorable, 18 percent with two points and four months prepaid interest for a loan term of one year. The interest from the first Trust Deed would be paid directly to my friend Bob. After four months, when the next payment became due and was not made, Bob started a foreclosure. An auction sale was held and the original owner of the Trust Deed, Jim bought the property at the foreclosure sale. This wiped out the second and third trust deed owners.

As Bob told me later, Jim didn't want to foreclose on the property due to the second and third trust deed holders being very good friends. In fact Jim had induced his friends to buy the second and third Trust Deeds. In this way he got Bob to do the dirty work and Jim ended up with the property for a very low price. Jim's friends didn't even know what had happened.

Really good friends are hard to find when money is involved.

Purchasing a hypothecated loan can be an acceptable method of investing money provided the property has a good LTV, the return is sufficient, and there is sufficient documentation protection.

There are several methods used in acquiring the benefits of a Trust Deed Note. One is to make the loan on the Trust Deed Note income stream. The Trust Deed Note is really personal property and can be dealt with contractually outside of the real estate. The trust deed monthly payments could be sent to an escrow company. The escrow company, in turn, would then disperse the funds minus a management fee. In the event the original borrower does not make payments or defaults on the terms of the Trust Deed Note, the original owner would assign the Trust Deed Note and Trust Deed to you. If this assignment of the personal property cannot be obtained, it can be obtained through a legal suit. This usually can take a minimum of thirty days under the Unified Commercial Code (UCC). After the Trust Deed is obtained, all the rights to foreclosure are available to you.

There is a problem that can occur when the hypothecated loan is funded by several lenders. Having all the lenders agree to the action to be taken and obtaining the funds to proceed can be exasperating.

The other problem that could occur is if the original owner of the Trust Deed or the new lender files bankruptcy. This will not give anyone a warm feeling.

In this type of investing, the documentation should be prepared by a real estate attorney to take care of most of the conceivable problems, civil code adherence, and case law impact. An escrow company, as in all loan funding, should be used.

The other method of obtaining the benefits of a Trust Deed Note is hypothecation. The replacement lender would receive the Trust Deed and Trust Deed Note for a specified period of time. This would provide for the receiving of payments directly from the borrower with full control. After a specified time, the Trust Deed and Trust Deed Note would be reassigned back to the original lender under the terms of a separate agreement. This by far is the best approach for you as an investor.

Hypothecation is different from *collateralizing* a loan using a Trust Deed. Collateralizing a loan does not give the investor total security. *Collateralizing* is the pledging of the repayment of a loan. Only when you have possession of the Trust Deed and Trust Deed Note and have the right to foreclose on the property will there be reasonable security. When a loan is to be funded, if the terms *contract, collateralizing,* or *derivative investment* are used, an investment is not being made, but rather a disbursement of money with the hope for its return. When a loan is collateralized, the agreement should be notarized and recorded.

There are other variations in the hypothecation of a Trust Deed and Trust Deed Note. However, caution should be your middle name.

MEZZANINE LOAN

There is an unsecured loan that is referred to as a mezzanine loan. These loans are on property but are junior to other loans and can be made even less secure by additional loans that are senior. In effect the loan is subordinated to additional funding. They are used primarily on rehab or construction loans, but they have been used in purchasing real estate. The security is an equity interest in the property. Typically the borrower is a limited liability corporation (LLC). This leaves very little recourse to the lender. These are extremely dangerous unless additional property is brought into the mix to provide tolerable security. They do provide a high rate of return due to the investment risk.

There is another version of the mezzanine type of loan called a junior trust deed mezzanine loan. There would be, as with a normal securing Trust Deed, a recorded junior Trust Deed. In this case the security is the future increase in property value. The LTV on this type of loan is larger than is normal for a second Trust Deed, an adventurous venture.

LINE OF CREDIT

There is a loan that is occasionally obtained on property called a line of credit, sometimes called a credit line. Most often it is placed on residential property but can be placed on other real estate. This loan usually has a low LTV, smaller than 65 percent. The loan allows the borrower to obtain money up to the line of credit limit. The borrower only has to pay interest on the borrowed funds. Line of credit loans by a hard-money lender can be made but with a lower interest rate than those that can be typically obtained with a conventional hard-money loan. These loans are very secure due to the low LTV. The borrower usually has good credit. If the borrower's credit is questionable, this presents an opportunity for the hard-money lender, providing he has funds accessible for future advances up to the credit line. It is a variation on a rehab or construction loan, where the loaned funds are held in an escrow account until needed. In the rehab or construction loan, interest is paid on the loaned funds even if they are in escrow. The controlled funds are released in stages after milestones are reached in the project. (See discussion on controlled funds in other sections.) With a line of credit, interest won't be paid until the funds are withdrawn.

Where the line of credit should be of concern is where a borrower wants to borrow using a typical hard-money loan. If there is a line of credit, typically in first position against the property, the new hard-money lender's loan is subject to this line of credit. The stated amount of debt usually is lower than the credit limit. If the borrower states that the amount owed is much lower than the credit limit, you should have a bad feeling. Prior to lending money where there is a line of credit, the maximum amount of the line of credit must be determined and used to accurately calculate the LTV.

OWNERSHIP OF PROPERTY

The ownership of the property that will be used as security should be verified carefully. Title insurance will provide some guarantee. A review of the title insurance policy will show the liens against a property and guarantee your loan position. In those cases where there are out buildings or a mobile home, special care should be taken to insure the borrower's ownership. If the loan is against these other properties, documentation must be generated that you as the lender have an encumbrance against these other properties. This would only apply if the other properties were needed to provide an adequate LTV. Some states use a *title search* to provide assurance of ownership. A *title search* is a review by a law office of all past transaction affecting ownership. There is argument on which is better, title search or title insurance. The major problem with title insurance is the title plant (facility that documents all legal transactions that can affect ownership) may not discover a fraudulent reconveyance or property transfer preformed in the past. The title insurance plant reviews just the operative recordings and could miss any fraud. However, they will indemnify for loss up to the policy limit providing all necessary action to prevent a loss is taken.

LOAN "ASSUMPTION/SUBJECT TO"

When a property is sold, there will be times that the loan is taken over as an *assumption* or a *subject to*. The *assumption* means the original owner transfers all obligations for the loan to the new owner. A *subject to* means that the terms of the original loan remain in place and the old owner retains the responsibility of making the loan payments in the event the new buyer doesn't make the payments. The original senior lender for both a subject to and an assumption sale must agree to the assumption if required by the Trust Deed Note. From a practical standpoint, there will be cases where a property is sold and the senior lender will not be told of the sale transfer.

The transfer of ownership will have to be evaluated on a case-by-case basis. There is the real danger that this can lead to a foreclosure by the existing senior lender if he hasn't agreed to a loan assumption (discussed later). In the case of the subject to sale, this will require that the loan be paid off by the original owner unless the new buyer can come to terms with the existing senior lender. These terms might include paying points, increasing the interest rate, and submitting an acceptable loan application by the new owner of the property. From a practical standpoint the original property owner usually doesn't have money to payoff the loan or won't and can't be found. He already has his money from the sale.

This issue becomes important if you are asked to lend on property that is being sold with assumption or subject to terms in the sales contract. The security of the loan would be reduced by the cost of borrowing funds to pay off a senior loan holder that may file a foreclosure, cost of refinancing the foreclosing loan, the payment for any prepayment penalty, and the cost of litigation that may occur.

There will be times when property ownership is being changed, and your loan is to be assumed. With an ownership change, you will need additional information to determine your degree of risk. This would occur because of the new owner's potential poor payment performance. Depending upon the market interest rate and creditworthiness of the new owner, it may be to your advantage to allow the loan to be assumed. This can be a true assumption or taking the property subject to.

CORPORATION LOANS

In the case of making a loan to a corporation, its financial resources or complexity of ownership can be prohibitively perplexing for new investors. (It appears that just about everyone is incorporating to provide financial isolation.) The potential for bankruptcy filing exists and there can be significant legal cost. If a Chapter 11 reorganization is filed—there should be some concern that money might be lost. In dealing with corporations, the officials very often are not dealing with their own money. When they decide to instigate a fight, they are basically playing Monopoly. They do not operate by normal rules. They could be proving a point in their office or impressing some of their underlings. As part of the loan package, a copy of the articles of incorporation should be obtained and reviewed by knowledgeable counsel.

For practical purposes, when a trust deed loan is made to a corporation, the property is the only real security. Any suit against the corporation could be very expensive and time consuming. It is therefore important that the property value be based on the property alone and not the business of the corporation. If a personal guarantee can be obtained from the corporation officials, it is prudent to obtain this guarantee. If a foreclosure is imminent, it is best to avert a fight with the legal expenses and try to come to terms.

Because of these considerations, when possible, it is often advisable to avoid loans with corporate borrowers. However, after your investment funds become large, this cannot be avoided. A real estate attorney should review all documentation when lending to a corporation.

LIVING REVOCABLE TRUST AND NONREVOCABLE TRUST LOANS

In the case of lending to a trust (i.e., revocable or irrevocable trust), a copy of the trust must be obtained. This will allow verifying the trustee names and their authority to act on behalf of the trust. The trust should provide the names of all individuals that can sign documents, their power under the trust, and all of the names of the trust beneficiaries. This can be very helpful if a foreclosure or bankruptcy is filed. One of the problems with lending to a trust is when the trustee or any of the beneficiaries of the trust files a bankruptcy, an *automatic stay*[3] occurs. This will stop your foreclosure and a *Relief from Stay* will have to be obtained. A *Relief from Stay* is a bankruptcy court order removing a property from the bankruptcy proceedings. The problems may not end there. The other trustees and beneficiaries named in the trust can then file subsequent serial bankruptcies.

A personal loan guarantee, when possible, should be obtained from the borrowers. This can be very helpful when one of the borrowers has deep pockets and a judicial foreclosure becomes necessary. Having the trust guarantee although helpful doesn't necessarily provide protection. If the trust is revocable, the assets can disappear. Finding the actual value of the assets in a non-revocable trust can be time consuming. When a guarantee is obtained, it should be from the trust, the trustees jointly and severally and all named subsequent trustees.

PARTNERSHIP LOANS

In the case of a partnership, if possible, a personal guarantee should be obtained from each of the partners. A copy of the partnership agreement, showing the powers of each partner, prior to funding the loan should be obtained in the event of a future foreclosure or bankruptcy. Documentation for the loan should be very clear with all signatures from the partners and those authorized to sign.

---

[3] An *automatic stay* places a hold on all associated legal actions.

Section 6

MARKET VALUE

An appraisal value is normally the highest and best use of property. This would take into account the market value (using comparable sales), land residual value, and income value. This is not always the value that is used when making a loan.

Figure 6. One person's junk is another's treasure.

From a trust deed investor's perspective, the appraisal is not the complete information needed for trust deed investing. What is also important to a trust deed investor is the sales price that can be realized in a fast sale with a willing buyer and a willing seller. This value may even be different for a buyer that is acquiring properties for future development or property that is to be rehabbed and then sold.

In determining the value of property, its location must be such that it can be personally viewed. This not only is to view the property but its surroundings. Being at the property site will give you the sights, sounds, and smells of your potential investment. It will also put you in close proximity to real estate brokers that should know the value of properties in the area.

Although a trusted agent might be able to report back to you, his perception and yours can be different. His perception can be different not only due to his values being dissimilar to yours, but could be different due to the fact that it is not his money that is being invested.

LAND VALUE INGREDIENT

From a trust deed investor's standpoint, the market value determination should include the elements of quantity and quality of the land associated with the property. Residential property with a significant amount of land can present a problem. An appraisal of property with a large portion of vacant land might show a high value. It would be difficult in a slow economy to sell at or near the appraised value. Alternately, the property would have to be sold at a significant discount to effect a fast sale because of the smaller number of buyers that want improved property with a significant amount of land.

The topography and zoning can also impact the land value. (What and how much can be built on it will influence the value.) When the land contains steep terrain, usually only a small portion is buildable. Land that needs extensive grading would have less value than a flat area of land. In some cases dirt must be imported or exported. This can add value in the case there is a needy, nearby land owner that will pay for the dirt movement. If the dirt that must be imported is some distance (and costly to transport), the land will be of less value. In the case where dirt must be moved, the plans and contracts to have this accomplished should be in place prior to making a loan.

If the zoning must be changed or the land subdivided, this will cost time, subdivision expense (engineering cost), application fees, and bonds. Changing zoning is probably the most difficult and therefore the most expensive effort. In some cases it can't be done or takes too long to accomplish.

The land location may require maintenance such as erosion abatement and removal of fire hazards. This would reduce the land value. Also if there is a large quantity of competing land available, this will reduce the land's value.

LAND RESIDUAL VALUE

Land value using a land residual method is a multi-step process.

An appraisal using the land residual method evaluates the property as if it were to be developed at its highest and best use. This would be a development permitted by zoning or anticipated zoning. In this approach, the value of the improved or developed property is first determined by using a market sales comparison method. The cost to rezone, provide bonds, subdivide the land, pay interest on loans, pay sale costs, pay for permits, pay any assessments, grade the land, and any profits are then removed. The amount remaining is the land residual value. A future increase in material, labor, or the reduction in the sales price due to future potential poor economic conditions on the improved property can cause the land value to be significantly less. If there is a discrepancy from other land comparable sales, (if they can be found), and the calculated land residual is significantly different—a careful evaluation should be done to determine the reason for the discrepancy. The discrepancy could be caused by a poor location, a flood plain, land contamination, or a major business closure. A decision can then be made on the amount to be loaned on the property or if a loan should be made.

ZONING CONFORMITY

Investments in improved substandard properties in violation of zoning regulations or variances, or that have been grandfathered can present special problems. If an improved property is destroyed by fire or other disaster, the property may not be permitted to retain its past form and use. Any restoration of the property would in all likelihood have to meet existing zoning and municipality building codes. If this is economically not practicable, this could leave an expensive (devalued) piece of dirt.

MARKET VALUE DEFINED

The construction cost of improved property isn't always the determining factor in market value. What is important is the price people are willing and able to pay. If the sum of total wages received by homeowners is pressured down, the market value of property will also be pressured down. This could also be caused by one of the two working parents being out of work, one of the parents elects to stay home and raise the children, higher taxes, higher fuel cost, higher mortgage rates, or an economic slowdown. This will result in families having a reduced monthly income. The portion that can be allocated to mortgage payments therefore will be reduced. It is only logical that property values could drop. Investment decisions must consider reality, not what politicians recite about jobs and the state of the economy.

One of the most significant factors in determining market value is the cost of money. This is the interest rate that is being offered by lenders. If the interest rate is very low, more buyers become available. This will push the price of property upward. Many have found that when cheap money is available, it is often cheaper to buy rather than rent. There is a downside to this cheap money. Oftentimes the money is loaned at a variable rate. When the cheap money disappears, interest rates and mortgage payments will increase. This usually puts more property on the market. Many property owners will not be able to sell the property to payoff their loan causing foreclosures to increase. This will further depress property values due to the excess of properties on the market.

Market value is defined as the price that a willing buyer and a willing seller agree to and are able to *close* (complete) an escrow. The fact that a buyer and seller agree on a price doesn't set a market value. Only after the escrow closes is a market value established. The factors that come into play when an escrow doesn't close are:

- buyers' or sellers' remorse,
- high or higher than expected interest rates where the buyer can't qualify,
- insufficient funds from the buyer to meet the lender's requirements,
- a change in the economy where the property value rapidly declines, and the buyer backs out,
- another property comes on the market that has more value to the buyer, and the buyer backs out of the deal,
- the escrow not closing within the required time frame per the terms of the agreement (contract),
- the price of property going up in value, and the seller backs out,
- the price of property going up in value with the seller wanting a higher price where the buyer refuses to ante up,
- defects in the property when the seller is unwilling or unable to make corrections,
- defects in the property when the buyer, the lender, or both are unwilling to accept the defects.

(Some of these reasons for an escrow not closing have legal implications and can cause litigation.)

APPRAISAL

There is an appraisal value and a market value. They will not necessarily agree and usually don't. This variation could be caused by the different date the value is set and variation of the value in the properties' features made by a buyer and an appraiser.

Appraisers on the surface are independent contractors. They are however, really working for the mortgage broker. If the appraiser makes the mortgage broker happy, there will be future appraisal requests. The mortgage broker has a need to have the appraisal high to make the loan and the appraiser also needs the appraisal high to obtain future business. Their interests are different but mutual. An appraiser can and often biases the valuation placed on property. If you ask appraisers if they modify their appraisals, they will emphatically state that they don't. But, after all, they are only human. Adjusting an appraisal is not too difficult to do. As an investor, you must critically review the appraisal and adjustments used on property.

In the case where an appraisal is significantly incorrect, an appraiser could be subject to a lawsuit to regain a loss due to a fraudulent appraisal. The facts should be very clear and the difference between the real value and the appraised value outrageous to permit a lawsuit to be successful. There is always the danger of property being *flipped* with a deceptive appraisal. *Flipped* is when a property is repeatedly sold or refinanced. When this happens, the higher appraisal will produce a gain to the seller or borrower. In the case of a borrower, he will just walk away with his ill-gotten gain, leaving the lender with the pain of a loan with inadequate security.

The appraiser must be licensed to legally function as an appraiser. He should also be a Member of the Appraisal Institute (MAI) but doesn't have to be to do appraising. Either of these situations does not insure an accurate appraisal but it does give a suggestion of the accuracy of the appraisal. Some mortgage brokers will use a real estate broker's comparative market value in presenting a loan package. This may not be an accurate market value. It should also be noted that some of these real estate brokers' comparative market value estimates could be more accurate than a licensed appraiser's value due to the broker being knowledgeable of buyers' desires.

The appraisal is a subjective process where estimates are made. This would include adjustment for comparing a small square footage home with a larger square footage home. The dollar per square foot for each different sized property can be different. The value of a view can be biased as well as the value of a pool that may or may not have deferred maintenance. Some appraisers will use a home located in a different neighborhood. There can be enormous differences in value if one of the comparable properties is in a prestigious neighborhood. Deferred maintenance cost is an estimated value and can be different from actual cost. Comparative properties that are used often have been prepared for sale. The cost to prepare a property for sale is not always deducted by the appraiser in determining the subject property value.

COMPARABLE SALES

Before accepting an appraisal, even when a full-blown appraisal is done, your own appraisal should be performed. Some of the appraiser's information can be used but with caution. The usable information would be the square footage of the improvements, number of bedrooms, number of bathrooms, other amenities, lot size, and general condition of the property. The sale price of comparable properties might be used. This however should be done with *due diligence* on your part to verify that there are not unintentional or intentional errors. One error to watch out for is the omission of lower-priced sales.

Due diligence is defined as reviewing all aspects of the loan including:

- character (ethics) of the mortgage broker,
- all appraisal documents,
- the subject property and comparable properties.

The comparable sales that are used should be *arms-length*[1] sales transactions. If the seller carries back paper or pays for the buyer's closing cost, this can show a higher market value. This is caused by the seller increasing the sales price to pay for this selling cost. If the seller carries back at a reduced interest rate, the sale price can be higher to adjust for the reduced value of the carryback Trust Deed. If the sale is a forced, distressed sale or

---

[1] An *arms-length* transaction is one in which the normal free market (i.e., no strings attached) allows the setting of the sales price without distortions.

a sale to a relative, the sales price might be lower than the market value. The forced-sale market value should not be in the appraisal unless there is some adjustment. The adjustment value would be very hard to determine. If there is adjustment, the adjusted sales value could be set too high.

If comparable sales cannot be found in the immediate neighborhood, this may be a loan to forget. An exception would be when the terms of the note are attractive and the estimated LTV is low. There will be times that comparable sales cannot be found due to the desirability of the neighborhood. All of the homeowners are happy with the location and don't want to move.

Your own appraisal can be done by obtaining a property profile from a title company and combining it with information on properties that are for sale in the immediate neighborhood. The property profile is important so the improvements can be verified with regard to the assessor's square footage and other improvements, such as a pool. If the assessor's description does not agree with the appraiser's description, there could be improvements that have been added without a permit. This would decrease the property value. Driving the neighborhood is important to find any recently listed properties and to determine the desirability of the location. The desirability of the location isn't necessarily where you would want to live but what is selling. A call to the listing agents on properties in the neighborhood can supply additional information about the property values.

Using the Internet site www.realtor.com (not realitor.com) will provide some information on property listings. There are other Internet sites that will also provide MLS listings (Realtor Multiple Listing Service). These presentations are puffed up to some extent, and only by viewing properties in person can a determination be made on value. The Web site www.zillow.com can also provide useful information about property values in the area of interest. Caution should be used in that there can be incorrect information and omissions on condition, features, and amenities.

APPRAISAL ADJUSTMENT

Your appraisal will include adding or subtracting value to the property under consideration, based on other properties' features and sale price. If the property under consideration has a good view and a good location, value can be added. Conversely, if the subject property under consideration doesn't have a view and a comparable property that had sold has a view, value must be subtracted. A $500,000 property with a view of mountains might have an added value of $100,000 if a comparable $500,000 property doesn't have the same view. After all the amenities, size, construction features, age, and condition of the properties have been considered and the subject property value adjusted, (up or down), a market value will have been approximated. The market value of amenities is in the eye of the beholder. This value can be approximated after having discussions with several informed real estate agents.

Finished Value

There are appraised values, specifically on projects under construction and rehab properties, that include impound or controlled funds held by a third party. This appraised value is based on the completed work. This appraisal is allowed under certain conditions up to $2,500,000 per Section 10238 of the *Business and Professions Code*. If the third party is reliable, this shouldn't present a problem, providing there is someone available to complete the project in the event of a default.

Personal Property

Personal property should not be considered in your appraisal. As covered previously, if there is a foreclosure, these items can disappear. Standard items such as built-in kitchen appliances might be considered even though an irate homeowner might potentially take these items in a foreclosure. Structures such as a mobile home or a storage shed that is external to a house probably shouldn't be considered in an appraisal.

However in generating a Trust Deed Note, each of these items should be listed as part of the property that is used as security for the loan.

The final appraisal value should take into account what will in all probability remain after a foreclosure sale. This would take into consideration the potential that landscape plants die, fruit trees die, appliances disappear, cabinets disappear, dishwashers disappear, heating and cooling systems disappear, doors disappear, and the possibility of property waste. This is not a common occurrence, but there is the potential for this happening. As discussed later, a financial inducement to the old homeowner to maintain the property and leave everything intact can be money well-spent.

IMPROVEMENTS

When improvements have been added to the property, special evaluation will have to be done. If the improvement is for front and back landscaping, there could be very little value added if the existing landscaping could have been spruced up. When tilt up garage doors are replaced with roll up doors, the added improvement is only the cost difference between the two. There is however the improved *curb appeal* [2] that will add an additional value that can be reflected in a final sales price. This may also be the case for replaced carpets, wallpaper, or flooring. If the improvements were to satisfy the owner's taste and not a true upgrade, the expense may not significantly increase the final sales price, especially if the changes don't appeal to potential buyers.

When the improvement is for the conversion of a garage to a living area, if there isn't another garage, there can be an actual decrease in value. This would be caused by the cost to restore the property. The conversion can also cause an increase in the homeowners' insurance due to the increase in living area. Most often, garage conversions are done without permits. Some municipalities will require that the property be in complete conformity to existing building permits before a sale can be made legally.

---

[2] *Curb appeal* is the first impression that a buyer experiences prior to entering the property.

Improvements that have been made a significant time ago could have been used up by the occupant's normal wear and tear. Logically these improvements cannot be added to the property value.

PROPERTIES THAT HAVE NOT SOLD

Other information that can be used in determining market value would be similar properties that are on the market and have not sold. This would include properties that have been on the market and have been withdrawn. These properties will provide a maximum value but not necessarily the market value.

Properties sometimes don't sell because the buying public isn't aware that the property is for sale, because of the poor condition or location of the property, or because the economic conditions are not conducive for a sale. Although there is always a price at which a property will sell, the price could still be set too low to reflect the true market value. With some small added value such as preparing the property, better advertising, or creative financing, the true market value might be realized.

DISTRESS SALE

There is another fact that should be considered in determining the market value. This is when there is a comparable property that has been sold as a *distress sale*. The reason for the lower price must be determined. A *distress sale* is a sale when the seller had to sell. This could be because of a foreclosure action, a forced relocation, a probate sale[3], a Drug Enforcement

---

[3] In a probate sale, the court will approve a sale that is at least 90 percent of the appraised value. Prior to the sale becoming final, the court, during a hearing, will approve the sale bid price. At this time an overbid can be submitted. The overbid can't just be the original bid price plus one dollar. The court sets the amount of overbid that will be acceptable. This can be a percentage such as 5 percent, a fixed amount, or a combination of both. Prohibiting an overbid of only one dollar avoids an auction with many overbids, something the court doesn't have time for.

Agency acquired-property sale, a tax sale, or a sheriff's sale. Although the distressed-sale property sale price can provide information, it can reduce the subject property's market value if used as a comparable sale. Some of the other reasons for a reported lower price are extensive deferred maintenance, a drug area, murder or suicide on the property, high crime area, and vandalism. A property acquired in a foreclosure could be in a similar situation so the distressed sale value might be the true market value for the neighborhood.

SPECIAL SALES

Included in the general classification of properties that are sold below market value are properties that are sold between friends and relatives. The sales price can be significantly low so as to distort the apparent market value. The determination of the reasons and amount of gift can be very difficult to determine.

A seller that does not know property value can impact comparable properties. Most of the time, these properties should not be used in determining market value.

There is another category of property that might be sold below market value. This would be the estate of someone that had been receiving governmental assistance. In this case the executor of the estate might sell the property at any price to quickly make a disposition. This would happen if he wouldn't receive anything from the sale due to the governmental agency receiving all of the proceeds, even if he were a beneficiary of the estate.

COMPETITIVE PRICING

In the evaluation of the market value, remember to ask local real estate brokers, "What is a fast sale price?" Critical in determining a fast sale price is having information about similar properties that are on the market and in competition with your potential future property. The first reality is your property won't bring a penny more than competing properties and possibly less, due to the condition of a foreclosed property. Discovering which property will sell first can often be determined by flipping a coin. The second reality is your similar property may only sell after the competing property is off the market.

The two best ways to have your property sell first is to add value such as curb appeal, the look of a property as viewed from the street curb. The second way is to set a price that is lower than your competition. This amount can be as little as $500. Don't delude yourself about your property. What you think about the market value is not relevant. Buyers that have been shopping know what the property is worth based on their value of the various features and their needs. This reduced price, or sales expense, should be used as part of your potential cost in a foreclosure. In calculating your LTV, the foreclosure expenses should be increased by this additional price reduction.

There are other low-cost improvements that might be done to help sell a property. These might include advertising on the Internet (with pictures), trimming trees to regain a view, painting, and general cleanup.

SITE VISIT

Evaluating property by looking at pictures, or an appraisal with descriptions cannot replace inspection of the property. There will be times that the interior of the property cannot be viewed. This may be because the property is occupied by a tenant that is not cooperative. The noncooperation can be due to a number of reasons. The inside is a mess, there are dogs inside that aren't allowed in a rental agreement, drugs in the house that the tenant wants to hide, or the privacy or control desires of a tenant. In this case the inspection will have to be done in a limited manner or by giving the tenant notice so the interior of the property can be viewed. When the LTV is not too high, not viewing the interior of the property may be acceptable. However, if the LTV is tight, a loan may not be prudent without an interior inspection.

In the inspection of the property, if there are dogs present, adjustments should be made to the appraised value. In too many cases the property inside and outside can be significantly destroyed by dogs. Refurbishment may require new carpets, replacement of doors or molding, and relandscaping. When inspecting the property, great care must be taken. Because of the territorial nature of dogs, an apparently friendly dog can become a mortal enemy when you enter its domain.

Visiting the property and talking with neighbors can provide information about nuisances such as dog barking, traffic noise, basketball hoops attached to properties, children always playing in the streets, bad neighbors, gangs, and graffiti. Knowing about these nuisances will allow for an adjustment to the market value or determine that the property is not acceptable for a loan.

PROPERTY SOUNDNESS

In the evaluation of a property, thoroughness must be used in checking the structural soundness. There are several things that should be done.

You can walk on the slab floors and check that the floor does not have a slight step-up or step-down. If there is a step-up or a step-down, there is a good probability of a cracked slab. If the floors are a raised foundation and bounce too much, this is an indication that the beams are not adequate or there is termite or dry rot damage.

Inspect the inside walls, outside walls, and internal ceilings of the structure. If there are any diagonal cracks or evidence that someone tried to hide them with filler and paint, there could be significant structural damage.

The outside of the building's concrete walks, driveways, and garage floors should be examined. If any cracks aim toward the house, further evaluation inside the house should be done. This can be done by pulling up the carpet in the suspected area. If the occupants do not allow this kind of inspection, they may be afraid damage could be done to the carpet. If the occupant takes this position and won't let a licensed inspector evaluate the property, they probably have something to hide. Alternately if the suspected crack is near an outside wall, inspection of the area might be done from the outside. If an inspection can't be done to your satisfaction, it would be better not to invest in this property.

HAZARDOUS MATERIALS

If there are hazardous waste materials on the surface or buried, such as would be found at a service station site, a hazardous materials dump, or manufacturing plant, the cost of inspection and cleanup could significantly reduce the property value. Adjacent properties that have hazardous materials also can affect neighboring property value. Contacting the responsible government agency and obtaining a Phase I Environmental Site Assessment about the property's hazardous waste status would be prudent action prior to making a loan. This would apply primarily on industrial and commercial property.

ASBESTOS

Asbestos is a generic name applied to a group of naturally occurring fibrous silicate minerals found in the earth's crust. It was used due to its insulation and tensile strength in the 1940s.

Repeated airborne exposure to asbestos has been found to cause fibrosis, or scarring of the lungs, eventually resulting in reduced lung capacity, mesothelioma, asbestosis, and lung cancer.

Asbestos has been used in insulation, residential and commercial siding, acoustic ceilings, and soundproofing of buildings. If there is evidence of its existence, the cost to remove or seal the problem should be taken into account.

Generally all regulated structures undergoing renovation or demolition must have an asbestos survey to identify asbestos materials. Materials identified as asbestos require notification to the local oversight agency prior to the removal by registered contractors. Cal-OSHA, Air Quality Management District (AQMD), and the Environmental Protection Agency (EPA) are the agencies that have developed survey, notification, removal, and disposal regulations to prevent asbestos exposures.

If the asbestos is intact and in good general condition, there are no regulations that require its removal. If there are renovations that can disturb the asbestos material, it must have proper removal before renovation or demolition can begin.

All commercial and some residential properties are regulated. Your local AQMD and OSHA can provide specifics.

HIGH-VOLTAGE TRANSMISSION LINES

High-voltage towers and wiring on, under, or near the property will impact property value. The impact of the high voltage to health is disputed. Even if evidence is found that there isn't a health problem, there will still be a portion of the public that will not believe the evidence. Their disbelief will be enough to impact property value.

PLASTIC PIPE PLUMBING

There is another potential problem that exists in some of the water plumbing in more than 100,000 properties built between June 1984 and December 1990. The construction industry used ABS plastic pipe with adhesive resins that, with time, deteriorate and cause significant water damage in ceilings and walls. In the evaluation of property, questions must be asked of the property owner about the plumbing status and a detailed examination done on the property. This would include the inspection of the walls, ceilings, attic, under sinks, and in the garage. Any evidence of water damage, mildew, mold, or a damp odor can be an indication of the plastic pipe problem. In most cases, the pipes are marked with the names indicated below.

The pipe types that exhibited the problem are: Centaur, Phoenix, Gable, Polaris, and Apache. The adhesive resin manufactured by Plastic Processing, Inc., and some of the pipe manufacturers used in making the union of these pipes resulted in a reaction that allowed the deterioration of the bond.

Repairs might have been made, but these may only be temporary fixes. There have been ongoing class action suits. The probability of obtaining funds from the class action suits in the event you come to own the defective property is low.

Until the problem is resolved and problems associated with the faulty plumbing corrected, the value of the property must be reduced. This reduction would be equal to the cost to correct or replace the plumbing, cost to repair any water damage to the property, and other associated temporary housing costs during repairs.

WATER PROBLEMS

Water problems can occur in a variety of ways. Poor site drainage, no rain gutters, no drip edge on roofs, broken pipes, streams and gullies that overflow during rain storms, leaky roofs and street gutters that plug-up during storms are all potential sources of water problems. In most of these situations, there may be some damage indication that can be seen during an inspection. The indicators would be mold or mildew odor or discolored walls or flooring.

Some of the other not-so-obvious water problems can occur due to planters that are higher than the property improvements, sunken rooms, or property that is lower than the surrounding property. These conditions can lead to water seeping into the improvements causing water damage, mold, dry rot, and termite infestation. Heavy rains can also cause the property foundation to crack or portions of the lot to disappear due to movement of slopes. A fence that is tilted or sags would be an indicator as well as sidewalks and patios that are cracked. Extensive drainage pipes in adjacent slopes and *French drains* could indicate past water problems and hill slippage. A *French drain* is created by installing a drainage pipe in a trench and filling the trench with gravel to create a water barrier and path to remove water.

LEAD-BASED PAINT

For pre-1978 properties, the existence of lead-based paint can become a factor in its sale. Owners of residential dwellings must provide a disclosure to renters and buyers. Disclosure is accomplished by providing an approved lead-based paint hazard pamphlet. The sales or rental contract must provide for a ten-day contingency clause. This contingency clause will provide for the buyer or renter an escape from the contract if the property is not acceptable. If the lead-based paint condition is corrected, the renter or buyer will be obligated to proceed if stated in the contract. The cost of any inspection is not the burden of the seller or landlord unless specified in the sales contract. There is new legislation that makes the seller and Real Estate Agent legally obligated to report the property condition.

There are exceptions to these requirements. Foreclosure sales by a bank or creditor are exempt from the disclosure and the ten-day inspection contingency mandate. Housing designed for elderly or disabled, or where children under the age of six are not expected to reside is also exempt from the coverage. Zero-bedroom dwellings such as studio apartments, efficiencies, and similar units where the sleeping area is not separate from the living area are also exempt. Short-term rents, less than 100 days, that are not renewable or extendable are also exempt. *Housing that is sold subsequent to a foreclosure sale would not be exempt from the requirements.*

Failure to comply with the rules could subject you to civil penalties up to $10,000. Criminal prosecution may occur. There can be a court-imposed award equal to three times any damages incurred by individuals buying or renting your property. Essential compliance information can be obtained by calling the environmental protection agency at 1-800-424-LEAD.

This law could have a significant impact on any Trust Deed that is being considered. In order to determine the impact, the construction date of the property should be obtained. Although the mortgage broker might give you the date, a review of property information from the County Tax Assessor's Office should be used. This information usually is part of a property profile or incorporated in a full appraisal of the property. If the properties are marginally close to 1978, the city's building permit information should also be checked. If the property is in an unincorporated area, the county's data will have to be used.

The other consideration when making a loan is the potential of owning the property. If after an acquisition in a foreclosure sale a new loan must be obtained, or the existing loan is to be assumed from a standard lender, and if the property was built prior to 1978, the lender in all likelihood would not lend on the property or allow the assumption of the loan until the lead hazard has been corrected. The lead paint law makes the acquisition of the property using a deed-in-lieu of foreclosure less desirable unless there has been an adjustment for lead hazard correction.

PRICE RANGE

Your evaluation should include the historic trends that higher-priced property and poorly located property will decrease faster in value than lower priced property in a slow or stagnate real estate market. Land also will decrease in value faster than improved property in a slow or stagnant real estate market.

ECONOMIC FACTORS

A constant evaluation of property value trends, typically available in local newspapers, can be helpful. If property values have been decreasing or increasing, don't look for a rapid change in this trend unless there is a significant event. This event could be a change in interest rates, change in tax law, a war, or a significant event where there is property damage because of an earthquake, major storm, mudslide, or an area fire.

Another important evaluation tool is noting the number of vacant properties in the area. Excessive vacancies could signal a deteriorating area with the potential for lower property value.

APPRAISAL DATE

The date of the appraisal is important. An appraisal is only good for that date of the appraisal. If there has been some significant time lapse, such as more than a month or two between your evaluation and the date of the appraisal, the borrower may have been *shopping the loan. Shopping the loan* means looking for a better deal, a lower interest rate, or fewer points to the lender or just someone to lend on the property. A property loan that has been shopped can have inherent defects or lack of equity that has turned off astute lenders.

PURCHASED PROPERTY PRICE

When a loan is to be made on newly purchased property or property that is to be purchased, there are several important considerations. Of utmost importance is obtaining a signed copy of the escrow instructions. This is to verify that all the terms are as reported. If *signed* escrow instructions are not available, this could be a warning sign that something may not be right.

The amount of down payment and the form of the down payment by the buyer are also important. If the down payment is less that 30 percent of the purchase price (where the LTV is 70 percent), this is a warning sign. If the form of the down payment is in gemstones, diamonds, options, oil leases, or other forms of questionable value, this is a warning sign. If the security on the loan is with a seller carryback on the sale and the buyer is not using his own money for the purchase, this is a warning sign. The important item in any transaction is that the borrower (buyer) should have a significant investment in the deal. When there is a seller carryback, the seller is the one providing additional loan security. This is not to say that these warning signs should stop you from making a loan. It means that further investigation is required to verify that the loan could still be a good one.

Often on a property that is to be refurbished, the buyer is getting a contracting job with you doing all of the financing. If there is an adequate upside to the property, adequate fund control, a good past contractor's performance, no detrimental government restrictions on the refurbishment, and a willingness on your part to monitor the contractor's performance, this type of loan can still be acceptable. It can however require a significant amount of your time. Often it is possible to have the mortgage broker monitor the construction progress and control the fund release. This can, at times, cause you pain because of the loss of some of the loan security. The funds don't belong to the mortgage broker and he might be too lenient in the release of funds. A good understanding with the mortgage broker must be obtained. The reason that the mortgage broker might be lenient is he doesn't want to do the required physical inspections, or he wants to keep the borrower happy, so he can make other loans with the contractor in the future.

SFR PROPERTY SQUARE FOOT COST

SFR properties typically have a value of roughly $100 to $500 per square foot depending on various factors. For a smaller house (1000 square feet or less), the value per square foot can be more than $300 per square foot. A larger house (2500 square foot or more) can have a value of less that $200 per square foot. This value of dollars per square foot must additionally be adjusted for quality, age, and location of improvements.

The amount of land, views, amenities, and condition on the property also adds to the mix. This number can be much higher, up to $1000 per square foot. This dollar per square foot is not the selling dollar per square foot but a rough estimate in evaluating properties. Cost per square foot is also used in quoting construction cost and often does not include land, surveys, roads, permits, and bonds.

If the improvement is overbuilt for the area, the cost of the improvement usually cannot be recovered in a sale. People tend to buy a house in similar surroundings. The exception is when a buyer wants to be king of the hill.

OTHER FACTORS IN EVALUATION

In the evaluation of property value, the future value needs to be considered. The future value might be based on appreciation due to economic conditions, but to be realistic, it should be based on tangible events. Appreciation due to economic conditions is very unpredictable, and forecasting should only be done by the gods. The events that could be considered include:

- rehabilitation of an improvement, adding square feet to an improvement, and building an improvement on a vacant lot,
- increasing rents as in apartments. This would increase the market value of the property,
- combining other properties, such as adding a parking structure or parking lot,
- dividing property into separate buildable lots,
- converting an apartment building into several condominiums,
- dividing a large factory or retail building into smaller units such as multistores, offices, or living quarters.

The final improved value might be used in determining the LTV and lendability. The cost of the improvements must be accounted for by either the borrower having an adequate investment in the property or the loan being used to make the changes is impounded and released as the construction phases are completed.

Section 7

TRUST DEED INVESTMENT CRITERIA

Figure 7. *Why is this mortgage broker being so good to me?*

The purchase of Trust Deeds or the lending on the equity of property should be based on the real world and not wishful thinking. Great care must be taken to accomplish this. Remember that your decision can cause the loss of part or all the money invested.

A trust deed investor is typically interested in a performing loan. This is a loan that provides a constant or lump sum return on an investment. The payments can come from improved property that can be rented or leased or from the borrower's income. Land normally does not produce income.

Lending on vacant land can still be an acceptable investment if the borrower has other income and doesn't need the cash flow from the property to make mortgage payments. In many cases the amount that is loaned includes prepaid interest. With the prepaid interest, you will have paid yourself when you make the loan, a good deal indeed. Some investors may even want a loan to default. If this happens, a jump rate clause included in the Trust Deed Note means the lender would receive a higher rate of return.

Some investors will lend on land at a 50 percent LTV. If they end up with the property in foreclosure, this isn't a problem. They hoped to own the property for appreciation or later development. In effect they have purchased the property at a discount. After the sale or development, the discounted amount becomes part of their investment return.

In evaluating a loan there are two items of importance. The foundation for lending is the value or potential value of the real estate property. Hard-money loans are secured by the property equity after deducting all anticipated cost. The second item is the honesty and stability of the borrower. The borrower's character comes into play due to your wanting a trouble-free loan. Some mortgage brokers will tell you that the important aspect in hard-money lending is the equity in the property. Although this on the surface is true, you don't want to deal with foreclosures, bankruptcies, legal filings, and writing notification letters to receive your interest and principal payment.

These two aspects more than anything else will determine the safety of and return of the investment. Safety is interrelated with return. If safety is the most important feature in an investment, a bank deposit or government treasury note might be a first consideration. There are even unsafe circumstances in bank deposits or government treasury notes. The effect of inflation and the potential of government default, confiscation through taxes, or devaluation of the dollar are real dangers. The return of the investment and on the investment is never a sure thing. Even when money is placed under a mattress, there is the threat of thieves, fire, or forgetting where it is hidden.

INVESTMENT EVALUATION

When investing in Trust Deeds, part of the evaluation should include the reality that the property may be acquired through foreclosure. With this type of acquisition of property, the sale of the property must be considered. Property usually is not owned forever by the same person or family.

The property owner should be questioned to detect if there are any hidden defects in the property. If possible, a written statement by the borrower should be obtained for the record. If a defect does become known in the future, your case, if there is a judicial foreclosure, would be strengthened. The existence of defects and cost to make repairs becomes part in the LTV calculation. How the property was or is being acquired can become important. If your new Trust Deed is going to be junior to an existing Trust Deed, and there is a due on sale (discussed later) or transfer clause in the senior loan, your loan could be put in jeopardy due to a potential demand for full payment by the senior lender. This may not be an issue if the subject property is one to four units and is owner (borrower) occupied. There are special cases where the due on sale clause can't be invoked. In general these cases are when the new owner or joint tenant occupies the property as a result of death or there has been a divorce. There is also the existing lender's and owner's actions that come into play. If payments have been accepted for a period of time, there is then a de facto (Latin for, in fact) acceptance of a junior Trust Deed.

LOAN-TO-VALUE (LTV) (See Section 10 for additional details on LTV.)

The loan-to-value ratio (LTV) is determined by dividing your determined market value into the final encumbrances (LTV = Encumbrances/Market Value). (The difference between the market value and encumbrances is the equity in the property.) When an encumbrance is being paid off using your loan or other sources of money, that lien should not be included in the calculation. The final encumbrances could include:

- all unpaid loans (including your loan),
- unpaid loan payments,
- early loan payoff fees (prepayment penalty),
- unpaid taxes, (including property, state, and federal income taxes that are or will become senior to your loan),
- judgment liens,
- association (condo) dues and assessments,
- ownership transfer fees,
- cost to repair defects,
- *Mello-Roos* lien[1].

Encumbrances, if a lien, will show up in the Title Report (see other discussions on Title Reports). If there are association dues and assessments, they may not have become a recorded lien. When there is an association, it is advisable to contact the association about assessments and the status of association dues.

---

[1] Not all Mello-Roos liens need to be included. They usually are not payable when ownership transfers. They are paid similarly to an association fee, on a monthly or quarterly bases. The lien could at some future date become due if not amortized. (In this case it would be included in the LTV calculation.) The existence of a Mello-Roos is usually reflected in the market value. Most buyers are aware of its existence and will pay less for the property after taking this cost into account. *Mello-Roos* is the name of legislation named after two California legislators. The legislation provides for the establishment of districts to bond various improvements that will be paid in the future by the property owners.

The decision to lend is driven by each lender's comfort level. This most often is based on the LTV and to some extent affected by the borrowers past credit rating and ability to make payments, including the final payoff of the loan.

If there is a high probability that a federal (and then a state) flat tax will be implemented, a smaller LTV might be used. The flat tax can potentially reduce property values due to the loss of deduction of property taxes and interest payments. If there is adequate compensation by taxing agencies, the adjustment to the LTV wouldn't be necessary.

TRUST DEED TERMS AND POSITION

A Trust Deed's recording date and time determines who has priority to the property's equity. This priority however could be changed by a senior trust deed owner subordinating his position. The fact that a Trust Deed is in first, second, third, or a lower junior position doesn't fully describe the vulnerability. If there is a lender that is junior to your Trust Deed, where there is adequate equity, should provide additional comfort. The hope exists that the junior lender will do all the dirty work if they acquiring the property in the event of a foreclosure. Before the acquisition, he will have to deal with the foreclosure, payments to all the senior lenders, and the potential bankruptcy. As a senior lender, when there is a bankruptcy filing, an attorney might still have to be hired to protect your interest.

The junior lender will have to deal with the property management, sale preparation, and sale responsibility after acquiring the property. They hopefully will continue to keep senior loans performing by making payments to the senior lenders.

If the junior lender on encumbered property doesn't have adequate protective equity, there is the high probability he will walk away from the loan, leaving the next least senior lender the dirty work. The higher interest rate reward, normally received by a junior trust deed holder, may not adequately compensate for this vulnerability when there is a likelihood of a default.

A Trust Deed in a first position with adequate equity is more desirable if the return is acceptable. Even if the return is lower, there is special protection. If the property value decreases, the total investment would in all probability not be lost. There would not be the need to make payments to a senior lender to stop a foreclosure.

The concern would be if the loan is on a condo or PUD. In this case the association can file a foreclosure on the property when overdue assessments are not paid even if you have a first Trust Deed. The present law establishes a threshold of $1800 before an association can file a foreclosure, providing some protection.

If there are unpaid property taxes, the County could take the property and sell it for the back taxes. This however is a lengthy process and can happen only after five years of nonpayment. This tax bill, even with large penalties, may remain unpaid if money is not available to make payments. This nonpayment of taxes would be considered a high interest loan, something that most likely is not desirable. After all, you are in the business of receiving payments, not making them.

Junior lenders have the distinct privilege of possibly losing all of their investment in a depressed market. This is one of the reasons that some institutional lenders will only lend on a first Trust Deed.

ASSUMABLE LOAN

There are a few loans that are assumable. These usually would be private loans and variable interest loans. To find out if a loan is assumable, a review of the Trust Deed Note will be required. A detailed examination does not always directly provide information if the loan is assumable. If the Trust Deed Note does not prohibit the assumption, the loan most likely is assumable.

When a loan is being funded and a senior loan will remain in place, a copy of the senior Trust Deed Note should be obtained. Obtaining the document after a foreclosure has started is often difficult or impossible.

The important loan terms shown in the Trust Deed Note would be:

- if the loan is fixed or variable,
- if there is a balloon payment,
- the starting date and maturity date,
- the nature of the payments (i.e., interest rate and payment increment),
- if there is a prepayment penalty,
- the original amount of the loan and payoff amount.

If the loan is not assumable, a refinance will probably be required after a foreclosure with the potential complexities indicated below.

In the case of variable interest loans, the lender requires that the loan assumption be approved. This requires submitting the typical loan application documents. The lender often charges a processing fee and a point for the privilege of assuming the loan. If the current market loan interest rate is higher than the note's interest rate, the approval process can be very harsh.

If the interest rate on a fixed rate note is higher than the current market interest rate, a lender may still allow the loan to be assumed even if the terms of the Trust Deed Note prohibit an assumption. The lender would in all probability still charge a processing fee and points as well as requiring an approval of the loan application.

The balloon payment is important due to the potential requirement of refinancing the loan. The loan can become due when there is a sale or transfer of ownership. This refinancing might cost the usual document processing fees, prepayment penalty, and points. Even if the loan were assumable, if there is still a balloon payment coming due, arrangements would have to be made to refinance or obtain an extension. This extension may cost several points.

Additional information on the amount of principal remaining on the senior loans can be obtained by reviewing the payment records that should be supplied by the borrower. This can be different from the Trust Deed Note's original loan amount. Usually the amount of principal will be less than the original loan when the principal-and-interest type of payments are made. There could be situations where additional funds have been loaned to the borrower. This will increase the principal but may not be reflected by the note. There could also have been payments that are less than the required amortized monthly payments. This loan would be a reverse mortgage loan where unpaid interest is added to the principal. In some circles this is called a walk-back loan or negatively-amortized loan. There may have been additional principal payments but not likely. All of this information will be required to calculate the outstanding balance due, so as to determine the true LTV.

The terms of loan payments could be:

- interest only,

- principal and interest (PI),

- principal, interest, taxes (PIT),

- principal, interest, taxes, insurance (PITI).

When the monthly payments contain taxes and insurance, these payments are often impounded (held in an escrow account) and accumulated until there is an adequate amount to pay the insurance and taxes when they become due.

RESALE POTENTIAL

Single-family residence properties that have negatives will require a longer marketing time and a lower price unless there isn't anything else available. These factors would include:

- building site below street level,
- next to a noisy freeway[2],
- under or near an airplane flight path or next to an airport,
- next to a proposed freeway, airport, commercial complex, industrial complex, apartment complex, or condo complex,
- located in a drug-infested neighborhood,
- located on a busy street with obvious problems of exit and entry.

The property should be in a conforming neighborhood. Neighbors should not have junky yards. Property could have problems but they should be easily corrected. The minor problems don't have to be necessarily corrected if it makes sense to own it for a while as a rental. If the property looks bad, and needs paint and landscaping, this should not prevent the investment. Properties that end up in a foreclosure, usually started out looking good, but end up looking poor by the time the foreclosure sale takes place and possession is obtained. Poor appearance of property does provide some information on the borrower's attitude about property, his ability to maintain property, and earning ability to pay for upkeep. The resale potential should be partially based on curb appeal or potential curb appeal. The potential curb appeal should only require a small amount of gardening, paint and minor repairs to make the property look presentable.

Properties that are in remote locations can take a longer time to sell. This is due to not as many people finding a remote location desirable. The exception would be a *bedroom community*. A *bedroom community* is one where the population uses the community to live, while working in another area. With the increase in the use of the

---

[2] Being close, but not too close to a freeway can be a positive feature, providing there isn't a noise problem. Freeway noise can be a problem if the property is downwind of the prevailing winds or sound walls aren't present. Many homeowners still want to be relatively close to a freeway because of ease of access.

Internet, and work-at-home employees, this rule might be broken if there are activities in the community that homeowners find appealing. This would also apply to a retirement community.

If adjacent property is zoned for multiresidential, industrial or commercial use in a residential community, the number of potential buyers can be decreased as could the resale market value. This would be due to the "not in my neighborhood" attitude that resists property development.

If the potential loan is for a commercial property that has poor access or poor street visibility, the property value will be less and the time to sell would increase. This would also be the case of a retail store that requires drop-in customers to be successful.

The criteria used in the Trust Deed purchase should not be based on property you would like to live in or own, but a property that can be promptly sold.

FIX-UP COST

The fix-up cost ideally should be low. The property should not have a cracked slab or appraisal to allow for an *as is*[3] sale or allocation for a cracked slab repair and approval. The roof condition should be noted and the market value adjusted to allow for repair or replacement. The cost of a resale can include the tenting and repair of the property in the event there are termites. This can be a gamble on the investor's part because of the inability to do a detailed inspection. There is some inspection for termite and dry rot that can be done by the investor. If there are sawdust-like droppings in the garage, or inside or outside of the house, this is an indication of termites. If there is soft wood (rotten wood) caused by constant contact by water, trees or shrubs touching the house or there is soft wood at the base of the house, at the base of doors, or the base of windows, this

---

[3] An *as is* sale means the property is being sold having no guarantees on its condition.

is an indication of dry rot or termite damage. In the event the property is acquired—tenting, replacement or reinforcement of damaged areas may have to be done. There may also be the need to paint all or part of the house to make the property salable in a short time. The owners of a property in foreclosure are often short of money and have greater problems than keeping the property well-maintained.

There is another fix-up cost that cannot be totally determined. This is the potential waste of the property by the owner when a foreclosure occurs. The owner could strip the property of items such as shutters, stove, built-ins, cabinets, furnace, air conditioning units, storm windows, screens, doors, and anything else that may come to mind. They also can destroy the property by filling the sewer system with concrete, punching holes in the walls, or cracking the driveway and sidewalks with a sledge-hammer. This fortunately doesn't happen too often. This is one of the reasons for a high interest rate on hard-money loans. If the interest rate was not high, the potential financial loss on average could not be recovered.

If vandalism takes place after the foreclosure sale, the old owner would be subject to criminal action if he were caught in the act, which is highly improbable. If there is a homeownership policy in place, some of the cost to repair the property can be recovered. The only defense to prevent this type of act is to offer a cash payment to the foreclosed owner when the property is delivered in good condition. It is important to receive the property with the keys at the street. Receiving the keys in this manner has the legal status of having the property turned over to you. Prior to making the cash payment, an inspection of the property should be made to insure the property is in *good condition* Do not be too severe in judging what is a *good condition*. If the judgment is not *reasonable*, there is always the danger that the old owner will visit the property at night and deliver an unpleasant message. Fortunately the message on walls can be covered with Kilz to prevent a bleed out of the message. (Kilz is the name of a primer paint manufactured by Masterchem Industries, Inc.) There are other paints that are coming on the market that will do the same covering job.

If the cost to refurbish the house is large, an as is sale might be a better approach. Buyers of fixer-upper houses can very often add *sweat equity* to have their purchase make sense. *Sweat equity* is the result of your generated sweat to improve the property.

TIME TO SELL

The time to sell a property will be affected by location, price, available financing, and the property's design. Ideally, the subject property's price should be at the low end for the community. The reason for suggesting the lower priced property is that there will be more potential buyers, so a faster sale can be realized. Unique houses with different floor plans, pink paint, or with a pool that needs repairs can be difficult to sell. If there is senior financing, it should ideally have an assumable loan. However, if the prevailing interest rate is low, this isn't critical. There is always the problem that when the property is ready for sale, the interest rates could be high. High interest is a relative term in the buyer's mind. If the interest rate has been high for some time, and the buyer can afford the payments, the interest rate really isn't too high. Ideally the property should have an appeal to a large number of buyers to speed the sale.

ECONOMIC CONDITIONS

Interest rates on senior assumable existing loans should not be too high. If the senior existing loan is a variable loan, the interest cap should be part of the evaluation. This is important if the property has to be carried for a significant time or rented due to a slow economy. In the event the loan has to be refinanced, finding cash for points and closing costs for the refinancing can be painful. Lenders for non-owner occupied properties usually will only lend up to 70 percent of the appraised value. If the equity is not there because the senior loan is too large, refinancing the loan may require adding cash to refinance to the 70 percent LTV. In slow economic conditions, banks are very stringent on issuing loans unless you are a true *"A" borrower*. An *"A" borrower* is someone that has a high FICA score and adequate equity in the securing property.

REFINANCING

Refinancing the property will require that you qualify for the loan. A good credit rating should be maintained. This can be accomplished with prompt payments on debts and an adequate income. A hard-money loan should be avoided except if it is used for a very short time. Hard-money loans can very quickly eat up the remaining equity in the property. A line of credit can sometimes be used. A line of credit is obtained from a lender so a future loan can be obtained using other properties that you own as collateral, or can be obtained using your credit and your verifiable income. A line of credit will have a maximum amount that can be borrowed. The rate of interest and the security used will vary from bank to bank, so shopping for the line of credit is important.

LOCATION

The property should not be in a depressed area. If it is in a poor location, there will be a shortage of qualified buyers, and it may be difficult to obtain a loan.

The property should be at a convenient driving distance from your residence. This is to allow ease of examining the property. The inspection would be to insure that the property is still occupied and that there isn't significant deferred maintenance. In the event the property is acquired, a short distance will help reduce the time to repair the property and therefore the time to sell or lease the property. Time not on the road can be used for working on the property.

Out-of-area properties, although they may have a good LTV, should be looked at very cautiously. There could be poor economic conditions due to a factory closing, military base closing, or just a gradual decay due to the demographics changing or an increase in crime. When you are not exposed to the happenings in an area from your newspapers or personal knowledge, poor decisions can happen. There is always the question when a loan is offered that is secured by an out-of-area property, "Why didn't a local hard-money lender make the loan?"

Out-of-state locations will have different foreclosure laws. This will require information on the state's foreclosure regulations to be able to make a proper evaluation of the investment's reward or loss. Remember that the borrower usually has an advantage. He most likely has more knowledge of the property in his area.

STRUCTURAL OR ECONOMIC OBSOLESCENCE

Ideally a single-family residence should have a two-car garage and more than one bathroom. A four bedroom, one bath, 2,500-square-foot house with a one-car garage can be a nightmare unless the sales price is low. Due to the structural obsolescence, the number of buyers will be reduced, reducing the market value. This isn't to say that a three bedroom, one bath, 1,000-square-foot house and no garage shouldn't be considered. The value can be very high due to location and demand.

The house improvements may be used up. A house that has decayed stucco and wood, decayed plaster, plaster in the bathroom that is crumbling or a kitchen that is disintegrated, or sidewalks and driveways that are cracked or decayed can significantly reduce market value.

This is not to say you should not make a loan on property that has some structural or economic obsolescence. These types of loans can be rewarding. Many hard-money lenders will turn their noses up at these properties. This can be their mistake due to a potential high rate of return that can be achieved. If reconditioning is required, there can be the potential for increased value if a fixer-upper buyer elects to buy the property *as is* and makes the required improvements. A *fixer upper* refers to a property that requires as little as a little paint to a major reconstruction project.

Everything has a market value. Your task is to accurately determine the value.

The downside with obsolete and used-up properties is that you may have to deal with renovation after your foreclosure. Due to this always being a possibility, the cost to subcontract the renovation of the improvements should be added into the equation to determine the market value. Although many hard-money lenders elect to do their own work, this usually should be left to those that have knowledge of construction and refurbishment methods along with physical stamina. The longer it takes to refurbish the property, the smaller the profit on your investment.

CONFORMING TO NEIGHBORHOOD

Improved property should be such that the marketability is not adversely affected. This would happen if the house were overbuilt for the neighborhood. A $600,000 property in a $200,000 neighborhood might be difficult to sell at full value. A house with a "unique" design for the neighborhood could be difficult to sell. The LTV should be low to allow for the undesirability of the property and potential long selling time. It isn't too difficult to be trapped into making a loan on a property with an odd configuration or a large square footage that had a high appraisal due to the lack of downward market value adjustment.

NON-CONFORMING USE

Improvements on land where the county or city zoning has been changed have special problems. In many cases the improvement is grandfathered. If the improvements were partially or totally destroyed, the improvement may not be allowed to be restored by the governing municipality.

This grandfathered category can significantly reduce the value of an investment. A single-family property with a zoning of R1 that has been changed to a higher density can be a problem. Although this type of change usually increases the value, this is not always the case. It may not be practical to build multiresidential units because of the lot size. The value as a SFR may have been decreased because of the closeness to multi-family or commercial units. A horse-breeding ranch could be downzoned for residential property or the amount of required land increased, thereby reducing the income-generating value. In some cases a residence, if destroyed may not be replaced because of the lack of sewer capability or because it is on too small of a lot. Additional evaluation by contacting the building department should be done when a property is in a nonconforming area.

Some older properties can be on a septic system that should have been or will have to be attached to a street sewer system. This can have significant cost to dig trenches and meet the city or county requirements. If the property were below the city sewer line, a pumping system would have to be added. It is not always easy to determine the status. There have been cases where a homeowner has been paying a sewer bill even though there hasn't been a connection to the city sewer line.

BUILDING PERMITS

There should be no nonpermitted additions unless the appraised value is adjusted downward along with the cost to remove the additions. Alternately, the cost to obtain permits and approvals of the additions should be deducted from the appraisal. Typically, cities will require properties with nonpermitted additions to have plans drawn and approved. A licensed contractor will have to be hired to certify that the property additions conform to the plans. Electrical and mechanical additions may have to be uncovered, inspected, and approved. There are double fees that may be imposed because of the *after the fact* plans and permits.

A call to the local planning department usually will provide information on the status of all building permits and square feet of the lot and improvements. The county assessor's office can also be contacted to verify that the square feet of the improvements agree with what was disclosed by the property owner's statements.

TENANT-OCCUPIED PROPERTY

In those cases where the property is tenant occupied, it is highly recommended to obtain a copy of the rental or lease agreement. This is easily done before lending money. It is also important to determine the appliances that belong to the owner and the ones owned by the tenant. If the property is foreclosed, tenants act in strange ways. They respond to a foreclosure as if there is a riot and pilfer the property. Without a clear accounting of the item ownership, appliances can disappear. Factors to determine in the rental agreement are length of lease, security deposit, number of occupants, if pets are permitted, rent amount, and rent escalation terms.

LABOR AND MATERIAL LIENS BY CONTRACTORS

In the event there has been recent construction or repair on the subject property, there could be a lien on the property that could take precedence over a new Trust Deed. This lien can be filed by a contractor, subcontractor, laborer, or material supplier.

A contractor's release and title insurance to insure the priority of your Trust Deed will be required. Any involved subcontractors, laborers, and material suppliers should also sign a release. This type of lien can develop when a loan is made to refurbish property. A problem would occur if the new loan has not been recorded prior to the start of any refurbishment.

CRACKED SLAB

There will be times when the subject property has a cracked slab or major construction flaw. This type of property trust deed investment is best left to the specialist or a lender that will be buying the property as a rental.

During the evaluation of the property, you as an investor should do a complete property inspection. This would include looking for cracks in flooring, driveways, outside foundation, and garage flooring. Very often a cracked slab can be detected by walking on carpeted floors. A slight step-up or step-down is an indication of a cracked slab. Diagonal cracks in walls are a good indication that the foundation has a major problem. If you are unsure of the condition of the property, a contractor should be retained to make an inspection and advise the cost of repairs. This repair cost should be included in the determination of the LTV.

The problem, with property having a major flaw, is obtaining new financing from a standard institutional lender. Most lenders will not lend on property in this condition. If a cracked slab has been repaired using a building permit and the work was done by a licensed contractor with final inspection approval, financing from a standard institutional lender can usually be obtained.

If you fund defective property and have to foreclose, be prepared to live with it until repairs are made, sell it as is or turn the property into a rental. If you elect to repair the defective property, savings may have to be available or a line of credit used.

SPECIAL LOCATION CONDITIONS

There are several special site conditions that must be considered. This is a location relative to earthquake faults, landslides, environmental pollution, and flood plains. There also should be a concern if there is fire danger because of the closeness of forests and brush. If there is poor drainage on the property, significant structural damage can occur. Natural land drainage should exist to avoid this potential problem. Typically, property should be graded to drain to the front of a lot. If the property drains to the rear, there has to be an adequate drainage system incorporated into the property. If it drains into other properties, easements for the drainage should be obtained.

If there is any concern about the property, contacting neighbors in the area about any problems should provide some information.

Part of the consideration should be the type of structure construction. This comes into play because of earthquake consequences. A tri-level or a multilevel structure is in greater danger as compared to a single level property. Tri-level structures have historically experienced more damage than a two-story structure. The existence of brick walls, a brick chimney, or property line block walls have more potential for damage from an earthquake. Commercial buildings that have inside first floor parking, also known as *soft construction*, can be susceptible to earthquakes. The exception to this would be construction that has special shear walls that have been designed and incorporated into the building to prevent damage from earthquakes.

If the property is in a flood plain, special federal insurance can be obtained. Water problems can still exist even if the property is not in a low-lying area. Sewer drains can become plugged, causing flooding and significant damage.

When property is in a fire zone and there are no firebreaks or barriers, there is a great danger of loss. Part of the loan terms should allocate funds to pay for the generation of firebreaks around the subject improvements. Unfortunately there can be environmental laws that prevent creation of adequate firebreaks. The type of roof is also important. A shake roof even with a fireproof coating can be vulnerable when there is a close fire. After a fire, there can be damage due to landslides and flooding caused by heavy rains. An evaluation of these dangers must be considered. This can be a difficult situation due to the problems in obtaining reasonably priced fire insurance.

If the property is in an environmentally sensitive area due to endangered plants, animals or birds, or near Indian burial grounds, construction on the property may be next to impossible. If the property has hazardous waste, this can prevent issuance of building permits until the site has been cleaned and certified. Any of these conditions can significantly slash the property value.

PROPERTY INSURANCE

There is a special concern that needs to be addressed. This is property insurance. The present policy of property insurance companies is to not insure properties that have had claims filed. This might be a claim for water damage due to a leaking roof, broken pipes, close to a fire hazard, or other loss. This usually occurs on older properties. They have been around for a while and things can start to go bad. In new construction of less than ten years, the builder would still be responsible and may correct the problem before a claim needs to be filed.

The insurance companies (90% of them) use a database called CLUE, the Comprehensive Loss Underwriting Exchange, provided by a company called Choice-Point, to determine if there have been any claims filed or even an inquiry about a loss. Future legislation may correct this problem.

Property under construction or being rehabbed requires a course-of-construction insurance policy. A California FAIR policy or similar type policy would have to be obtained at a high premium with a high deductible amount. The deductible amount could be several thousand dollars. This deductible portion wouldn't be paid when a claim is filed. The coverage is bare bones, so a renter's policy might be advisable to cover the contents of the property. Knowing the past history of claims on a property is therefore important. There is an additional impact of this new insurance company policy. If the property owner filed a claim during the period of your loan, or just reported a loss and didn't file a claim, the insurance could be canceled and your problems, if the owner doesn't pick up the tab, increased. If you end up owning the property in a foreclosure, this would be an additional cost to you. Selling the property, because of the higher insurance premium, would most likely be at a sale price significantly below market value.

DO YOU WANT TO BUY THIS PROPERTY?

The final decision on the investing in a Trust Deed should be based upon all the factors. The final question that must be asked is, do I want to own this property at the new encumbered level? If the answer is no, you will want to walk away from the loan. It hasn't cost any real money up to this time. It has only cost time for the evaluation.

If the Trust Deed has been offered to other investors or has been available for some time by a *secondary mortgage broker*[4], there may be something potentially wrong with the investment. The fact that the investment has not been grabbed quickly is an indication that other lenders have determined something is wrong. After a Trust Deed has been around for a while, there is an increase in the chance that the broker will deceive you or not fully disclose everything about the investment. After the broker has offered the Trust Deed to others, and the Trust Deed has not been grabbed, the broker learns what not to say or what to say to improve the chances for the sale of the Trust Deed to an investor.

---

[4] A *secondary mortgage broker* is one that is not the originating mortgage broker. This may occur when the originating broker doesn't have lenders with enough funds and allows other brokers to sell the Trust Deed. Often the Trust Deed is questionable and difficult to place. The secondary mortgage broker may be located in a different area or even a different state. If the loan is for property out of the area, the question must be asked, why hasn't a lender in that area made the loan?

CONTROLLED FUNDS

When lending money for rehabbing or repairs on properties, controlled funds (often called an impounded account and held by an escrow company, a trusted mortgage broker, or yourself) should be seriously considered. In making loans, knowing the borrower and his financial responsibility is important. This however does not preclude the borrower from occasionally taking money out of the controlled funds and not performing the repair work. The repair work should be done in phases that are inspected and approved. In this manner, if the borrower has not performed the work as agreed, there will still be some controlled funds available after taking over the property. Hopefully the remaining funds will cover most of the required work and allow for the sale of the property without a loss of and on the investment. The controlled impound account should be set up so the lender can claim the impounded account if a foreclosure is required. One of the Trust Deed Note terms would include the statement that any construction work should be done in a timely manner.

There may be impound accounts that are to be used for street improvements on offset locations that will be paid to municipalities. These impounds might be created in the form of checks. The checks should be set up so they can be paid to the municipality only and nontransferable. To do otherwise would potentially allow the borrower to obtain control of the fund, thereby removing equity from the property. This would be similar to a stack of lumber being removed by the borrower or a thief.

When disbursements are being made from an impound account, there should be a statement on the back of checks as follows:

POSITIVE I.D. REQUIRED

THIRD PARTY ENDORSEMENT PROHIBITED

Issued without recourse to the drawer and as absolute payment of any and all underlying obligations.

BORROWER'S INVESTMENT

The borrower should have a significant interest in the property. If the borrower is buying a property with nothing down, there is no reason for this borrower not to walk if things are not going his way. The only incentive would be that his credit rating would suffer. Often someone buying in this manner has a credit rating that isn't too good to start with. When a loan is made on property that has appreciated, there is some inducement for the borrower to save this equity. There will be times where a borrower will have inherited the property. There is a tendency for this borrower not to consider the equity as hard-earned money. Therefore, there is a probability that this property will eventually be investor owned through a foreclosure. This isn't a big problem provided there is adequate LTV.

COST TO SELL

In addition to the above-mentioned costs, there is one that all too often is forgotten—the sales commission. Although many properties can be sold by hard-money lenders, if time is important, listing the property can save you money. Real estate brokers have access to many more buyers than what newspaper ads can generate. Many buyers won't buy from owners due to the complexities and personal interaction between buyer and seller that happens when real estate is sold. It doesn't take too many escrows that don't close to eat up any savings in the sales commission. Typically the sales commission is 6 percent on residential property, 10 percent on land, 10 percent on mobile homes, and 6 percent on commercial property. If the property is a very high price, these commission rates can often be reduced. As in the case with everything, commission rates are always negotiable.

Section 8

BORROWER'S PROFILE

Figure 8. *Trust me, I won't file bankruptcy this time.*

EARNING ABILITY

A borrower's earning ability isn't as important as the property equity. However, it is still important to evaluate the borrower's ability and willingness to make payments.

Ideally, the borrower should have income to cover the payments on all of his obligations. This would include all senior loans and your potential new loan. The monthly payments could include PITI (principal, interest, taxes, and insurance), association fees, and property assessments. There should be enough income to cover his other living expenses. The total monthly payments should therefore be equal to roughly one-third of the borrower's monthly income. When the property has a low LTV, income isn't as important to protect the investment. With the new federal high-rate loan law, payments on an owner-occupied property cannot exceed 50 percent of the borrower's income.

If the borrower has an employer, his income can be verified with payment stubs. In the case where the borrower is self-employed, income tax returns for the prior two years should be obtained and reviewed. Very often the borrower will claim higher income because he has not declared all of his income. This higher income would be difficult to believe even if the borrower has a second set of books. If the borrower has cheated on his income taxes, there is no reason to believe that he would provide an accurate picture in a loan application. The borrower, in effect, has cheated himself, and may not be able to obtain a loan with favorable terms.

Even with a copy of income tax returns there is a potential problem. With computer tax return software, a false return can easily be generated. Asking for canceled tax payment checks to the IRS to verify the tax returns would be helpful.

In those cases, where tax return information is not available, the property should have a low LTV to cover a potential foreclosure and bankruptcy. If the LTV is not low, additional property of the borrower might be added to cross-collateralize the loan. This hard position should be taken when there is some indication that the borrower has questionable business practices. If the borrower's credibility is in question, a cosigner with good credit can be requested.

If there is a questionable source of money for the borrower's down payment on a purchase, a copy of bank deposits should be requested. If there are significant deposits and withdrawals, there should be a satisfactory explanation. If the explanation is not satisfactory, this could be a drug money laundering operation, something that must be avoided.

A hard-money loan may be used as a swing loan. In these cases the borrower only needs money to purchase another property. The loan will be paid back when the securing property is sold. A swing loan is a temporary short-term loan lasting typically 30 to 120 days. A copy of a listing agreement should be reviewed to verify that the property is listed and that the loan is really a swing loan. Here, the earning ability isn't too important providing there is an active real estate market, the property to be sold is priced realistically, and the money provided will carry the borrower for the marketing and escrow period. It is sometimes better to lend an additional amount to allow for contingencies, providing there is adequate security. The swing loan is exempt from some of the predatory lending laws.

A swing loan doesn't have to be against only one property. However, using cross-collateralization can be asking for complexity, where there is already enough to go around. Cross-collateralization may still be necessary to provide an adequate cushion.

In hard-money loans, the income of the borrower is important from the standpoint of being able to make payments on the loan. If the income or potential income of the borrower is not there, the loan will be in trouble in a short time. A short time is interpreted to mean, the period that is required to spend the funds that the borrower received after deduction of points and other loan costs.

If the loan is for refinancing a previous loan that has gotten into trouble, this new loan probably will be in the same type of trouble very soon, only compounded. This will be due to the reduced equity in the property. In the case where the borrower will not be able to carry the weight of the loan with his earning power, it is recommended to lend only on property that can take another refinancing. This should provide a highly desirable safe investment. The borrower will still be able to refinance or sell the property prior to your loan becoming due.

For the case where the property does not have enough equity for a refinance, there will be a high probability the property will be acquired through foreclosure with the associated fix-up and sales cost. However, the loan can still be acceptable if you don't mind owning the property. Remember, there would still be the cost of the foreclosure and potential bankruptcy that will reduce the apparent equity before you can take possession.

TRUSTWORTHINESS

Trustworthiness is difficult to judge. Borrowers who sound too good to be true probably are too good to be true. If a trouble-free performing loan is required, the borrower should have a past performance of earnings and making payments. *What has happened in the past will probably happen in the future* can be your general rule. If he has lied once, he will probably lie again. If he failed to make payments on obligations, he will most likely do it again.

A strawman might be used to give the appearance of a sound borrower. Only by being objective in the review of the property appraisal and checking the sales on the properties in area to verify the validity of the security can you protect yourself against this type of deception.

Past performance isn't necessarily the total story. An engineer or computer designer who has been successful in the past won't necessarily have the same earning capacity if industrial needs change and his expertise isn't in demand. A movie producer may not have a new production. A policeman who has been fired is not the best wage earner. A drug addict or alcoholic probably won't have any money left for the payments on the Trust Deed after his habit is satisfied. A real estate agent who is just starting out, or who has had a good past performance record may be unable to earn a living in a slow market. Real estate agents and other sales types have a high burnout so a judgment will have to be made on their performance potential.

If the borrower has been involved in illegal acts, this can portend problems for you. This type of borrower can become unstable and potentially hurt you or your family if a loan is made that goes into default. Borrowers often will blame you for their problems. A credit report might provide some information. A search on the Internet of the borrowing company and the principal borrowers could provide shocking information.

The use of the loan money is important, but not the most important item. If the loan is to make improvements on the house, this is an indication of a good loan. This will provide additional equity. Don't always believe what the borrower puts down on the loan application. He may be deceptive or the mortgage broker will tell the borrower some good reasons to write into his loan application. The mortgage broker knows what lenders like to hear.

FILED BANKRUPTCY

Anyone who has received bankruptcy counseling *and* filed a bankruptcy is a credit risk. This person can have poor business judgment, be a gambler, an alcoholic, a drug user, or someone who doesn't believe in meeting his obligations or can't handle his money. If the property has good equity, this can justify the loan. The LTV should be better than from a borrower that has not filed a bankruptcy. Anyone who has filed a bankruptcy will know that a filing doesn't necessarily protect them from foreclosure. This unfortunately will not stop the individual from filing to gain time to delay a foreclosure or a foreclosure sale.

The bankruptcy procedure will usually only absorb equity. The borrower will try, with the bankruptcy, to bleed the remaining equity from the property by either collecting rents or just to have a place to live. The filing of a bankruptcy is like getting a divorce, after the first one, it's not as difficult the second time. The bankruptcy can remain on the borrower's record for ten years.

FILED HOMESTEAD

The homestead exemption (Civil Codes 704.710 through *704.995*) is a statutory protection where a homeowner's equity (value above the sum of Trust Deeds or mortgages) in his residence may be protected from judgments, liens, and creditors. The amount of protection in a court judgment is:

- $50,000 for single homeowners,
- $75,000 for families,

- $100,000 for seniors, disabled, and low-income homeowners (earning $15,000 or less annually).

Only one homestead exemption is allowed at a time. The homestead exemption will not prevent foreclosure by a lender, mechanic's lien, seizure and sale for back taxes, or to avoid paying child support or alimony.

Many people believe that filing a homestead will keep their property from being lost in a foreclosure. This is not the case. When considering funding a new Trust Deed when a homestead has been filed, have the borrower file an abandonment of the homestead to provide an additional defense in the event bankruptcy is filed. Although this is not necessary, it raises the borrower's awareness that there isn't homestead protection from the debt being generated. In reality, a homestead filing is a voluntary lien by the borrower and will not jeopardize the senior position of a new loan. The Preliminary Title Report should show the homestead exemption status.

There are a number of companies that have made a business of frightening homeowners into filing a homestead exemption for a fee. This type of operation is considered legal but unethical.

In practice, a homeowner, if he finds himself in financial trouble, can file a homestead exemption, just prior to a court judgment. This approach will avoid the perception of planning to default on debts. In filing a declaration of homestead, the borrower has implied that they have an expectation that a judgment may be made against them.

Filing of a homestead exemption can be an impediment to a homeowner obtaining a loan. If a trust-deed-secured loan is given on the home equity, the points and interest can be slightly higher because of the loan default implication. Lenders might believe the borrower does not plan on paying his debt. Additionally, in a foreclosure auction, any overbid above the credit bid on the property might be slightly less if a homestead exemption has been filed. This would leave the property owner with less due to not receiving as much money from an overbid. There is the perception that the old homeowner could find a lawyer who could make a case that the property is valued much higher than the bid price. The buyer in fore-closure would have to defeat the lawsuit, thereby incurring additional expenses that could happen.

PAYS DEBTS

The credit report will provide an indication of the borrower's attitude on payment of debts or the borrower's ability to budget. If a borrower has been sloppy on his payments, the late fee clause in the Trust Deed Note might help. The paying pattern of the borrower usually doesn't change, so don't hold your breath for timely payments if the borrower has been late in the past.

JUDGMENTS

Part of the reason that a credit report must be obtained is to learn the past performance of the borrower. Past performance usually will happen in the future. The credit report should show judgments and liens against the borrower.

If the borrower has had a history of lawsuits and judgments, and there is adequate equity in the property, there shouldn't be a problem. The only problem, with past suits and judgments, is the borrower will have gotten use to them and the trepidation about them isn't a big deal. They can also rationalize reasons they shouldn't make payments or they are quick to hire an attorney. Be prepared to write a lot of nonpayment notices, file foreclo-sures, challenge bankruptcies, attend depositions, and appear in court if there are lawsuits and judgments in the borrower's history.

Past judgments and present lawsuits can be a significant problem. Although the recording date is very important to establish the priority of liens, a lien with a temporary restraining order (TRO) on the disposition of the property will delay a foreclosure sale. Legal counsel may be required to remove the TRO and to establish your equity position.

PREVIOUS FORECLOSURE

A Preliminary Title Report will show if a Notice of Default (NOD) and a Notice of Trustee Sale (NOS) have been filed on the property. These prior actions can still be acceptable if the property has a good LTV or the property is one that you want to own. Remember, hard-money loans are made to people that don't have the best loan history. If there are any Notice of Defaults and foreclosure proceedings, these must be rescinded before the loan is finalized. This can be handled in the escrow instructions by including the statements that defaults and foreclosure procedures will be removed and agreed upon when existing loans are paid off. There is one problem that can occur after the Notice of Default is removed with your loan—the borrower may, in a short time, refinance the loan at better terms. This will result in very little payment for your effort. A prepayment penalty (if allowed) should be included in the terms of your loan. If the prepayment isn't allowable, a processing fee or points should be charged so your efforts can be rewarded.

When dealing with borrowers that have had foreclosures, you need to consider the value of your time and money spent filing a foreclosure and chasing the borrower out of bankruptcy before a loan is made.

TYPE OF PERSON

The borrower ideally should be common folk, someone who has a sense of responsibility to family and work. This may not make him the most interesting person, but he will probably make his loan payments. The borrower should also be intelligent enough to understand the importance of the Trust Deed, Trust Deed Note, and terms.

Part of the evaluation of the borrower should include his housekeeping traits. If the yard and the inside of the house are poorly maintained, then the lifestyle and payment performance may also be poor. If the window coverings are bed sheets, this is a possible indication there is insensitivity to keep their life in order or inadequate money to meet obligations. Past actions are an indication of future actions.

There is one type of borrower that should be treated with the utmost of care. This is the elderly. If you suspect the mortgage broker is working this type of borrower to obtain commissions, or when there are questionable serial loans, you should not become involved. You may want to report the incident to the Department of Real Estate. When dealing with the elderly, if you are a party to the transaction, you could be party to elder abuse, and consequently a lawsuit. One way to avoid elder abuse is to have one of their children appointed as a conservator or have their children obtain power of attorney to conduct the loan transaction. This could still present problems if the children don't use all of the funds for their parents' benefit.

WORK SKILLS

The borrower should have work skills that are in demand now. An aeronautical engineer working outside of his profession due to the reduced demand for his skills might have a reduced income. Real estate agents and brokers need to have verifiable past and present income performance. A business degree or a degree in government is not always highly marketable. Some attorneys should be avoided. If they have filed lawsuits in the past, there is a high probability they will do so again. They can file and refile lawsuits easily and make life a torment.

The impact of change in taxes also can affect the earning ability of borrowers. For restaurant owners, the reduction of the deductibility of meals from 85 to 50 percent can have an effect on their business. This would create the possibility of the borrower having to file a bankruptcy in the future if his income is reduced.

In the case of lending funds for the rehab of a property or construction of a new building, the borrower's past performance is extremely important. Viewing the borrower's completed projects, even if the drive is substantial, can, in the long run save you enormous time and pain.

FAMILY AFFILIATION

The borrower should have family responsibility and a willingness to meet his responsibilities. He should also show a willingness and ability to make a living and pay the bills.

FRIENDS AND RELATIVES

Loans should not be made to friends or relatives! If a hard-money loan is made to a friend, usually it will be because they critically need money. There is always the probability that the friend will not be able to make the payments or pay off the loan. In this case, the friend will not only be lost, but there is a high likelihood that an enemy will be made.

When lending to a relative, the same logic should apply to that of lending to a friend. There is the additional problem that relatives will take sides and not only will the borrower become an enemy, but there could be a splitting of the relatives over the transaction.

Lending to strangers is difficult enough when a loan is not paid. Complicating the transaction by lending to a friend or relative not only will complicate your life, it also can reduce your wealth because of the possibility that the loan will not be paid.

REASONS FOR MONEY

Business

When the loan is for business purposes, this should not affect your decision. Often a loan application will show the purpose to be for a business venture. This is often not the real purpose for the loan. The property must still be the security for the loan. The loan must not be a business loan. Even if the true purpose of the loan is for a business, many start-up businesses and expansions of businesses fail.

One business that a borrower will conduct is to rehab property. A rehab can consist of a large patchwork of improvements. This can include simple painting to major work on the property. Work such as repairing a cracked slab, remodeling kitchens and bathrooms, reroofing, replumbing, rewiring (with a new service box), and restuccoing may be required. There will be times when a property was vandalized to the extent that the inside drywall must be repaired. This may require removing the old drywall or drywalling over the old drywall. This last repair method will require shimming windows and door moldings. The cost of all of these repairs can be estimated, so an adjustment to the LTV can be made.

The loan usually will be used to purchase a property and then the buyer will do the rehab. This type of loan can be satisfactory. It should be remembered that the borrower is applying for a job—the job of rehabbing property. You as an investor are hiring the borrower to do a job. As with any employer, it is critical to control the release of funds to the worker. If you, as an investor, do the fund control, you are now a manager. As a manager, your return should be more than just the interest on a loan. The easiest method to control funds is to have a lender in a junior position provide funds for the rehab. In this case the junior lien holder will deal with the worker management. If the project goes bad, the junior lender stands to lose all of his investment. The mortgage broker on the loan might be used, if they have knowledge of rehab projects; and they are willing to monitor the project and control the funds. Mortgage brokers however have their business to run and don't have as much invested in the project, so funds might be released without adequate verification that scheduled work has been completed. If the rehab is substantial, a project manager might be considered. This however will deplete your return unless the borrower foots the cost. In this case, the manager owes his allegiance to the borrower, not you, and bad decisions might be made.

It is important with rehab projects that the borrower has a reasonable amount of his own money in the project. In some cases the borrower will purchase the property with his own funds and only need the additional funds to rehab the property. This puts the borrower at a greater risk and you in a safer position.

Every so often you will find a borrower that needs money to rehab a building. This could be a sham if the borrower only plans to do a minor facial change. The borrower may really be using the money to keep the property out of foreclosure. This is often the case where there is a large senior loan that will remain in place.

Pay Off Trust Deed Loan in Foreclosure

If the loan is to pay off a loan in foreclosure (refinance), an evaluation should be made more on the property than the borrower. The property should appraise to provide a lower than normal LTV. The lower LTV is to allow for a new refinance, unless the lender hopes to own the property. This position should be taken because of the high probability that the property will be in a new foreclosure and require refinancing in a short time.

Illness

This can be a difficult loan to evaluate. If a copy of the medical bills can be viewed, you might want to look at them. You should be careful about this. The borrower could be in an emotionally charged state and you would be dealing with privacy issues.

If the illness is of a short duration there shouldn't be any problems. If the illness is projected to be of a long duration or terminal, unless there is a disability mortgage insurance, life insurance, or PMI (Private Mortgage Insurance) policy to cover the loan, there might be a foreclosure in your future. If the borrowers are realistic, when there is a lack of income to make payments, they will know that the property may have to be sold. If they don't recognize the problem, the loan can be very difficult to service. When there is enough equity for payment of bills and the payment of interest, this type of loan can be acceptable.

Buy a Car or Truck

A loan that will be used for a car or truck purchase can be a good indication. This is a sign that the borrower wants to write off the loan on his income tax. Borrowing the money using real estate instead of the vehicle as security makes the loan tax deductible. Under these conditions, the borrower is probably committed to a payoff of the loan.

CREDIT APPLICATION

The loan application submitted by the borrower(s) should be reviewed in detail. The application should show any bankruptcies, foreclosures, judgments, debts, and income. If the income looks too high, a copy of the borrower's income tax returns for the previous two years should be requested. A handy man usually doesn't earn $150,000 per year. Remember, all of the applicants (owners of the property) for the loan must sign the application.

Very often the application will have omissions. This is a sign that there may be facts the borrower doesn't want you to know. If all the application is not filled out or the document is not signed (under civil and criminal penalties), there is deception happening.

The credit application should agree with the credit report and Preliminary Title Report. If there are discrepancies that are not adequately explained, do yourself a favor by walking away from the loan.

CREDIT REPORT

Credit reports are available from various companies. They are similar in form and describe the payment performance of the borrower. There will be variations due to their using different data. The three main credit reporting companies are as follows:

- Experian (Experian/Fair, Isaac risk model score, FICO)—(888) 397-3742; Web site: http://www.experian.com,

- Equifax (Beacon credit score, $9.95 per copy per year for individuals)— (800) 685-1111; Web site: http://www.equifax.com,

- Trans Union Corporation (Empirica score, $9.95 per copy per year for individuals)—(800) 888-4213, (800) 916-8800; Web site: http://www.truecredit.com.

There are other companies that offer various programs that monitor your credit using the information of the three companies named above. The fee is approximately $44 to $80. A few companies offer a big package but don't provide easy access to just a credit report. The yearly programs were introduced as a help to spot identity theft and errors on your credit report. These programs will most likely keep changing as companies jockey for market share. It isn't necessary to call each credit reporting company. A centralized point has been established by the three named companies above. The free credit reports can be obtained once a year by calling (877) 322-8228 or online at the Web site: www.annualcreditreport.com.

Other local credit-reporting companies are available. Apartment owners use a separate evaluation of renters that will show tenants' past performance. All credit reports require a signed customer release to obtain the report.

The mortgage broker usually will obtain the release authorization for the credit reports. A credit report supplied by a borrower should not be used. With copy machine quality, it is too easy to make up a credit report that hides important information. The reports for all the borrowers on the property should be reviewed in detail to determine the borrowers' acceptability.

The payment performance is shown as "C" as current: "1," "2," and so on, describing the number of months a payment is late. A payment is late if not made within thirty days of the due date.

Most credit reports provide a score number. This would be on a sliding scale where a low rating number would be the worst credit. Other credit reports will show a percentage for a probable default. This doesn't mean too much if the borrower defaults on your loan. However, a low default percentage is desirable.

The credit reports will show a Beacon credit score, Experian/fair, Isaac/fair, Isaac risk mode, FICO score, or an Empirica score. A score of 300 (the lowest score) would be very poor, 500 fair, 600 good, 700 very good, and 850 (the top score) excellent. When the score is high and the borrower is looking for a hard-money loan, you should be a little suspicious. The borrower with a high number should be able to obtain a conventional loan with low interest and low points.

There are valid reasons for a borrower with a high FICO score to obtain a hard-money loan. This might be to obtain a fast loan, the borrower's income wouldn't cover the loan servicing, the property won't qualify for a conventional loan, the loan amount relative to property value LTV is too large, there are major defects (but hopefully correctable) in the property, or the property use is grandfathered. These problems, although unacceptable to a conventional lender, might still make a property lendable providing the terms of the loan are configured properly.

The credit report should also show bankruptcies, foreclosures, judgments, not-responsible notices, tax liens, tax releases paid, lawsuits, and any wage assignments against the borrower.

The credit reporting agency is required to remove bankruptcies after ten years and foreclosures after seven years. The borrower could be cute and not report these negative items on his loan application if they occurred after these periods, knowing you probably wouldn't be able to find out about them. If he is keeping his credit clean after these events, he is probably now an acceptable credit risk.

The credit report will show the outstanding balance on the various charge accounts. An evaluation must be made to establish that this won't be a problem with the trust deed investment. If there are lawsuits and recorded judgments against the borrower, it is very important that the property have a good LTV to pay off these judgments.

When there are a number of judgments, unpaid back taxes, foreclosures, or bankruptcies, there is a probability that a foreclosure will have to be filed in the future. If the borrower has a significant amount of outstanding debt, and the loan is not being used to pay it off, there is a high likelihood that the borrower is preparing to file a bankruptcy. If a request that the outstanding liens be paid is refused by the borrower, the loan in all probability should be refused. If the borrower agrees to pay the debts, the loaned money should be paid directly out of escrow for the debts. Needless to say, the property should have a LTV to withstand a foreclosure, unpaid taxes, and bankruptcy.

When the loan applicant or one of the property owners is a member of the military (either male or female), this can have a profound effect on the income generation of a Trust Deed. This will come more into play if a foreclosure must be filed and there is or has recently been a declared war. The loan interest and foreclosure will be put on hold because of the Soldiers' and Sailors' Civil Relief Act. This also will apply to someone in the reserves that has been called up to service. A notarized affidavit of non-military involvement should be obtained if you suspect that the borrower is in the service or suspect he will be called into service. If you have made a loan that is impacted by this law, an attorney that has dealt with this issue should be retained. The provisions of the law do give you some redress.

In evaluating the credit report, verify that the report is a recent one. If it is old, there should be some suspicion that the borrower has been shopping around for a long time for a loan or there is a recent event the borrower is trying to conceal.

Section 9

LOANS

Figure 9. *Which one of these dogs should I select?*

LOAN RESTRICTIONS AND INFLATION

Present law provides that on a loan less than $20,000, a balloon payment is not allowed during the first five years. Loans can be amortized for periods less than five years to avoid the balloon payment limitation. Interest-only loans, therefore, should normally be above $20,000 to avoid this problem. The problem with a five year or longer period is the ever present threat of inflation and the reduced purchasing power. (See additional restrictions on high-rate loans for owner-occupied property.)

Because of the threat of inflation, it is advisable to keep loan period short. If the inflation rate is low, less than 5 percent per year, it is advised to keep the loan period less than three years. If an inflation rate is 5 to 10 percent, it is advised to keep the loan period less than two years. If the inflation rate is 10 to 20 percent, it is advised to keep the loan period less than one year. As a quick approximation, the inflation rate usually is the rate of long-term bonds or the interest rate on thirty-year loans, less 3 to 4 percent. These guidelines are only that. Deviations should be made based on the loan's merits, such as a very good LTV or a high rate of return, or both.

There are news reports that claim the inflation rate is much higher than reported by the government. This is due to the government's inflation rate not including all of the living costs. This presents a difficult decision on the rate that should be charged on hard-money loans. Having said this, the interest rate that can be charged will be dictated by the marketplace rate.

The marketplace rate not only is defined by the economic condition interest rate, but also by the economic condition of mortgage brokers. When the number of available loans begins to decrease, mortgage brokers, who are in competition with each other, offer better terms to borrowers. In order to be more competitive, the number of points received and the interest rate charged is reduced. The reduced number of points also will impact the hard-money lender. There won't be points available to you as the hard-money lender. The major impact, when there is increased competition, will be the lower loan interest rate you will be able to receive. This interest rate will be less than the rate available in times of abundant Trust Deeds. This will also be impacted by the stock market. If the stock market is increasing in value, investors will invest in stocks reducing the amount of money that will be available to fund Trust Deeds.

If a hard-money rate of 14.5 percent is charged, and the actual inflation is 9.5 percent, with the total tax rate of 40 percent (federal and state), this would produce a return of only 3 percent ((14.5% – 9.5 %) × 0.60). This return doesn't provide bragging rights. This analysis can be carried even further. Consider that the government spends 1.8 dollars for every dollar collected—the actual tax rate is 1.8 times the amount paid. This tax may not be collected, but that does not mean that there isn't a *tax* At some point, inflation resulting from the government *printing* money will increase. Including the 1.8 factor in the equation would provide a return of ((14.5% – 9.5%) × (1.00 – (.4 × 1.8))) or 1.4 percent, a rate of return that is embarrassing.

These guides also should apply to IRA accounts that may be kept for a long time. In any self-directed IRA, there are charges by the bank to set up the account, putting a foreclosure property into the account, owning the real estate, and the reconveyance of a Trust Deed. These expenses would have to be balanced out against the rate of return. There are other special considerations in an IRA account. The beneficiary can *only direct* the IRA fund holder on how funds are to be used and *cannot control* the use of the IRA funds. This is because the beneficiary is a prohibited person. Trust deeds in the account cannot be used as security for a loan. To do so would cause the Trust Deed to be treated as a distribution.

If there is going to be a foreclosure, it may be desirable to sell the Trust Deed to a third party, most likely at a discount, to avoid the problems of a foreclosure and a potential bankruptcy. If the property is acquired in a foreclosure, it will become part of the IRA account. There will be an additional IRA account holder charge of roughly $500.

There is much discussion by politicians and the news media that hard-money lenders are gouging the public. When the actual spendable return is calculated, this is hardly the case. One of the tenets in trust deed investing is to preserve the investment. Hard-money lending requires high interest rates to offset loss from inflation, your management costs, foreclosures, and bankruptcy.

Unfortunately, an investment that provides an apparent high rate of return is sometimes difficult to find, or the safety of the loan is questionable. It would not be prudent to invest in a very high rate of return Trust Deed if there isn't a good expectation of return of and on the investment. Remember that one of the most important aspects in investing is preservation of capital. Proper hard-money lending can usually accomplish this.

HIGH-RATE LOANS (SECTION 32)

Recent federal law has added additional complications to the interest rate that can be charged, the points that can be received, the loan duration, prepayment penalty, and several other loan terms. A general guide is detailed below. (Loans obtained from mortgage brokers that are not intimate with the details of high-rate loans should be avoided. This is due to the large penalty that can be imposed on you as a lender.)

HOMEOWNERSHIP AND EQUITY PROTECTION ACT OF 1994

The lender and mortgage broker must comply with the Federal Truth in Lending Act (Regulation Z). In general the Federal Regulation Z restrictions are similar to the *California Financial Code* with a few other peculiarities such as jump rate, prepayment penalty, amortization, and ability to make payments.

Special rules apply if lenders make two or more high-rate loans or one or more through a mortgage broker in a twelve-month period.

This does not apply to:

- a non-owner occupied property,
- equity lines of credit,
- a loan to purchase a home.

High-rate loans are triggered by the following:

1. The first-lien loan (first Trust Deed) annual percentage rate[1] (APR) is greater than 8 percent plus the treasury security rate on fifteenth of the month prior to loan application for a like period. For example if the loan is for five years, the treasury rate for five years must be used. (The 8 percent rate may be changed in the future to between 8 and 12 percent.) If the rate works out to 13 percent, the rate to be used to avoid triggering the high-rate loan should be a lower rate such as 12.99 percent. The triggering rate for a second-lien loan (junior Trust Deed) is 10 percent plus the treasury security rate.

The loan amount is defined by Regulation Z. This amount can be less due to points and other costs, unless excluded. The actual interest rate and point can be higher, making the loan a high-rate loan.

2. The fees are greater than $510 (for 2005) or 8 percent of the loan amount.

   A. The amount will be adjusted annually on January 1, based on the consumer price index increase from the previous year's June to subsequent year's June.

   B. The amount includes points, fees and third party charges that are not reasonable. This could include direct or indirect compensation for an appraisal, credit report, and title insurance.

When high-rate loans are triggered, the following apply:

1. There is a mandatory three-business-day (cooling off) rescission period for loan disclosure. The three days exclude holidays, Saturday, and Sunday. This requires that the borrower sign and be provided with the

---

[1] *Annual percentage rate* is the interest rate a borrower pays when fees such as interest, points, and other charges are included. Lenders differ in the loan fees that are included in the calculation.

obligations that will be imposed prior to the cooling off period. (There are exceptions if an emergency exists.)

2. There is a requirement for disclosure, in conspicuous type size, of potential loss of home with the following statement.

   "You are not required to complete this agreement merely because you have received these disclosures or have signed a loan application" and "if you obtain this loan, the lender will have a Mortgage on your home. You could lose your home, and any money you have put into it, if you do not meet your obligations under the loan."

   These disclosure obligations also are imposed on a creditor (lender) making one or more high cost mortgages through a mortgage broker.

3. There is a requirement for disclosure of annual percentage rate and regular monthly payment.

4. There cannot be a change to the loan contract unless it is predisclosed with a three-day rescission clause. The three days are defined as calendar days (excluding Sunday). After these three days, the loan can be funded.

5. No prepayment penalty unless permitted by state law, and all loan payments are no greater than 50 percent of the borrower's monthly gross income. If refinanced by the same lender or affiliate, there shall be no prepayment penalty.

   No prepayment penalty after five years. (Note the difference from California law.)

6. A loan cannot be based solely on collateral without regard to the consumer's repayment ability, including the consumer's current and expected income, current obligations, and employment. (The law and regulations do not additionally clarify ability.)

7. Home improvement must be jointly payable to the consumer and the home improvement contractor (or third-party escrow agent).

8. There shall be no jump rate in the interest charged if property is put into foreclosure, nor any post-default interest rates that are higher than the contract rate.

9. There shall be no balloon payment for the first five years.

   There is a narrowly drawn exemption from the balloon payment limitation for mortgage loans with a maturity less than one year, if the purpose of the loan is a bridge loan connected with the acquisition of a dwelling intended to become the consumer's principal dwelling.

10. There shall be no negative amortization (i.e., monthly payments that result in an increase of the amount owed).

11. The prepaid interest cannot be for more than two months.

12. There is an absolute liability on assignees for all claims and defenses the consumer has against the original creditor, unless the assignee demonstrates that he could not have determined that the transaction was indeed a high-risk mortgage loan. This amount is limited to the sum of the remaining debt and amounts previously paid on the loan.

13. Failure to comply with the act could trigger a private lawsuit or state attorney general action for actual damages, together with all finance charges and fees paid by consumer plus reasonable attorneys' fees.

14. A borrower's rescission attempt (after the rescission period) must be contested within twenty days or the lender must satisfy the mortgage and return all finance charges and other amounts paid by borrower in connection with the loan.

Predatory Lending Law (effective July1, 2002)

There is a more stringent California law, *Financial Code, Chapter 732, Division 1.6, (Sections 4970* through *4979.8)* that imposes greater restrictions *on owner-occupied one to four unit* properties located in California and covers loans that exceed the loan rate by 8 percent as defined by item 1 of the law, when the original principal balance is less than $250,000 and when the total points and fees payable by the borrower will exceed 6 percent of the total amount of the loan. Excluded from the law are reverse mortgages (on first liens only with proper disclosure of terms), open lines of credit, loans secured by rental property, or second homes and bridge loans (discussed later).

California law prohibits payment of a prepayment penalty after three years. A prepayment penalty may be included for the first thirty-six months only under specified conditions. There is a probation of a new loan having a prepayment if originated by the same person. The loan shall not have negative amortization, unless it is a first Trust Deed with disclosures. The borrower in a loan transaction of one to four residential units may not be required to pay interest on the principal for a period of more than one day prior to recording the Mortgage or Trust Deed.

Loans with terms of five years or less must be fully amortized.

Advance payments required to be paid from the proceeds are prohibited.

A covered loan will not impose the prepayment fee or penalty if the covered loan is accelerated as a result of default. The person who originates the covered loan shall also have offered the consumer a choice of another product without a prepayment fee or penalty.

Increasing the interest rate as the result of a default is prohibited.

Persons originating covered loans must reasonably believe that the consumers obtaining the loan will be able to make the specified payments from resources other than the consumer's equity in the dwelling. The law establishes criteria upon which the person may rely.

Payments from the proceeds of the loan made directly to a contractor under a home improvement contract are prohibited. Payments made jointly to consumer and contractor or into a third party escrow are allowed with specified requirements.

Encouraging or recommending to the consumer to default on the existing loan or other debt is prohibited.

A loan that contains a call provision that permits the lender, in its sole discretion, to accelerate the indebtedness unless under specified conditions is prohibited.

Refinancing that does not result in an identifiable, tangible benefit to the consumer is prohibited.

A specified Consumer Caution and Home-ownership Counseling notice must be given to the consumer no later than three days prior to the signing of the loan documents.

Steering, counseling, or directing a consumer to accept a loan product with a risk grade less favorable than the consumer would otherwise qualify for, or with higher costs than the consumer would qualify for is prohibited.

Structuring the transaction as an open line of credit, or otherwise, in an attempt to avoid or circumvent the statute is prohibited.

Acting in a manner that constitutes fraud is prohibited.

Additional details can be obtained on the Web site http://www.dre.ca.gov/relaw.htm. Information requires the Acrobat Reader, which can be downloaded from this site.

If the above is confusing, consider also that the legislated law and implemented regulations are slightly different. There are ongoing changes to the regulations, and case law is starting to make an impact. Your mortgage broker should be fully aware of the regulations or hopefully have access to an updated computer software package that deals with the lending regulations.

Due to the confusing language of the lending laws, some mortgage brokers only process loans over $250,000 or loans on non-owner occupied one to four units to bypass some of the predatory lending laws. This unfortunately may make it difficult for some borrowers in need to find a lender.

If the loan you are considering is borderline, a restructuring would be appropriate to avoid violating the state and federal laws.

USURY

Lending of money as a private individual has legal restrictions. The major restriction is a maximum interest rate of 10 percent. (See previous discussion on limits.) This does not restrict the seller of real estate from charging more than 10 percent or buying a note that has a higher rate than the 10 percent. If the note has a higher rate than 10 percent, the generation of the note must adhere to the legal restrictions in place when the note was generated.

ESCROW HOLDER

The selection of an escrow holder can have a major impact on the disposition of funds. If the escrow holder is a real estate broker, he is controlled by the Department of Real Estate. The Department of Real Estate specifies how funds shall be controlled. Once the funds are put into the real estate broker's trust account, they cannot be returned unless both parties, borrower and lender, are in agreement. This applies even though the escrow instructions have not been signed by either party.

In the case where the escrow holder is controlled by the Department of Corporation, only after both the borrower and lender have signed the escrow instructions would both parties have to agree on the disbursement of funds.

To avoid problems, it is important that all paper work such as escrow instructions, Trust Deed, and Trust Deed Note be correct and terms properly defined before funding.

Funding should only be made to a known and proven escrow company. (See other sections about contacting the Department of Corporation on escrow company status.)

LOAN TERMS

In the setup of a loan, don't ask for something you can't possibly receive from the borrower. Asking for the impossible can result in turning the borrower or the mortgage broker off so you will not be able to get the terms you really want, or you will not be offered a good loan.

On the other hand don't be afraid to ask for terms. After completing the negotiation stage, favorable terms usually cannot be obtained. During the negotiation, asking for several terms including some terms that are not important (throwaway terms) can often result in obtaining the terms that you really want.

There is also a legal potential problem, due to the lender being in a stronger position. If there are unreasonable terms, they could be disallowed or become unenforceable by the courts if a lawsuit is filed. This would be caused due to the *reasonable expectation* of the borrower that is the weaker party to the loan transaction.

Rate of Return

The rate of return for a second Trust Deed should ideally be 12 to 17 percent with an inflation rate of 3 to 4 percent per year. The rate of return for a first Trust Deed might be 1 to 3 percent lower. The amount that would be changed depends on the terms and various features of the loan. This would include LTV, length of the loan, inflation rate, creditworthiness of the borrower, location of property, type and condition of the property, and general economic conditions at the time of the loan. The rate is also affected by instability of the stock market and other investment vehicles. Instability, decline, or no upward movement of the stock market can cause investors to move into cash and look for Trust Deeds for their investments, driving the interest rates down.

If a variable interest rate is negotiated, this ideally should be tied to one of the standard money index rates, such as the prime rate.

There are several methods to evaluate the rate of return. The simplest is the note's stated rate. However, when a note is discounted, has prepaid interest, or nonconstant payments, the actual rate is not always easy to determine. A calculator can be used to figure out the interest rate, but it is a complicated process. A business calculator will make the task easier, but this requires, reading the instruction book.

The easier method is to do the calculation using a commercially available business software program's internal rate of return on your personal computer. The internal rate of return assumes that payments received are reinvested immediately at the same interest rate. This virtually never happens. However, the calculation can still be useful in the evaluation of a loan.

Discounted Note

When a note has an interest rate below the market rate, it sometimes is sold at a price lower than the note's face value. This obviously will provide a higher rate of return on the investment than the note's stated interest rate.

A good rate of return can be obtained by buying a purchase-money second Trust Deed or a first Trust Deed from the seller of property. For example, if the Trust Deed Note is for $10,000 at a note interest rate of 8 percent and interest only for five years, the note might be sold for $8,000. The resulting interest rate would be 13.53 percent (internal rate of return). However, the LTV can be as poor as 90 percent in the case of a second Trust Deed. This does not provide very much cushion if the market drops or the borrowers lose their jobs and can't make the payments.

In the case when an owner sells his property and is required to carry back (receive) a Trust Deed for his equity in the property, the seller's credit check may not have been as comprehensive as with a standard lender. In these cases, if an investment of this purchase-money Trust Deed is considered, it is important that a complete evaluation be conducted, the same as with any hard-money loan.

Prepaid Interest

Loans that have prepaid interest also increase the internal rate of return. This is because the amount of the loan funding is less than the note's face value. The reduced amount is equal to the face amount less the prepaid interest on the note amount. This will allow for the investment of the difference (between the note value and the loaned amount) in another venture. However, if the difference is not invested, there isn't an actual increase in the yield, only a mathematical increase.

As an example how a loan with a prepaid interest can increase the yield, consider a loan of $20,000, for one year, at 15 percent, with all the monthly payments made when the loan is initially made. The prepaid interest for 12 months is $3,000 (interest of 15 percent on $20,000 for one year). This will require an investment of only $17,000. The net effect will be to increase the rate of internal return from 15 percent to 16.36 percent.

Another example is a three-year note with a face value of $96,000, an interest rate of 13 percent, and a prepaid interest of one year. The effective interest rate based on an internal rate of return will be 13.36 percent. Obviously, if the borrower pays the three years interest up front, the rate of return will be much higher. Here, if the interest were prepaid for the three years, the yield would be more than 17 percent. (Home Ownership and Equity Protection Act of 1994 (HOEPA), Section 32 of Regulation Z, for owner-occupied property does not allow for prepaid interest for a period greater than two months.) After the loan has run for a period, there is nothing in Section 32 that prohibits a later payment for a longer period. If the terms of the loan note calls for a payment that is longer than two months, you would be on thin ice to accept the payment.

The interest rate allowed by law for a private citizen is a maximum of 10 percent. (See previous discussion on limits.) Any rate above this is usury. However, if a controlled institute arranges the loan, the rate can be the market rate. Real estate brokers and lawyers that arrange financing also can charge the interest market rate when arranging a loan. There is a unique exception to using the market rate for real estate brokers. They are restricted to a maximum rate of 5 percent above the Federal Reserve index rate of San Francisco reserve when their personal funds are used.

Money loaned on the sale of a property by standard lenders or hard-money lenders (using a mortgage broker) is classified as *purchased money*. The rate that can be charged is the market rate. This could, but usually does not, exceed the 10 percent usury rate for a good borrower. (See previous discussion on usury limits.) Purchase money, carryback by seller, and second Trust Deeds usually have an interest rate lower than hard-money rates. This is partially due to the buyer having to qualify for the first Trust Deed and therefore being a better credit risk. His creditworthiness is much better than a typical hard-money borrower.

This lower rate of return on a carryback junior Trust Deed Note has always been peculiar. The lower rate is usually due to the buyer of the property having reasonable credit, assuming the purchase-money loan was a conventional loan. There is a second reason for the low interest rate. Sellers that are highly motivated will sell the property with favorable terms. He typically only adds the face value of the Trust Deed Note and the cash he will receive to determine the amount the property is selling for. The seller may not realize that the trust deed market interest rate is higher than the interest rate he is willing to accept. He will have to discount the Trust Deed Note if he elects to sell it in the marketplace.

The higher interest rate that can be realized in hard-money lending is due to the borrower not having a choice. It is the only game in town. Although the rates may be high, the risk for the lender is also high. This is a lending service that is being offered. The compensation is justified by the high risk that a hard-money lender takes. As long as the government doesn't put unreasonable restrictions on lenders and chase them out of the business, the interest rates charged will be adequate to compensate for the risk. If the government puts too many requirements and restrictions on hard-money lenders, a black market could develop in lending.

Net Funding

Some mortgage brokers do *not* net fund. This means that when a loan is funded, the full loan amount is paid. After the loan escrow is closed, the amount of the loan discount, prepaid interest, and points to be paid is then sent to you, the lender.

Due on Sale

The Trust Deed Note for the loan should contain a due on sale clause. This clause provides for the full payment of the loan when the title is transferred. In some cases it may not be desirable to demand full payment of the loan when a property is sold. If the new owners have a good credit rating and a potentially better payment record, a more secure loan would result.

A due on sale clause is very important in an economic period where there is high inflation or expected high inflation in the near term. This will provide for a payoff of the loan and a reinvestment at the higher prevailing interest rates if the property is sold. If the loan can be assumed, there probably wouldn't be a payoff. Your loan investment would deteriorate in value and the borrower could make payments and a final payoff with cheap money. If a foreclosure is required, ownership of the property might be desired. This would allow for payment of senior loans with cheap money if you were in a junior position. If you are in a senior position, loans junior to your loan will be wiped out in your foreclosure. In reality they would most likely bring your loan current and file their own foreclosure.

If payment is accepted from the new owner, and it is later decided to invoke the due on sale clause, the payment acceptance is an implied acceptance of the new owner. If the borrower takes the case to court, the lender's defense will be weak.

If payments start to be delinquent, the property is being wasted, or the property is poorly cared for, a request for full payment or a foreclosure may be necessary. It should be noted that when interest rates are high, it becomes difficult to sell a property at full value.

There are cases where a demand for full payment is not allowed when there is a transfer of ownership. These are when:

- the new owner is a surviving joint tenant,
- an owner by action of transfer by inheritance (except where the property is not occupied as residential property),
- a change of ownership caused by a transfer due to a divorce, either to the children or spouse,
- the ownership changes due to a transfer into a trust.

Jump Rate

A jump-rate clause in the Trust Deed Note calls for a jump in the interest rate in the event the property is put into foreclosure. This clause provides compensation for the potential loss and effort necessary in a foreclosure. (Regulation Z on high-rate loans prohibits jump rates in the interest charged if property is put into foreclosure or post-default interest rates that are higher than the contract rate.)

Most mortgage companies will put this clause into the note, although some mortgage brokers feel that the clause is illegal. The jump rate can be as much as 5 percent. This would be in addition to the existing Trust Deed Note interest rate. This increased rate starts when the loan is put into foreclosure and not when the terms of the loan are violated.

A fee can be used instead of an increase in the interest rate. For example, if the property must be put into foreclosure, a fee amount of $500 might be charged. If the property is included in a bankruptcy, an additional fee of $1500 might be charged. A schedule must be included in the Trust Deed Note before these fees can be charged.

Late Payment Fee

The late payment fee is usually 10 percent of the payment after a ten-day grace period. (If the loan is purchased money, the late fee is usually 6 percent after fifteen days on residential property.) When a payment is received, check the postmark on the received letter to verify that the payment was sent by the tenth day. On purchased money, the period usually is fifteen days. Some hard-money lenders use the date the payment is in hand, similar to lending institutions.

The late payment can only be charged once. It cannot be added to the principal unless stated otherwise in the Trust Deed Note. If the property is put into foreclosure, the unpaid late payments can be treated as an advance with an interest charge.

Prepay Interest Penalty for Involuntary or Voluntary Payoff

The rationale for the prepay interest penalty is to provide some compensation to the lender in the event the loan is paid off earlier than provided by the note. The lender must find another loan that will pay a similar or market interest rate. Locating a similar loan can take significant time. The need for the involuntary[2] and voluntary[3] prepay interest penalty clause in a Trust Deed Note is to provide for this payment when there is a foreclosure. If the note does not contain the involuntary clause, and there is a foreclosure, a prepay penalty could not be included in the credit bid in a statutory foreclosure or collected if litigated in a judicial foreclosure.

On four or less residential units, the prepay fee is limited to six months interest on 80 percent of the unpaid loan. The borrower is allowed to prepay up to 20 percent of the loan in any prior twelve-month period. The amount of the prepay fee can be less than this amount if the borrower is astute enough to negotiate something less. A prepay fee is not allowed after five years on four or less units of residential property. If high-rate loan criteria apply, there are other restrictions. (See high-rate restrictions.)

---

[2] *Involuntary* is the result of an action that occurs where the borrower has not agreed to the action or wasn't aware of a contractual requirement.

[3] A *voluntary* clause in the Trust Deed Note is also important. If a foreclosure is filed, without the voluntary clause, there would not be any prepay fee allowed if the borrower elected to payoff the loan prior to the foreclosure auction.

Ideally, there should be a prepaid penalty for the full term of the loan, if it can be obtained. If the property is for sale, it may be difficult to get a prepay penalty, except for a few months. There are situations where the borrower only plans to keep the property for a couple of years. Here, the prepay may only be for two years on a three-year loan. Some notes will contain a clause that will limit the prepayment penalty to the interest remaining on the loan. For example, if the remaining loan period were two months, only two months prepayment penalty interest would be due. In this case, the interest amount due would be on 80 percent of the remaining loan amount because the borrower would be allowed to pay 20 percent of the principal without the prepayment penalty.

ADDITIONAL PROVISIONS IN TRUST DEED NOTES

Personal Guarantee

When the security for a loan is inadequate, a guarantor can be added to the mix. This can be a friend or relative of the borrower or even the mortgage broker. If the guarantor doesn't have any assets or the assets have been used to guarantee other loans, the guarantee doesn't have much value.

When the property being loaned on is in the borrower's name and not a corporation or limited liability corporation (LLC), there is a type of guarantee if the borrower has other assets. If a foreclosure becomes necessary, a judicial foreclosure can provide some access to the borrower's other property or assets. (Purchase-money loans provide substantial immunity to the borrower's other assets.)

Loan Extension

This provides the borrower the right to extend the loan period. There may be a charge to exercise this privilege in the form of a fee (points), a change in the interest rate, or modification of other terms. A loan extension clause without compensation, adjustment of interest rate being tied to an index, would be similar to giving money away.

Right of First Refusal

This provides the borrower with the option of purchasing the Trust Deed Note (paying the note off) at a discounted price. If the sale price is lower than the face value of the Trust Deed Note, the borrower has just saved himself the discounted amount. This would only occur when the lender decides to sell his note. This typically might happen when the lender needs all or a part of the value of the Trust Deed Note, the security has decreased in value, or the note's interest rate is below the prevailing market interest rate.

Legal Precedent

This clause specifies the state or county laws that will be used to interpret the terms of the Trust Deed and Trust Deed Note.

This list does not tick off all of the loan terms that might be used. Each loan is unique as well as the needs of the lender and borrower. Occasionally a special Trust Deed Note and Trust Deed may need to be drafted to meet a unique situation. It should be remembered that if a new document is written, its interpretation could take on unpredictable consequences.

RECEIVING POINTS FOR LENDING MONEY

If possible, the lender should try to receive points for lending money. The number of points available varies and can be nothing to three points or more depending on the difficulty the mortgage broker has in finding a lender. When the loan is brokered out, a case where there are several brokers involved, there is less likelihood of receiving points. When there are several real estate brokers involved, logically there will be fewer points to go around. Part of determining if points are available is to directly ask the mortgage broker if he is the originating broker. In a brokered loan, there would be an originating loan broker who will give the loan to a broker that has lenders. This is done very often when a loan is difficult to fund.

These loans often are ones not to be excited about. Brokered loans can have a poorer quality. If the quality is good, the originating broker could sell it very quickly. One of the exceptions to this general rule is if the loan amount is large. The originating loan broker often does not have enough lender contacts, and an outside broker would have to be used to fully fund the loan.

There is another source of money for lending. This is when there is a shortage of money from hard-money lenders. Mortgage brokers will pay for your keeping funds available for a loan that is being prepared for funding. Under these conditions, interest on the money would be paid even though the loan has not been funded. There should still be the opportunity to use due diligence and not accept the loan and still receive the interest. The compensation might be points instead of interest or both depending on the availability of hard-money funds in the marketplace.

How points and interest are received can impact your taxes. If points and prepaid interest are paid to you immediately after the loan is funded, this can be interpreted as earned income or interest. Adding to the mix is if the loan is funded by the mortgage broker or directly by you. How this payment is treated will depend on the type of 1099 form that is issued by the payer. If the 1099 is issued as a 1099-Misc, this might be reported to the taxman as earned income. When treated as earned income, there is an additional FICA tax assessed. If the 1099 is issued as 1099-Int, this must be reported as interest. How interest and points are handled should be reviewed by your tax accountant.

TITLE INSURANCE POLICY

The title insurance policy on the loan should be American Land Title Association Loan Policy (ALTA). This could be the standard or extended coverage. (See Section 10 for additional information).

FIRE INSURANCE AND HOME OWNER'S POLICY

The insurance should cover the total loan or full property replacement cost. The insurance must cover any senior loans and your new trust deed investment. Loans that are junior to your loan must have their own insurance. For example, if the senior loan is $100,000 and your loan is for $20,000, the insurance should be for $120,000, or full replacement cost up to $120,000. There are some fire policies that prorate the coverage. This means that the insurance will only pay part of the property value. These types of policies must be avoided because of the full replacement of the property (improvements) not being covered.

There are policies with exclusions on the coverage that do not provide for the rebuilding of the property to existing codes. On newer properties, this shouldn't be too much of a problem, because newer properties are most likely built to existing codes. However, with older properties, the insurance would not necessarily cover the actual rebuilding cost, because the rebuilding permits require building to code. Code-compliant, full replacement coverage insurance policies can be obtained. The cost is not too expensive so it may be prudent to have a policy with this rider. The fire insurance policy can have a reasonably large deduction. This will provide a lower premium. The other reason for the large deductibility is that small losses would not be claimed. If too many small claims are made, the danger of the insurance company terminating the insurance is very real.

The insurance for the property should correctly reflect the property status, owner-occupied or non-owner occupied. There is an additional property occupancy status. This occurs when the property is uninhabited. This would happen if the property were being refurbished or just vacant for a long period of time. Under this category, a very special insurance would be required. This can cost up to twelve times the insurance of an occupied property. Without this course-of-construction insurance policy, you as the lender would be exposed to a total loss except for the land value. The only recourse for an uninsured loss would be if a judicial foreclosure could be pursued successfully. This action would only be successful when the borrower has deep pockets and the loan was not purchased money on four or fewer units.

The escrow instruction for the loan can be used to define the amount of insurance coverage required. If the instructions state that the property must be adequately insured, this can be interpreted as a full replacement value, prorated improvement value, or improvements only. If the escrow company makes the incorrect selection, the loan may not be properly covered if the property is totally destroyed.

Part of the value of the property is the land. Land usually cannot be destroyed. The land value however can be reduced significantly if there is a fire storm where there are several homes destroyed. The bad press from this event will make the neighborhood less desirable and therefore less valuable.

The effect of zoning, covenants, conditions, and restrictions (CC&R), or government action can come into play in determining the land value. If there are changes to the property's status, rebuilding to the old configuration may not be possible. If the land has to be sold, it would have to be at a discounted price after a long listing period. The safest method of handling the amount of fire insurance is to specify it as the loan value or full replacement cost. This request may not be honored if the borrower wants to contest the amount. When an initial loan is being made, the borrower will usually fulfill your request. After the insurance policy period has expired, the borrower may change the insurance terms without your being informed of this change.

In the evaluation of Trust Deeds, it is important to verify that the loan is not on property that is grandfathered. If the improvements are destroyed, the land value could be lower because of the building restrictions caused by the zoning. The grandfathered condition allows the property to exist only as long as the improvements continue to exist. An appraisal may not adjust for this reduction in value. When investing in property that is grandfathered, the zoning and potential future value must be determined.

When a loan is made on an owner-occupied property, and then changed to a tenant-occupied property, the property may not be appropriately insured. The coverage can be determined by contacting the insurance company. When the coverage cannot be changed using the existing insurance company, a separate insurance policy should be obtained. Foreclosure can be started if the borrower does not pay for the insurance. If the mortgage payments are made on time, it may not be desirable to foreclose. The new insurance policy can be issued and the cost recovered, when the loan is paid off. The cost of a tenant-occupied policy is less than an owner-occupied policy. In a tenant-occupied property, the tenant's personal property is not insured. Usually a tenant will obtain his own insurance policy to cover his personal property.

In the case where a senior loan is being paid off or refinanced, the property owner should sign an authorization to remove the senior lender listed on the policy. There are insurance companies that will not remove the old senior lender without the borrower's authorization. Although this may not be a problem, it can cause displeasure if there is a claim of loss filed.

When an owner has trouble paying for the insurance or taxes, there should be a suspicion that the borrower is not making payments on senior loans. It is advisable to check with the senior lender to determine if payments are current. Do not depend on the senior institutional lenders to provide fire insurance to cover junior loans. Some lenders are self-insured for only their loan amount. If this is the case, and usually it is, insurance will have to be obtained to cover your exposure.

Note that some insurance companies will only insure owner-occupied property. If there is a change to this occupancy status, insurance will have to be immediately obtained from a different insurance company.

The period of fire insurance coverage on a new Trust Deed or purchase-money Trust Deed should have at least six months coverage remaining. Ideally the coverage should be for a full year. If the coverage is less, the mortgage company that is processing the sale of the Trust Deed should obtain additional insurance out of the loan proceeds. Every so often the borrower will run short of cash and only pay for the first quarter. This may be acceptable but will require your monitoring the situation to ensure the next quarter's payment is made in a timely fashion.

When an insurance policy is placed on property, the mortgage holder's name will also be placed on the policy. If the policy is going to be terminated, you will be notified of this event. If the borrower doesn't make the payments, you will have to do this and add it to the Trust Deed Note as an advance. The insurance policy termination has a thirty-day grace period to accomplish all of your actions. The thirty days isn't a long time when a notification letter and the borrower's response (or nonresponse) occurs. A call to the Insurance agent oftentimes is required to determine the present status.

OTHER DETAILS OF THE TRUST DEED NOTE AND TRUST DEED

The details of the Trust Deed Note and Trust Deed should be checked for accuracy, specifically; names, address, property tax number, loan amount, interest rate, monthly payment amount, prepay penalty, jump rate, late payment fee, and other terms that are pertinent to the loan.

The borrower that receives the loan must be the only owner of the subject property. If there is another recorded or unrecorded interest in the property, such as a spouse, this can create a significant problem. If a loan is made to only one of the owners of the property, there is a good chance of litigation and potential loss of some of your investment. This can happen when a foreclosure is necessary and you become a part owner with another individual. Even if there isn't a foreclosure, there are other unforeseen disagreements that can occur with the other owners. Unless there is a signed agreement on future intent, such as the collection of rents and sale of the property with the other owners, the issue could become a costly civil litigation to force an agreement.

REQUEST FOR NOTICE OF DEFAULT

A Request for Notice of Default should be included in the escrow instruction for your loan and recorded with the County Recorder's Office. This filing, with your correct mailing address, will provide a prompt notice if a foreclosure has been recorded by any of the other lien holders of the property. Any change to your address should be recorded with the County Recorder's Office to avoid an incorrect mailing. Inasmuch as the address provided is a matter of public record, a P. O. Box should be used. This is to avoid being personally contacted by borrowers. It is very disconcerting to have an unhappy borrower knock or kick at your door at all hours.

By statute, this Notice of Default should be mailed to you by certified mail within ten days of the recording of the foreclosure.

A notification of the filing of a foreclosure would eventually be sent to you even if a Request for Notice has not been recorded. This later notice however would only be sent within one month after a foreclosure filing. Although the delay might be acceptable, you could lose some interest on advances used to bring a senior loan current or delay the filing of your foreclosure. The advances on a senior lender are highly recommended to avoid your being shutout if the senior lender takes the foreclosure to completion. Your immediate filing of a foreclosure is recommended. If there is a suspicion that the borrower might file a bankruptcy you will want to race to your foreclosure company. When there is a bankruptcy, you would not be able to start your foreclosure until a Relief from Stay is obtained or the bankruptcy is completed. The senior lender that had filed prior to the bankruptcy will have the clock running on their foreclosure and require you to make up all of the arrears, probably sooner than you would like, to protect your loan.

INTEREST PAYMENT

Verify the details of payments in the Trust Deed Note[4]. This would include:

- the date of the first payment and amount,
- interest rate,
- date of the last payment,
- the payoff amount,
- the grace period for late payments.

The actual payment date usually isn't entered on the note until after the loan is funded. In those cases where there is a date, it should be verified. The payments ideally should be prorated to the first of the month. This provides for an easy check of payments when there are several loans in your portfolio. As your portfolio grows, it will become very difficult to remember the due dates if the payment dates are different. In the cases where payments are late, letters can be sent out at one time. This will provide free time for the rest of the month.

Payments on trust deed loans are usually made after the borrower has had the use of the money. Therefore, when the loan is set up, payment of interest is for the previous month. In calculating prorated interest the payment usually is for the upcoming days when a loan is originally funded. There can be variations when the payments are to be made, and a calendar is very useful to visualize the payment days.

To determine the prorated amount, first determine the loan payment per day. Consider the case where the normal payment is on the seventeenth

---

[4] There are different types of payments such as: amortized (where the payments are incremental until the loan is paid off), straight-interest-only (where only interest is paid) or different combinations and payment amounts when payments must be made.

of each month and the payment is to be prorated to the first of the month. If the original payment on a loan is due on February 17, divide the payment by 28 (for a 28-day February). For a monthly payment of $280, this would be $10 per day. To prorate the amount to be paid (or additional amount to be paid) March 1, multiply 11 times $10. This would make the prorated payment for March 1, $110. If the payment is to also include the previous month's interest the amount would be $390 (280 + 110).

A calculation will need to be made when an existing loan is purchased. This is to ensure that both the lender and the seller of the Trust Deed receive the proper amount of interest. The arithmetic is similar to the above example. For the note seller, the interest not received by the borrower will have to be added to the amount paid for the note. This is because the next interest payment has not been made and this payment will include the interest during the note seller's ownership. In the case where the payments are not prorated to the first of the month, the calculations will be adjusted to the actual Trust Deed Note payment date.

PARTITIONED LOAN

There is a special configuration of Trust Deeds that is occasionally done. This is the dividing of a loan into a first and a second Trust Deed. This allows the first Trust Deed to have a lower interest rate and a second Trust Deed with a higher interest rate. The payment on the combination could be lower or the same as one Trust Deed but allows the lending by a standard institutional lender at the lower rate. The second Trust Deed can also have the interest payment prepaid and points to the lender for making the loan. This allows the mortgage broker to advertise the second Trust Deed at a very high interest rate when the interest rate is calculated. For example, a loan of $100,000 at 14 percent for one year, prepaid interest for one year, and two points to the lender would produce a net rate of return of 19 percent. In this type of loan, due to the high interest rate, provisions must be included in the Trust Deed Note to realize a return for the full or near full term of the loan. This provision such as a prepayment fee or points for making the loan would be required due to the possibility of the high interest rate loan being paid off early, negating the high interest return on your money.

INTEREST RATE AFTER LOAN MATURITY DATE

The Trust Deed Note should contain a clause to provide an interest rate increase in the event that the loan is not paid off as required. This amount is the Trust Deed Note interest plus an additional interest rate. The terms could have a graduated interest rate. This interest could start at 1 percent and increase by 1 percent per month up to a 7.5 percent limit. *This increased rate may not be applicable if the required statutory notice has not been sent to the borrower, with a proof of mailing, 90 days and not in excess of 150 days prior to the payoff due date for one to four units of residential property* (Civil Code 2924i). It is still a good practice to send out a maturity notice letter for loans on all properties—and would be required—if specified in the Trust Deed documentation.

INTEREST RATE ON ADVANCED FUNDS

In a foreclosure, any advance funds to cover your cost may be charged at an additional interest rate. This additional interest rate is called a jump rate. These advanced funds could be payments to a foreclosure company, a senior lender, an insurance company, or a lawyer. This jump rate interest can only be as high as allowed by the terms of the Trust Deed Note. Typically the jump rate can be 5 percent. Some of the standard note forms obtained in stationery stores call for a lower rate. Every attempt should be made to use the higher rate when negotiating the loan. If there is no interest rate specified, the interest rate on advances can only be the legal limit of 10 percent.

In the event forbearance (an extension of the loan) is given on a loan that has come due, senior and junior lenders on the property should be notified. This notification is not an option, but required by law. To insure that all lenders are notified, a Preliminary Title Report should be obtained. The cost of the report can be charged to the borrower. The borrower can also be charged for the extension of the loan. The amount should be reasonable and comparable to the cost the borrower might have to pay in the marketplace. Knowing the borrower's payment history should allow you to be very competitive with the market points. It is better to be reasonable so as to retain the loan, if it's a desirable loan. The borrower might be able to find a low interest rate with a few points if he has established an institutional credit rating or the property has increased in value. If the borrower has been a slow or poor payer or the property has decreased in value, high points might be requested to offset these problems. These harsher terms should encourage the borrower to find another lender. Good judgment will have to be exercised on how you proceed. If there isn't too much of an equity cushion, it might be better not to charge any points so the loan continues to be performing. When forbearance is given, a mortgage broker should be used so interest doesn't become usury. If a demand is given and subsequent forbearance given, there is an interpretation of the law that only 7.5 percent interest can be charged, if there is an absence of an agreement. The terms of a Trust Deed Note would probably supercede this condition due to notes normally making some provision for nonpayment upon demand.

COLLECTION OF RENTS

It is important to have the Trust Deed Note contain a collection of rent's clause. The problem with the standard pre-1997 collection of rent's clause, found in older standard Trust Deed Notes, is that a court order may be required prior to the collection of rents. This can be an expensive and time-consuming procedure. When a post-1997 collection of rent's clause is used, the lender can collect the rents directly from the tenants. This will require sending a notification to other lien holders. Both the borrower and tenants must be notified. Payments would then have to be made to senior and junior lenders as well as for utilities, taxes, maintenance, and insurance. This might be better handled by an experienced receiver or property manager that can send out notifications, disburse funds, and provide the required accounting.

There is some question on the impact of collecting rents on a foreclosure without court approval. Consultation with an attorney is recommended to avoid having to restart the foreclosure procedure if rents are collected and the foreclosure is challenged by the borrower due to your accepting payments.

PROPERTY OWNERSHIP

There is a potential problem of property ownership that should be avoided. This is when the property is owned by only one of the spouses. This is a different situation than when both spouses are on title. The problem occurs when there is a divorce and the non-owner spouse makes a claim on the property. The claim could be senior to any subsequent Trust Deed. The situation could be complicated if one of the spouses files a bankruptcy and a foreclosure is filed. Most of these problems can be partially avoided by having a reliable title insurance company underwrite the title insurance. If not properly dealt with, a court procedure would be required. There also could be a problem obtaining the Trustee Sale Guarantee Policy (TSG, foreclosure title insurance) when these complications exist.

This normally shouldn't be a problem if handled properly. Before lending on property in this category, the non-owner spouse must sign a Quitclaim Deed and have it notarized. The Quitclaim Deed transfers any and all interest in a Trust Deed Note (or property) to the recipient. By having the Quitclaim Deed signed, the potential ownership cloud is avoided. The title company usually will detect the existence of a spouse and require the necessary signature.

Lending to a foreign corporation has special problems. There is the potential problem that the foreign corporation is laundering money, something that must be avoided in lending money. The foreign corporation could also be a shell corporation. However, the property is still the security and if all the legitimate officers of the corporation sign the necessary documents, your problems should be minimized.

Lending to a trust or property with several owners can become a nightmare. If the payments stop, it could be due to a disagreement between the owners. If a foreclosure has to be started, the owners can start filing serial bankruptcies. It could take forever to finish the foreclosure.

All of these problems can be minimized by using due diligence, having title insurance with a good property profile to show the loan position. The property profile should also show an address to which notices can be mailed. If required by statute, a proof of mailing and delivery confirmation should be obtained. The note should also state that payments are to be made in the United States and in U.S. dollars.

TRUST DEED POSITION

The position of the Trust Deed is all important. It will determine your security (degree of safety) and the interest that can be charged on the trust deed loan. A first position is the safest position providing there is adequate equity in the property. As the loan becomes less senior the safety is reduced. The exception is the case where there is more than adequate equity. If there has to be a foreclosure, there is enough money to pay all the lenders.

Junior trust deed lenders usually will protect senior lenders. This is because the junior lender does not want senior lenders to file a foreclosure with the associated accumulating cost and potentially be auctioned out of the picture. However, this protection can disappear if the junior lender determines there is no equity to pay off his loan, and walks away from the loan.

When a senior loan is paid off, the junior lender moves into the senior position. This position might be changed by the junior lender subordinating his loan to a new senior loan. Usually this is done to accommodate a construction loan. Very often there will be some compensation for the subordination. This could be up to several points or an increase in the interest rate. There is the advantage for the junior lender not only for the additional compensation, but the knowledge that the property is being improved, thereby increasing the equity. The exception would be when improvements on the property are removed to accommodate the construction.

There are situations, such as in a divorce or where two lenders want a senior position, but that position cannot be resolved. This can be dealt with by recording the loan(s) at equal position. On the surface this appears acceptable. There are, however, several potential problems. One of these problems is in a foreclosure. Who will be responsible for the payment on the cost of a foreclosure? Although a separate agreement could be drafted, this would have an implied partnership, something that would have to be avoided because of the legal entanglements. There also would be the question of ownership status after the foreclosure. Would both own the property as tenants in common? Would the person who did not file the foreclosure only have a Trust Deed on the property? These complex potential problems dictate that a real estate attorney with experience in partnership and real estate law be employed, someone who would be difficult to find. However, the potential problems can be avoided by not becoming involved with this type of Trust Deed.

SUBORDINATION

There should be some concern when you are asked to subordinate your loan. This may happen when the loan is first funded, during the life of the loan, or later when the loan is being extended. It often happens when interest rates have decreased and the borrower wants to refinance with a senior loan to take advantage of the lower interest rate. The borrower might also want to pull some equity from the property. The terms that are available in a senior position are more favorable to the borrower than a loan that is in a junior position to your loan. The refinance usually isn't possible unless you subordinated your loan.

The main issue is the security of your loan after subordination. Your security will have decreased in value, and you would be on solid ground to ask for compensation due to the increased vulnerability. When subordination is asked for, compensation should be paid. This could be in the form of a higher interest rate, several points, or a combination of the two. Depending upon the LTV that would exist after subordinating, you may not want to subordinate. The other terms of the loan, such as a prepayment penalty or shorter loan term to provide compensation might also be incorporated into the modified Trust Deed Note. There is also the issue of an implied increase in the yield that you would receive on your loan. If the points or interest on the loan make the loan a high interest loan and the security is on four or less owner-occupied residential units, you could be violating lending laws. When an existing loan is subordinated, a title insurance binder should be obtained, paid by the borrower, to verify that there are no other encumbrances or liens that will take precedence over your loan. An appraisal may also be required to verify that there hasn't been a reduced property value, placing you in a poor position with a potential loss.

If your loan is rewritten, and it is a loan of more than 10 percent interest, without a mortgage broker involved, you would be violating the usury law. (See discussion on limits.) The mortgage broker should also be able to advise you on the limits to the terms that you would like to receive.

Section 10

LOAN-TO-VALUE

Figure 10. *When everyone plays fair, no one will get hurt.*

The loan-to-value ratio (LTV) is computed by adding any outstanding assessments, liens, amounts of senior loans, and the amount that will be invested divided by the appraised value times 100. This calculation is the LTV expressed as a percentage. ((Senior liens + new loans)/(appraised value)) times 100. Changes to the calculated LTV should be made when the assessments or other encumbrances will be paid by escrow from the loan funds. This would be similar to a refinance of an existing loan. Your money pays off the existing loan, leaving only your Trust Deed against the property. However, your money usually pays for the escrow cost and points to the mortgage broker and could result in a larger Trust Deed than the original Trust Deed. (It is highly advised not to plan on the borrower making payments on liens after the close of escrow. His *promise* does not guarantee that the payments will be made.)

This new LTV will be the final situation after the loan is funded and any liens agreed upon, paid. The computation of the LTV provides a rough estimate of the remaining equity in the property. This remaining equity provides coverage for various costs to repossess the property, prepare for sale, adjustment for decrease in value due to waste, economic downturn, payoff of all liens, and the time to sell. The time to sell can be equated to your having equity in the subject property without receiving any interest on your money unless there is cash out after the sale. If there is cash out after all costs are paid that is equal or greater than your total normal interest payments you will have received your interest.

This calculation does not necessarily show a true LTV. A more practical method would consider all senior loans, the new loan, senior liens (shown in the table below), major improvement costs (such as roof replacement, carpets, paint), and selling costs, divided by market value times 100. This approach would not be used if the appraiser has made adjustments in the appraisal for the difference of comparable properties. For example, if the appraiser deducted the corrective work that must be done on the subject property to make it equal to the comparable properties, additional adjustments would not be necessary.

CHECK LIENS

It is important to check the Title Report for liens against property. Some borrowers forget, aren't aware, or don't want to disclose all of the liens against their property in the loan application. Those recorded will have priority over a new trust deed loan. The LTV may not be adequate if these liens are not removed when the loan is funded.

It would be prudent to review the loan escrow documents and include in the instructions that the loan funds will be used to pay off any agreed-upon liens. Your loan position after recording of the Trust Deed should also be stated in the escrow instructions.

The only exception where liens may not be paid is a swing loan, sometimes called a *bridge* or *gap* loan. A *bridge* or *gap* loan is an interim loan allowing a buyer to purchase a property using the equity of the new purchase or the property that is being sold. Here, the borrower should be able to prove that there will be funds in the future from a solid source such as an escrow closing or the sale of the securing property. This source should be reviewed for the amount of equity that will be available. A review of a listing agreement, sales contract, and any escrow instructions is in order as well. The loan should still be cross-collateralized to provide additional protection if necessary.

UNRECORDED LIENS

The lien that can be most troublesome is a mechanic's lien. This can be senior to a new Trust Deed, even if it has not been recorded. There would be a *constructive notice*, by virtue of any work being done on the property that you can see at the building site. A constructive notice can also be a legal recording, a provable written notice, or a court decree. If work has been done at the property, verification will be necessary to insure that all construction labor and construction material have been paid in full. The contractor has ninety days after the completion of construction to file a mechanic's lien with the County Recorder's Office. If the contractor has filed a notice of completion on the property, the original contractor has sixty days to file a mechanic's lien. If no court action is initiated, the mechanic's lien will automatically expire unless an extension of the lien is recorded. There are other notices such as a preliminary twenty-day notice, release of mechanic's lien, and satisfaction of judgment that can be filed. If there has been new construction on the property or mechanic's lien filings, legal counsel should be obtained. If the title insurance does not insure against a mechanic's lien, the lien has not been paid, or the time periods have not passed to nullify any mechanic's work, adjustment must be made in calculating the property's LTV to determine the safety of a loan.

Mechanic's lien status can be obtained by contacting a title insurance company or personally contacting the County Recorder's Office. The information may become available on the Internet in the near term. (Mechanic's liens are covered by Civil Code Sections 3109–3154.)

The other type of lien that can cause a problem is a lease on the property. This would come into play if you as a lender are aware of its existence or acknowledged the lien at the time a loan is made. If you were aware of the lease, it would remain in effect after a foreclosure even if the lease has not been recorded with the County Recorder's Office.

SENIOR TRUST DEEDS

A copy of all senior loans should be obtained from the borrower. They will show: terms, interest rates, types of loans (i.e., fixed, adjustable-rate, VA, FHA, CalVet, conventional, or a seller carryback), and due dates. The existence of senior liens can be determined from the title insurance company's Title Report. When the senior Trust Deed and Trust Deed Note is being reviewed, a copy should be retained for your file. Although a copy of the Trust Deed can be obtained from the County Recorder's Office later, it is convenient to have a copy in your file. Trust Deed Notes usually are not recorded. Obtaining a copy of Trust Deed Notes for your file is important not only for review but to have them available in the event a foreclosure is required.

Some of the terms and clauses that you should be aware of in an adjustable-rate mortgage (ARM) are:

> *Cap*—This is a limit to the amount of the increase to the interest rate. Each increase can be as much as 2 percent. There is a separate interest rate cap over the life of the loan. This is typically 5 to 6 percent.

Index—This is the basis for the interest rate increase. Some of the indexes are the One Year Treasury Index or the 11th District Cost of Funds Index.

Conversion Clause—This is a provision that allows the conversion from an adjustable-rate mortgage to a fixed conventional loan. There is a time limit to do this and a fee may be charged.

Discount—This is an initial reduction in the interest rate to induce a borrower to accept an ARM. The period for this discounted interest rate is typically short.

Negative Amortization—This is also sometimes called a loan that walks back. For these loans, the monthly payments that are made do not cover the full monthly interest. This can occur initially when the loan is made or the indexed interest rate has increased such that a fixed monthly payment does not cover the new indexed monthly interest. The shortfall is added to the principal thereby increasing the loan amount.

Special consideration should be given to senior liens that have prepayment penalties. This would become an expense if the property were owned after a foreclosure. When the property is sold, this prepayment penalty may have to be paid.

Usually the payments and remaining principal on senior loans are noted on the senior loan payment stub. If there is any question about the interest rate and remaining senior loan amount, a computation can be done with a business calculator or computer software using the payments and original loan amount.

Ideally, the interest rate on senior loans should be low. The payments should not exceed your ability to make the payment in the event of a foreclosure sale. The payment would have to come from your income and contingency reserves. Often, because the foreclosure takes about 120 days, payment on the senior Trust Deeds is advisable if the borrower hasn't kept payments current. This is to avoid the additional cost if the senior lenders start their foreclosure. Late payment fees can be annoying but usually aren't the driving issue.

The good news with making the monthly payments on senior loans is the payments can be treated as an advance. If the junior Trust Deed Note contains a clause providing for interest payments on advances and hopefully includes a jump rate, this should provide a sufficient return on the advance if funds need to be borrowed.

The importance in making payments on the senior loans is to avoid having to bid on the senior loan in their foreclosure. This would be necessary to protect your junior Trust Deed position. The major problem that can occur in this situation, where the senior loan is auctioned at foreclosure, is having enough cash or a certified check available to bid the credit bid of the senior lender, something you should avoid because of the unknowns at a foreclosure auction such as overbids.

Part of the evaluation of a junior Trust Deed is whether the senior loan can be assumed. Senior loans might not be assumable after a foreclosure sale. This will depend on the terms of the senior Trust Deed Note and the attitude of the senior lender. It should be noted that a CalVet loan is a contract loan and not a Trust Deed secured loan. This is because the state of California owns the property, not the California veteran. CalVet loans can only be assumed by a qualifying California veteran.

In general, loans that can be assumed with the senior lender's approval include variable conventional, VA (government guaranteed), and FHA (government insured). Fixed conventional loans are usually not assumable. Seller's carryback Trust Deed Notes often do not contain a due on sale clause and can be assumed without the note holder's approval. The existing terms and interest rates transfer to the successful bidder in a foreclosure sale, subject to the terms of the Trust Deed and Trust Deed Note. The existing interest rate therefore is important. In the event the property is to be retained, the rate should be affordable. In those cases where the note's interest rate is high compared to the present available interest rate, a refinance is sometimes desired if the property is to be held for a lengthy period.

There are several problems with a refinance. First, the amount of a new loan is usually only 70 to 75 percent of the appraised value and often is a variable interest term loan. This limitation on the loan amount can be a problem if the property has lost value due to market conditions. The refinanced loan may not be large enough to allow for the payoff of the old loan. If you wanted to proceed with a loan, money would have to be added to the escrow to pay off existing loans. If the property was acquired with a deed-in-lieu of foreclosure, any junior loans would slide into a senior position. A subordination agreement from junior lenders would be required to avoid this problem. This may cost some points or an interest rate increase to allow a refinance loan to be placed in a first position.

The second potential problem is that a refinanced loan loses the protection against a judicial foreclosure, unlike a purchase-money loan. The new borrower (you) will be potentially vulnerable to a judicial foreclosure by the new lender in the event of a default on your Trust Deed Note. This would come into play if the property has lost significant value. There is also the loss of bargaining power to obtain a short sale from the lender when you sell the property. Walking away from the property has the added problem of incurring a poor credit status as well as not meeting one's moral debt.

There is an additional problem with a refinanced loan. This is when a larger loan is obtained. If there is a short sale or an abandonment of the property with a resulting foreclosure, there would be debt relief. The amount of the debt relief is taxable by the IRS. There has been an attempt to by pass this debt relief by selling the property to a company that claims to avoid the debt relief by purchasing your property. Although the fee is only 1 percent, the IRS considers this a tax avoidance sham and could put you in a position of still being subject to taxes on the debt relief.

A short sale can occur if a property decreases in value. The buyer can request that the existing lender reduce the amount owed. This will come into play only when the property is being purchased. Lenders will not reduce the amount that is owed before a sale. This, not only is due to the loss of money to the bank but because of the cost to evaluate the property, the borrower, and the loan. If there is not an event such as nonpayment on the loan, there is no motivation for the lender to act on a loan reduction request. The bank's motivation to accept a short sale is to convert a non-performing loan to a performing loan or remove the loan from their "books." This is necessary to make the bank's loan portfolio look good.

When an owner that occupies one to four units takes a short sale when the loan is nonrecourse (purchase-money loan), there is usually no gain that can be taxed. Only when the loan is refinanced is the loan turned into a recourse loan that could cause the debt relief to be taxable. This usually happens when the homeowner receives money from a refinance of an existing loan or obtains a new loan against the property.

There are many situations where there is a taxable event. The general guideline that might be used is when the property owner has a gain such as might happen from a tax write-off from depreciation, reduction in the amount of debt owed, or a refinance with cash and the property is sold. However, conditions of property transfers such as a deed-in-lieu of fore-closure, foreclosure, bankruptcy *discharge* court order, voluntary sale, and discharge of indebtedness can also impact the gain or loss. *Discharge* in a bankruptcy filing is the forgiveness of debts. Also affecting the gain or loss is the basis of the property and if an increase or decrease in value has occurred. Due to the complexity of the tax law, an experienced tax accountant should be employed prior to committing and completing a transaction. Filling out the federal tax form 1040D for your transfer will supply some guidance as to a gain or loss. You should however be prepared to spend time learning the definitions that are used by the IRS.

One of the more desirable hard-money loans is a CalVet second mort-gage. The California Department of Veterans Affairs will only allow this owner-occupied *home-loan contract*[1] to be assumed or taken over by a qualified California veteran. This does not present a major problem to you as a non-California veteran hard-money lender. If the mortgage is foreclosed on, the California Department of Veterans Affairs will purchase the foreclosing junior loan at full face value. The loan in effect is guaranteed by the State of California.

When the property is in foreclosure, CalVet will notify the holder of the junior Trust Deed of the various options. If there is substantial equity in the property after computing the cost of the sale, and you as the lien holder have enough cash to pay off the CalVet loan, ending up with the property may be desirable. The payoff on the CalVet loan will be done after the foreclosure sale. This has been the California's CalVet past policy. However, policies can change, so it would be wise to verify that the aforementioned policy still applies before money is loaned on property with a CalVet loan.

ASSESSMENTS

Assessments on the property can be from city, state, the common area associations on some single-family homes, condos (subdivision in air), planned unit development (PUD), Mello-Roos, or stock ownership. The treatment of these assessments is similar to liens. To learn if there are any assessments, a call to the association's service company can be made to find out the status. There also can be federal, state, or county tax liens (property tax). The only one of these that can be easily determined is the property tax from the county tax assessor's office. If the assessment is significant, the liens should be paid when a loan is being made or, if not due, allowance made in the LTV calculation.

---

[1] The *home-loan contract* is similar to a home purchase except the Department of Veterans Affairs purchases the property and contracts with the veteran to make installment payments. Upon the completion of the installment payments, the property is then owned by the veteran.

SUPPLEMENTAL TAX

There is an additional tax that is created in a property transfer called a supplemental tax. This is a property tax that is imposed on property and usually will not have been paid. The tax is the result of the property being sold at a higher sales price or the county's new appraised value being increased. The additional tax is for the period between when the property is sold and the next property tax assessment period. These supplemental taxes are assigned a separate property tax number, but cross-referenced to the subject property. Fortunately the supplemental tax isn't too large in a slow market. If the property value has increased significantly, the supplemental tax could be large. It might be desirable to file an appeal with the County Tax Assessor to have the amount reduced if his appraisal is too high.

In addition to the normal property tax and supplemental tax is an estate tax that can be assessed. The estate tax can be a result of a personal tax, property improvement tax, business tax, or a *deferred tax*[2] from an estate. The deferred property tax could be from an elderly property owner with a low income who has elected not to pay the taxes until the owner-ship is transferred. Some of these taxes, charged to the property, may be questionable, except for the county's deferred taxes that are justifiably assessed to the property.

The property tax lien will be senior to any Trust Deed. This lien will be senior even if it is recorded after recording of a Trust Deed. A review of the preliminary property profile should show if the taxes are current (paid).

AUTHORIZATION TO RECEIVE INFORMATION

The California statute requires that all senior and junior lenders, upon request, provide information to the holder of a Trust Deed on the property. Additional authorization is not required. Senior lenders oftentimes

---

[2] *Deferred taxes* occur when property owners, due to their low income or status, have applied to defer payment of their taxes until the property is sold or they are deceased.

will provide loan status with a phone request. Some will require a written request and a copy of your Trust Deed and Trust Deed Note.

TAX LIENS

Needless to say, any income tax lien may impact the trust deed loan security. If the income tax liens have not been paid, this fact may not show up in a Preliminary Title Report. However in a foreclosure cycle, if there is an income tax lien, the IRS or State Franchise Tax Board will provide notification. There are consequences to such a notification that a good foreclosure company can clarify. This will include time periods of appeals and usually actions that will be taken by the taxing agency.

In the case of a federal tax lien, if the government recorded (filed) the lien before the recording of a new Trust Deed, only then would it have priority. This would be a constructive notice of the lien. The title company would not issue a title policy insuring the loan against this lien. They would require that the federal tax lien be paid first or exclude it from the policy. This is similar to a constructive notice that is senior to a new trust deed loan. If the title company did not pick up these liens in its title search, the title company would be responsible.

Statutory provisions, when there is a federal lien, can cause a time delay before a foreclosure sale can proceed. The government, if they feel that there is sufficient equity in the property, may claim a portion of the equity to cover their lien. There are, however, procedures that the foreclosure company should be able to handle. This, by the way, is one of the questions that can be asked of a potential foreclosure company to find out about its knowledge. If the company is aware of the details that are required in processing a foreclosure with a government lien, this is a good indication of their competence.

ASSOCIATION FEES

Monthly (sometimes quarterly or yearly) association fees on condos or homes that have an association fee should be considered in the LTV determination. The fee ideally should be small. The fee amount must also be considered when determining the required cash flow in the event of a foreclosure. If the assessment fee is significantly overdue by more than two months, the escrow instructions should state that it would be paid from the escrow funds.

BONDS

Some newer properties have Mello-Roos bonds that have been used or will be used to construct services. This would be a special improvement tax that would be used for roads, sidewalks, sewer lines, water lines, power lines, schools, and other improvements. These fees are senior to all other liens. Adjustments must be made to the property value when these fees are present. The fees can be a monthly amount where the bond is amortized, or a fixed amount that is due at some future date. These bonds should be treated as a senior existing loan that reduce the equity in the property.

COST TO SELL

The cost to sell the property can be expressed as a percentage. Typically this will be 8 percent plus other fix-up costs. This cost is not normally added into the computation of the LTV. The unused equity, the amount in excess of all liens and encumbrances will usually provide coverage of this cost in a foreclosure unless the process is protracted. Other potential costs to sell the property are prepayment penalties of existing senior loans that usually must be paid off. This amount is normally 80 percent of six months interest.

DISTRESSED SALE

There is a special case in dealing with LTV. This is the case where the property was acquired or is to be acquired in foreclosure, a probate sale, or a deed-in-lieu of foreclosure. If the property is to be acquired in these types of sales, and the mortgage broker states the market value is much higher, you should be suspicious. An appraisal would have to be obtained to determine the true situation. If there is a significant discrepancy in the appraised value and the acquisition price, there may be other factors that are not being disclosed. These could include hazardous materials, a planned highway, a shopping center moving in or out of the area, a dynamic change in the ground stability, or environmental requirements.

PRIORITY OF LIENS

Listed below is a table showing the priority of liens on property after a foreclosure sale:

Type of lien	Recorded prior to loan	Recorded after loan
Senior loans	senior	
Property tax	senior	
Homestead[3]	junior	junior
Business tax lien	senior	junior
IRS tax lien[4]	senior	junior
State tax lien	senior	junior
Association lien	senior	
Condo fees[5]	senior	
Assessment fee lien	senior	
Construction lien	senior	junior
Judicial lien[6]	senior	junior
Bonds	senior	
Bond payments	senior	
Mechanics' lien	senior	junior
Bankruptcy[7]	senior	junior
Easements	senior	junior[8]
Lease	senior[9]	junior

3 A homestead lien is junior to a trust deed loan due to the borrower voluntarily agreeing to the terms of the loan. A judgment lien on property has a special characteristic with regard to a homestead filing due to its not being a voluntary lien. The homestead would only afford protection to these lien types if filed prior to the filing of the judgment lien. (See limits to the amount of protection.)

4 There is a special 120-day injunction on the property in foreclosure when there is an IRS lien. After this period, the injunction will be automatically removed. An application for an earlier removal of the injunction can be submitted. This removal could happen if the equity isn't sufficient to pay the IRS lien.

5 The priority of condo fees and condo assessments can vary depending upon the CC&R's and the bankruptcy's specific chapter that has been filed. Usually this can be resolved by discussions and negotiations with the management firm that is authorized to represent the condo association.

6 These court liens can be various types of judgment liens placed on property. They can include child support, actual and punitive damages, and legal fees.

7 A foreclosure cannot proceed until authorization to proceed is received from the court that has jurisdiction. This is usually done by obtaining a Relief from Stay. There are other authorizations, so it is advised to have a bankruptcy attorney provide guidance.

8 There are easements authorized by government agencies that will take priority even if recorded after the recording of a Trust Deed.

9 When such has been recorded or the investor is cognizant of its existence. It should be noted that before the County Recorder's Office will accept documents that remove or release a lien, they must be notarized.

ADDITIONAL FUNDS ON EXISTING TRUST DEED

Every so often a borrower will want to borrow additional funds. This can be handled in two ways. The existing loan can be increased or a new junior Trust Deed generated. There are potential dangers in either approach.

In the case of modifying the existing first Trust Deed, if there is an existing junior lien on the property, the first Trust Deed could become a junior lien. This would come into play if a junior lien holder contested the position of the modified Trust Deed and the method used to fund additional funds. The best method to use is to have a clause in the Trust Deed Note to allow additional funds to be advanced. If this has not been done, a new Trust Deed should be generated using a mortgage broker. The need for the mortgage broker is to allow an interest rate charge above 10 percent without being considered usury. (See previous discussion on interest limit.)

In the case of generating a new Trust Deed in the refinancing of an existing Trust Deed, there might be an encumbrance that was generated after the existing Trust Deed was created. This new encumbrance would become senior to any new loan unless a subordination agreement was obtained. To avoid any unknown junior encumbrance that could become senior, title insurance should be obtained to determine if there are any junior liens and insure that your new Trust Deed is in a senior position.

The types of encumbrances that could have occurred would be a preliminary mechanic's lien notice (must have been filed within three weeks of the start of services by subcontractors), recorded mechanic's liens, construction loans, income tax lien, and any judgments. For mechanic's liens, the obligation does not necessarily have to be recorded to take precedence over a new loan. If there has been any type of work on the property, a release from the contractor and material supplier must be obtained before lending funds. Title companies in all likelihood will not insure the loan without mechanic's release if there has been construction work. Mechanic's liens, similar to property taxes, go with the property and can take precedence over other encumbrances. (There are statutory time periods that apply to mechanic's liens that can void their effect. See unrecorded liens above for details.) If a title company does provide insurance, they would probably exclude construction liens unless there is a release.

There is sometimes an advantage with a new separate junior Trust Deed. In the event a foreclosure is required and you want to own the property, an overbid on the Trust Deed is less costly because of the smaller amount of a certified check that may be required at the auction for overbids. Additionally, if you elect a small trust deed loan, it can be more readily sold. If sold, this junior Trust Deed can add protection to your senior loan. This would be more likely if the buyer of the Trust Deed is interested in the property and hopes it can be acquired in foreclosure. In this case he will be willing to make senior loan trust deed payments, thereby making your senior loan a performing loan. The purchaser of the junior Trust Deed, if he acquires the property, may pay off your senior loan. If there were a prepayment penalty in your Trust Deed Note, there would be an increase in the yield of your senior loan. Unfortunately, this doesn't happen very often.

There may even be cases where the property is over encumbered. If the borrower wants to retain his good credit, a new loan might be written with more favorable terms to the borrower, just to keep the loan performing. Hopefully the property value will increase or the borrower will pay off the loan in the future so you can salvage your investment.

Whenever additional funds are advanced, the following points should be reviewed:

- The new junior trust deed loan should also have title insurance. The cost, because of the smaller loan amount, would be small in comparison to the original loan title insurance,
- The title insurance policy should be reviewed in detail for any encumbrances that would become senior to your new loan,
- Fire insurance on the property would have to be revised to assure that the additional loaned funds are covered,
- An appraisal, which is recommended in a changing market, should be obtained,

- The LTV should be low, less than 70 percent, unless there are other factors that add value. It is important to determine the LTV by additionally doing your own appraisal. The appraisal can be done by using recent sales, expired listings, and properties that are presently on the market,
- A new borrower's credit report, to determine if the borrower is getting into trouble or has legal action pending, might also be obtained,
- Adjustments should be made for changes in square footage, deferred maintenance (such as poor carpets, poor roofing, poor landscaping, required stucco work, painting, and a cracked slab), removal of non-permitted structures, and other repair costs,
- Market value and the market interest rate and terms, should be taken into account,
- In the case where the market interest rates have increased or the property value has decreased, consideration should be given to changing the terms of the Trust Deed and obtaining additional security if needed,
- Any borrower problems should be analyzed to decide the final terms and rate to be offered.

Section 11

TITLE INSURANCE

Title insurance coverage is important to protect your investment. The title company will insure that the borrower has ownership of the property, that a valid Trust Deed is recorded, and that the trust deed position is correct. Without this coverage and title company research, your loan could be in a junior position without any equity security. Additional coverage can be added to your title insurance policy when there are other concerns.

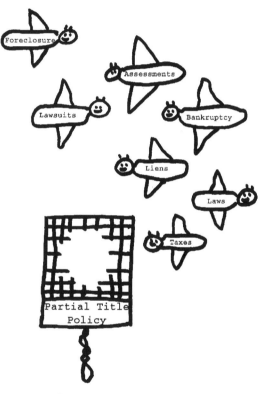

Figure 11. *House vermin.*

Not all title insurance companies are equal. In many cases, a title insurance company only issues a policy for an underwriting title insurance company. There are a few title insurance companies that serve as their own underwriters and have their own title plant. (A title plant has a record of all documents affecting property.) The only way that you might be able to find the better title insurance company is to talk to *several* foreclosure companies and obtain their recommendations. This does not guarantee a valid recommendation based on performance. Title insurance companies offer free services to foreclosure companies (as well as real estate offices) such as pickup and delivery of documents and coffee cups to obtain their business.

Title insurance is an indemnity policy that will only pay when it can be shown that there is a loss, the same as fire insurance. The loss often can only be demonstrated by the full cycle of foreclosure and ultimate sale of the property. The problems that occur along the way are numerous. Any misstep can give a title insurance company grounds for not paying for your loss. There is also the arbitration clause that most policies have included. This requires that disputes be resolved by arbitration. Although there can be grounds to bypass the arbitration requirement, this rarely happens. One of the problems in arbitration is the possible bias of the arbitrator. His future job can depend on how the title company views his performance. It is important to note that the title insurance covers conditions prior to the issuance date of the policy, unlike other insurance that covers events after the issuance date.

PRELIMINARY TITLE REPORT

Part of the trust deed lending cycle is obtaining a Preliminary Title Report. A review of this Preliminary Title Report must be made. The report, also called a prelim, will show the status of most of the property liens. In the event there are displeasing conditions that show up in the report, they must be corrected or an allowance made in the property's equity value. It is best to have any unacceptable conditions such as a homestead filing eliminated before funding. Other liens that are to be paid off should be addressed in the escrow instructions.

The Preliminary Title Report usually shows:

- the estate or interest of the property owners,

- the recorded owners,

- the assessor's parcel number, legal description, street address, and any clarifications,

- any liens, encumbrances, and priorities as of the date and time of the report,
- assessed valuation,
- any notices of default (NOD), notices of trustee's sale (NOS), and Requests for Notice of Default,
- any recorded lawsuit or bankruptcy relative to property,
- any *lis pendens* (notice that a lawsuit is pending).

The Preliminary Title Report does not cover:

- easements not of public record,
- boundary disputes not in the public record,
- improvements owned by a neighbor on the parcel,
- it does not provide a guarantee against errors in the report. It is used only to facilitate a subsequent issuance of a title insurance policy and may not cover all liens. *It is not a title insurance policy.*

There is also a similar type of policy called limited coverage policy (LCP). It can be obtained for about $100. It provides information on the status of a Trust Deed at the time the policy is issued. Many don't consider this type of policy worth the cost, but it does give some information about the Trust Deed.

The report will show (if recorded):

- property taxes,
- tax delinquencies,
- supplemental tax liens,
- easements (if any),
- covenants, conditions, and restrictions (CC&R),
- deeds of trusts against the property,
- homestead filing.

TITLE INSURANCE TYPES

There are two general types of title insurance. Title insurance for the buyer (borrower) on a new loan (ALTA) and title insurance for the seller on the property (CLTA). These title insurance policies can be either the standard or the extended coverage. Also available is a Trustee Sale Guarantee Policy (TSG).

American Land Title Loan Policy, ALTA (Insures Loan)

The borrower's form of ownership is of special concern. The title insurance company should ensure that there are no other persons, partnerships, or corporations that have an interest in the property so that there will not be other claims on the property. This would typically be a married borrower who takes (holds) the property as his sole and separate property. If this condition were to exist, the other person in the marriage or partnership would have to sign a Quitclaim Deed.

The title insurance for the new loan is usually paid by the buyer on a purchase-money loan or the borrower on a hard-money loan. The buyer doesn't receive anything of value directly for paying for this insurance. The buyer's only benefit is being able to obtain a loan. Lenders require the insurance, and most often won't make the loan without it. The title insurance policy does not insure a borrower against any title risk but insures that the lender will not incur a loss.

American Land Title Association Extended Coverage Loan Policy (Insures Loan)

The extended coverage, if referred in the policy, is Form 100. This endorsement provides added insurance to cover such items as covenants, conditions, and restrictions (CC&R), encroachments, and the right to use the land for mineral development (if not previously deeded away). It also insures that the CC&Rs do not contain any enforceable reversions (where the previous owners' sale conditions are violated, thereby allowing their claiming the property), right of reentry, or power of termination. There are other forms of title insurance that can be purchased to cover other conditions. The extended policy only covers the lender. Its advantage to the lender lies in the protection of matters that are not generally public record.

If there has been recent construction or refurbishment, a contractor's endorsement should be added to the policy. The borrower should show proof that materials and workers have been paid. An indemnification agreement against any material or worker claims should be provided by the contractor.

A variation of the ALTA is now being used. This variation is ALTA-R. The cost is usually the same as the ALTA, but requires the title company to physically inspect the property site.

California Land Title Association Standard Coverage Policy, CLTA (Insures Property)

The CLTA insurance of property in a sale is usually paid by the seller. It covers vesting, lien or encumbrance, and other operational procedures. It does not cover eminent domain, defects, certain liens created by the insured, and other operations of the federal bankruptcy, state insolvency, or similar creditor's rights laws.

Trustee Sale Guarantee, TSG (Used in Foreclosure)

The TSG type of policy is used by a foreclosure company during the foreclosure process. With this policy, the title insurance company will provide information on the vesting of title as to the interest, the encumbrances to the land, the name and addresses of individuals and entities who must, under state law, receive notice of the foreclosure, the newspapers qualified to publish notice of the foreclosure proceedings, and the municipality or judicial district where the property is located.

> Note: There are additional types of title insurance with special riders. If there are special situations about a loan, such as a leasehold property, and land not in a standard

subdivision, additional coverage may be required. The above information is only provided as a general outline, a title company should be contacted to determine proper coverage and if special insurance or riders are warranted. The coverage may vary between title companies, so it is important to check in detail the coverage that is being offered by the specific title company.

FRAUD

Even when a title insurance policy is obtained, there is always the danger of a fraudulent transfer of ownership. The crooks are all too often very devious. They can, by knowing notary public, county recorder office, title insurance or escrow company procedures, circumvent safeguards. A method that is sometimes used is to fraudulently record a Full Reconveyance of an existing Trust Deed. This would make your new loan appear to be in a senior position, but in reality it would be a junior Trust Deed. The crooks can also place several Trust Deeds on a property and not file them with the County Recorder's Office. They could also obtain a loan on property with a Trust Deed, file it with the County Recorder's Office and the real owner wouldn't know about it for some time.

One should be vigilant on properties that have a small first Trust Deed or no Trust Deed. Properties that are vacant, tenant occupied, or where the owner is out of the area, could be vulnerable. If the deal looks too good, this should raise your antennas to possible danger. Only by dealing with reputable mortgage brokers, title companies, escrow companies, and borrowers that provide a credit report (not a copy) can there be some degree of safety.

Section 12

OWNERSHIP TITLE

When dealing with Trust Deeds on property, it is important to talk with your tax accountant and attorney to decide the best method to take title on property. This comes into play when a married couple holds ownership. Holding ownership

Figure 12. *Don't be intimidated by titles.*

as tenants in common, joint tenants, or community property can have legal, income tax, and inheritance ramifications.

The loan security (Trust Deed Note and Trust Deed) pledged as collateral should be in the lender's (your) name and not a servicing organization. In this way, you can retain full control. To do otherwise could put your investment in jeopardy. The exception is fractionalized loans. In these cases, there is joint ownership of the Trust Deed. This ownership should be shown on the Trust Deed and Trust Deed Note as well as the title insurance policy. Typically, decisions are made based on a majority of the owners. This can be delusional in that many owners are swayed by the mortgage broker that services the loan. The mortgage broker's benefit often is in keeping the borrowers happy so additional loans with points can be obtained in the future.

The forms of ownership usually fall into the categories described below.

SOLE OWNERSHIP

This ownership form can be as a trust, single man, an unmarried woman, an unmarried man, a widower, or a married person as his sole and separate property. Because California is a community property state, the sole and separate property ownership of a married couple must not have any mixing of funds as to the source to maintain this status. There is a presumption that property obtained during a marriage is community property. The methods to maintain a sole and separate property are to have the property ownership prior to marriage, maintain a *clean paper trail*[1], and have the spouse acknowledge the property is a sole and separate property through the use of legal declaration. A typical method is to generate a Quitclaim Deed on the subject Trust Deed Note. A trust is another method to isolate the ownership. This is due to the trust being a different type of ownership. Even with a trust, a clean paper trail needs to be maintained.

MARRIED COUPLE OWNERSHIPS

The trust deed ownership can be set up as a married couple with tenancy in common, joint tenant (HWJT) or a husband and wife as community property (HWCP). The HWCP from a taxation standpoint provides a property value step-up basis in the event of the death of either partner. The HWJT would have only a one-half stepped-up base in the event of the death of either partner. The step-up basis means that an appraised property value for tax purposes is set at the time of death of the deceased. There is a downside to the community property status. In the event of the death of one of the spouse, the death tax can come into play. The amount of the deceased spouse's community property over a statutory value might

---

[1] A *clean paper trail* can be achieved by having all funding and payments made from your sole and separate bank account.

be taxed. (This would apply to high value property. The statutory amount is changing. See estate tax table for the statutory amount and changes.)

DOMESTIC PARTNER OWNERSHIP

As of January 2005, with some important exceptions, a domestic partnership is much like a marriage. Like married couples, domestic partners will become financially responsible for each other, both during the relationship and possibly after it ends. Domestic partners will be responsible for each other's debts. If one partner takes out a loan for a new car and fails to pay, the bank could come after the other partner. If there is a split up, a court would treat the breakup like a divorce and could order the payment of financial support to the other partner.

California community property system will also apply to domestic partnerships. So a partner therefore would automatically be entitled to a half interest in any property purchased after the forming of the domestic partnership. If there is a break up, all the community property will be divided equally between the partners. Of course, this also means that you as an investor have the right to use the court system to claim assets. This new law is in its infancy and case law can create a significant impact to the trust deed investor's handling of foreclosure and bankruptcy actions if the uninvolved same sex or different sex partner doesn't sign and have notarized, a property transferring Quitclaim Deed.

JOINT TENANCY WITH RIGHT-OF-SURVIVORSHIP OWNERSHIP

A joint tenancy can have any number of people. The ownership interest must be equal. The transfer by any one co-owner without the other owner(s) will dissolve the joint tenancy. This transfer by one owner would apply, providing it was recorded prior to death of the owner. In the event of the death of one or more of the owners, the ownership would convey to the remaining survivors. The interest of any part owner can be claimed by creditors and sold to satisfy any judgment. The remainder ownership will revert to a Tenancy in Common for the remaining owners.

There is a variation of this ownership that can provide some protection from judgments. This is a tenancy by entirety. A lien cannot be placed on the other owner's interest. There is a right of survivorship. Any one of the owners' portions cannot be willed away.

TENANCY-IN-COMMON OWNERSHIP

This form of ownership can be for any number of unrelated people or related people. The percentage of ownership can be equal or unequal. The interest of each owner can be disposed of separately.

CONSERVATORSHIP OWNERSHIP

The ownership of a Trust Deed by a minor child or a person officially designated as incompetent has special problems. Although the Trust Deed and Trust Deed Note is personal property and can be owned by a minor or incompetent, this form of property can transfer to real property in the event of a foreclosure. This would require a court appointed guardian. A court appointed guardian would be required to sign any legal transaction. This would include a reconveyance, substitution of trustee, and filing of a foreclosure procedure. A title company would also require a legal guardian's signature to recognize any transaction.

The appointment of a guardian by the court would be an annoyance, time consuming, and would have a cost factor due to an attorney being required to petition the court to assign a guardian. The guardian would have to report back to the court on the financial transactions annually, or less frequently if the court so approved. The guardian would in all probability be the parent or, in the case of aged parent, a younger person. This would work part of the time, but could become a disaster in the case of a divorce. The uncertainty in a divorce would be the control of the property of the minor or incompetent. The minor, after becoming an adult, can have control of the property. If the minor, after reaching 16 years of age, obtains a court approved emancipation, he can also have control of the property.

PARTNERSHIP OWNERSHIP

Partnership ownership can be for two or more people. It is best to have a lawyer familiar with partnership law involved before taking ownership in this form. This is due to the complex legal implications.

Another type of ownership that will affect a loan is that of same-sex couples. This is becoming an issue and will become more extensive with legislation and case law. Due to the dynamics and changing legal status, care should be exercised when this appears to be an issue. An attorney may be required to safeguard your loans if this is a possibility.

LIMITED LIABILITY CORPORATION (LLC)

A *limited liability corporation* is a simplified corporation generally set up for legal protection and tax considerations. The LLC is provided for by all states.

POWER OF ATTORNEY AND CONSERVATORSHIP

Although this is not a form of ownership, it is of great concern for lenders. The individual with the power of attorney or a conservatorship has legal powers similar to those of the owner of properties and accounts.

When a loan is made to someone with the power of attorney, verification must be made with the actual owners that this person has permission to act with regard to this matter and that the owners are aware of the loan. There are different powers of attorney categories with significant differences. In general terms, there is the durable power of attorney, special power of attorney, general power of attorney, and specific power of attorney. Each of these categories has different meanings with regard to authority. There would also be a difference with regard to authority after the death of the property owner. Contacting legal counsel is recommended when dealing with power of attorney.

In the case of a conservatorship, verification should be made that the court has issued the authorization for someone to act as a conservator.

Even with title insurance, there is great danger that the money is not being used for the benefit of the true owners of the property.

TRUSTS, REVOCABLE AND NONREVOCABLE

In simple terms there are two basic types of trusts. These have a large number of subgroups, such as a charitable trust or an AB trust that will not be covered due to their complexity. Living trusts can be revocable, meaning the trust can be dissolved. A nonrevocable trust provides that once the document is signed, it cannot be dissolved.

The trusts will have a trustee or several trustees usually with a secondary trustee who can become the acting trustee in the event the primary trustees cannot act. The existence of a trust can become a problem in trust deed investing. You will need to know who has the power to act and his authority. It would be similar to having the power of attorney for an estate. The powers of a trustee can be limited. To determine the extent of the trustee's powers, the original document needs to be reviewed. Use caution in this matter because it is too easy with modern copy machines to have a trust modified for your deception.

When there is a fractionalized loan, some of the lenders may in reality be a trust. The broker's responsibility, and by default yours, requires a verification that the parties to the loan are authorized to act as the trustee of the trust. Title companies also have this responsibility when they insure a loan. Unfortunately not all title companies are equal. Some may miss some details in their authentications of a trustee. The issue can become more difficult when there is litigation, a bankruptcy, or even serial bankruptcies by any of the trustees or beneficiaries of the trust. The problem could be compounded if a loan is not performing and there are out of pocket costs for an attorney to litigate the problem.

Section 13

TRUST DEED PURCHASE, SALE AND RESALE

Figure 13. *I would like 6 months prepayment penalty, late fee, points, full prepaid interest, and one pound of flesh.*

TRUST DEED VALUE

Don't expect to receive all of the loan terms that you would like. This will seldom happen.

Trust Deeds should sell at face value on most standard hard-money loans, providing the terms and interest rate are similar to what is available in the marketplace. When buying a Trust Deed, an attempt should be made to purchase it at a discount or with points to provide a higher rate of return. In the case of a newly created Trust Deed, negotiating with the mortgage broker and the borrower can result in more favorable terms. In order to find the real rate of return, standard software programs are available for use on personal computers to find the internal rate of return. The internal rate of return, although not an actual rate of return from a practical sense, will give a relative rate of return in comparison to other loans. The most widespread software used is Microsoft Excel and Corel Quattro Pro. If these are not available, a good business calculator can be used.

POINTS

When hard money is loaned through a mortgage broker or directly to a borrower (using a mortgage broker), points can be charged. These points often may not be available to the lender when the mortgage broker has found and arranged the loan. The number of points can be anywhere from zero to five points or more. The number of points usually is a function of the desirability of the loan. If the loan is poor (high risk), the points can be high. When the loan is very desirable, points usually aren't available, but there is no harm in asking. However, a desirable loan should be bought immediately before another lender jumps at it. Excellent loans are hard to find.

There are times when a poor loan will not have any points offered. This can be due to the loan being originated by another mortgage broker. When several mortgage brokers are involved with the loan, the points usually are spread very thin. These poor loans usually are shopped between various mortgage brokers until a buyer is found. If others have refused the loan, you may want to do the same.

LOAN DISCOUNT

A Trust Deed that was previously created may have an interest rate lower than the present market rate. The purchase terms may not be favorable, such as no prepay fee, no jump rate, or a long term. The LTV also may be high (more than 70 percent). This could be due to the Trust Deed being created by a seller carryback, decreased property value, or deferred maintenance. Added to this, the borrower's credit may have been downgraded due to a foreclosure, bankruptcy, or nonpayment on the loan.

If any or all these conditions exist, the loan's vulnerability could be significant. It is reasonable to ask and expect to receive a discount to increase the loan's yield. There should be caution if the loan's quality has decreased too much. It may be one that should not be considered at any price. This would especially be true if the loan is a junior Trust Deed.

SEASONED TRUST DEEDS

A *seasoned Trust Deed* is one that has had monthly payments paid on time for at least six months without any late payments. The longer the seasoning, the better. If seasoned, the Trust Deed could sell at a higher than face value because of the proven track record. If a voluntary or involuntary statement is present in the due on sale clause, the salability is improved. Also, if there is a jump rate or a late fee clause, the Trust Deed can be more readily sold. If a seasoned Trust Deed is being purchased, it would be wise to verify the amount of the unpaid balance and the date the loan was obtained from the borrower. The address and telephone number of the borrower should be obtained independently from the seller of the Trust Deed Note. A signed statement from the borrower stipulating the terms and remaining amount of the loan should be obtained. There is one warning on paying more than the face value of a Trust Deed. If the interest received or there isn't an enforceable prepayment penalty covering the discounted amount, you could end up with an early payoff with a net loss to you.

There is one caveat that you need to consider. There are mortgage brokers that configure Trust Deeds with prepaid interest. This prepaid interest does not season a loan. The borrower has not demonstrated his ability or inclination to make payments on time. Asking detailed questions of the mortgage broker and obtaining a credit report on the borrower may provide some real information. If there is a major concern, a copy of the originating escrow instructions should be requested and reviewed to find out if there has been prepaid interest.

ESCROW USE

When purchasing a Trust Deed, an escrow with escrow instructions should be used. The escrow instructions must contain provisions for title insurance, fire insurance, and payoff of all liens that are agreed upon. Payment of delinquent property taxes, and other judgment debts should be paid even if not presently a lien. If there is adequate equity and a low LTV, it may not be necessary to pay off all of the liens (debts). The escrow instructions must be reviewed and approved by you before any funds are provided to the escrow company.

The funds to be loaned should be in the form of a cashier's check, made out to the escrow company, the title company, or the mortgage broker's trust account. The need for the cashier's check is to expedite processing of the loan. If the check were a personal check, escrow would not be able to process the loan until the check is cleared through the bank. Alternately the loan can be funded with a bank wire. The cost of wiring the money should be paid by the borrower from funds held in the escrow account. The escrow company or title company would provide the necessary information to wire the funds. The escrow number and your name should be referenced on the wiring instructions as with the cashier's check.

The escrow cost should be between $100 and $300. This normally is paid by the borrower. This amount does not include many of the other fees that need to be paid such as title insurance, loan fees, property taxes, and *junk fees. Junk fees* are those other costs that are required to process the escrow. In the case where an existing Trust Deed is being sold, the cost is borne by the trust deed buyer unless the seller is highly motivated and pressed to pay the cost. However, if the deal is a good one, don't blow it for a few dollars. Using an escrow should provide protection in money transactions in this questionable new-world business environment.

ASSIGNMENT OF TRUST DEED

When a Trust Deed and Trust Deed Note is purchased, there will be times where the mortgage broker will have previously funded the loan. In this type of transaction, all of the reviews stated above, must still be accomplished.

There is a special restriction on assignment of Trust Deeds by a real estate licensee who is not the lender. When the loan is on one to four units of residential real estate, the recording of the Trust Deed in his own name is a violation of Business and Professions Codes (BPC) §10234, unless the lender has given written authorization to do otherwise. If an authorization is given, the Trust Deed and Assignment of Trust Deed shall be recorded within ten days or delivered to the lender with a written recommendation that it be recorded within ten days following release of funds. The exception is for properties larger than four units, unimproved real property, or commercial property.

Purchasing an existing Trust Deed is accomplished by assigning the Trust Deed and Trust Deed Note to the new hard-money lender. The Assignment of Trust Deed must be recorded to provide constructive notice. If the Trust Deed Note is not also assigned, you haven't made a complete purchase.

Usually the Trust Deed Note is assigned as a nonrecourse transfer. Although this on the surface absolves the broker, the broker is still liable in the generation and preparation of the loan. He must also provide all significant information to you on the loan. This would include any and all information that he is aware of or should have been aware of that could cause you a loss.

If the Trust Deed Note were transferred with recourse, the trust deed owner (usually the mortgage broker) of the note would be responsible if the loan is not paid as prescribed. In the case where you sell a Trust Deed Note to a third party, it is recommended that the note be assigned *without recourse* for you to avoid any future payment obligations.

There will be times when the Trust Deed includes an assignment of rent's clause. This is similar to a separate assignment of rent's document.

You will sometimes find a trust deed holder that had a Trust Deed for a period of time, and wants to sell his Trust Deed. This could be due to the trust deed holder needing cash for other transactions, the Trust Deed has been an annoyance in the collection of payments, or other problems with the property.

The sale is accomplished by assigning the Trust Deed and Trust Deed Note to you the buyer. The back of the Trust Deed Note can be used to do this. A statement assigning the Trust Deed Note, without recourse should be signed by the owners of the Trust Deed Note. Alternately, a separate document can be used and signed by the owners of the Trust Deed Note. There is also an assignment document for the Trust Deed. This must be signed, notarized, and recorded. The County Recorder's Office will not record any document unless notarized. This includes a trust deed assignment document.

When a Trust Deed is purchased in this fashion, you must still use due diligence. This includes verifying all aspects of the original loan and the property that is the security. If the seller of the Trust Deed claims that the loan is seasoned, you will have to review all of the payment records and verify with the borrower that the payments were made as claimed.

In summary, the assignment of a Trust Deed is accomplished by:

1. Assign the Trust Deed to the new hard-money lender with a specialized Assignment of Trust Deed form. This form must be signed, notarized, and recorded by the County Recorder's Office. It is important *not* to assign the Trust Deed using a Grant Deed. A Grant Deed has significant legal implications. These implications include your obligation to defend the title. In the event there are challenges to the ownership or claims against the property, the resulting cost can be significant.

When funding is from your trust, the assignment usually will be to the name of the trust.

2. Endorse and transfer all interest in the Trust Deed Note by having the original hard-money lender sign the back of the original Trust Deed Note or use a separate document that assigns the Trust Deed Note. When funding from a self-directed IRA, the assignment is to the IRA institution with you as the beneficiary of the IRA.

It is important to receive the original Trust Deed documents such as:

- Assignment of Trust Deed,
- original Trust Deed Note,
- Assignment of Trust Deed Note

and keep them on file.

If this is an IRA-funded transaction, the Trust Deed, trust deed assignment, the Trust Deed Note, and the Trust Deed Note assignment are usually sent to the IRA institution. A copy should be made for your file.

The assigned Trust Deed must be sent (with the filing fee) or hand carried to the County Recorder's Office for filing (and paying the filing fee). If there isn't a mortgage broker or escrow or title company involved, you should hand carry the trust deed assignment to the County Recorder's Office to insure that the document meets all of the recorder's requirements. If there is the smallest error, the recorder will not record the document. This will require having the document corrected by the Trust Deed Note seller or mortgage broker and resubmitted to the County Recorder's Office. If you are doing the recording at the County Recorder's Office, a copy can be obtained, at the time of recording, for a small fee. A certified copy can also be obtained but at a much higher cost.

As part of this process, verify that the County Recorder's Office's return mailing instructions on the Assignment of Trust Deed form has the correct mailing address. This is to insure that after the recording, the original document is returned to you. Another reason to have the correct address is in the event there are any legal actions on the property, notifications will be sent correctly to you.

When funding from a self-directed IRA, the County Recorder's Office's mailing instructions on the Assignment of Trust Deed should show that the document is to be sent to the IRA institution.

3. Obtain the original copy of the title insurance. A Title Insurance 805 endorsement is recommended. This can usually be obtained for less than $100. When the endorsement is obtained, the title company will do the filing with the County Recorder's Office.

4. Obtain a copy of the fire or home owner's insurance policy on the property. Check the policy's effective date to make certain that the property is insured. Verify that the amount of insurance coverage will insure the property to cover the loan amount or the property's full replacement cost. The coverage will have to be large enough to include any senior loans. A letter or call will have to be made to the insurance company, changing the name of the lender. The notification of the insurance company is usually done by the mortgage broker. If a revised notice is not received in about thirty days, a call to the insurance company should be made to verify that the insurance company's records are correct.

5. Documents such as the Trust Deed, Assignment of Trust Deed, Trust Deed Note, Assignment of Trust Deed Note, title insurance policy or endorsement of existing title policy, and the fire or home owner's insurance documentation should be placed in a safe fireproof location.

Note: There is no reason for a mortgage broker to retain the original documents. This is the case even if the mortgage broker will be servicing the loan. Having the mortgage broker service the loan can be convenient but there is a cost for this service. The expense can be in the actual service cost and a potential delay in filing a foreclosure if payments are not received.

The major danger in not having the Trust Deed documents in your possession is the risk to your wealth. There is always the remote possibility, that a dishonest mortgage broker, might use your Trust Deed documents to float a loan, and then decide to take a trip to Las Vegas or have a party. You may be paying for his amusement.

LOAN BROKER INFORMATION

When purchasing a Trust Deed from a mortgage broker or using the mortgage broker to arrange the purchase of a Trust Deed, it is important to obtain the broker's real estate license number or, in the case of a Corporation Commission (CLS) lender, his license number. Very often the agent working the loan is a real estate salesperson and not the broker of record. It is prudent to obtain the salesperson's real estate license number as well as the real estate broker's license number. Verify that the license has not expired by noting the expiration date.

The agent's claim to be licensed is not a guarantee that he is legitimate. The validity of the real estate license can be checked by calling the Department of Real Estate or using the Internet. A call to the Department of Real Estate or the Corporation Commission in the case of a CLS licensee will also provide information about the agent's status and if there have been complaints.

There is a special danger when dealing with a real estate broker or agent who is unknown. He could be using a counterfeit license or someone else's license. If this is the case, there can be little protection. It would be wise to ask for the names of other real estate brokers that he knows, so calls can be made to check the ethics of the agent.

When a loan is made, a completed lender/purchaser disclosure statement (LPDS) is required by the Department of Real Estate and should include a full disclosure about the loan. The document will require your acknowledgment (signature) to complete the broker's file. The acknowledgment is accomplished by signing the broker's disclosure documents. This file is subject to the Department of Real Estate's periodic review. You should also receive signed copies at this time.

LOAN GUARANTEE

The mortgage broker may offer a guarantee on a loan. Its value depends on how the guarantee is written and the mortgage broker's estate value. If the guarantee is for the total loan and the mortgage broker has a substantial estate, this can be well worth the effort. The concern here is if the mortgage broker offers a guarantee to everyone. He may have guaranteed more than the value of his estate. Not every loan can go bad, so there is still some guarantee. You should not use the guarantee to replace good judgment in determining where you place your funds. The loan must still have good bones.

Alternately an agreement with the mortgage broker might be obtained to purchase the Trust Deed from you after a period of time such as six months or one year. Here again the mortgage broker should have adequate funds to make the purchase or be willing to sell the Trust Deed to another investor.

The mortgage broker must have a real estate broker's license, must have a securities endorsement to guarantee a loan, post a surety bond, and adhere to all disclosures and reporting, as required by the DRE and the State Department of Corporation.

Shown below is an example of a loan (recourse) guarantee agreement that might be used between a mortgage broker and a lender.

LOAN GUARANTEE

This agreement is entered into this____ day of _____, 200__ by and between _____(mortgage broker or borrower), hereafter referred to as guarantor and _____(lender) hereafter referred to as lender.

In consideration of beneficiary (lender) funding _____(name of borrower) for a loan secured by a Trust Deed and Trust Deed Note in the amount of _____(amount of funding) secured in _____ (position of Trust Deed) by the property located at _____(address or tax parcel number(s)); the guarantor agrees to indemnify and pay for any loss sustained by the beneficiary should default occur. The guarantor shall additionally deposit with beneficiary the sum of _____ (typically 5 percent of funding) upon default of the second consecutive Trust Deed Note installment.

Said deposit shall be credited toward the purchase of said property by the mortgage broker should it revert to the beneficiary at a foreclosure sale. The mortgage broker's purchase price of the property to indemnify the beneficiary shall cover the principal balance, interest not paid, all late charges, legal fees, foreclosure costs, property disposition costs, and advances made by the beneficiary to protect the integrity of the collateral less previous deposits by guarantor.

Date: _____   Date: _____

_____   _____

Guarantor   Beneficiary

Section 14

CHECKLIST, TRUST DEED PURCHASE

Figure 14. *Check, check and recheck.*

The following copies of documentation should be obtained, reviewed, and kept in your files before funding:

- loan application (with borrowers' social security and phone number),
- senior Trust Deed Note and Trust Deed,
- property appraisal,
- escrow instructions,
- trust documents,

- partnership agreements,
- lease contract on property with names of present tenants,
- insurance policy with contact information,
- condo CC&R,
- current tax bill,
- Preliminary Title Report,
- income tax returns,
- credit report of borrowers.

If you don't ask and demand the above documents, don't expect the mortgage broker to supply them. The request calls for the mortgage broker to do additional work. In many cases, they will be reluctant to supply all of the copies.

Many mortgage brokers will provide a one or two page executive summary of a loan. Unfortunately, oftentimes, this document only highlights the loan, showing mostly the positive features. Included in some of the mortgage broker's package can be voluminous information that may be confusing and extraneous to the security of the loan. It is very important to still review the package due to a negative detail that could be buried in the pages. Included in a loan package can be appraisal, qualifications of the appraiser, rent schedules, credit report, project schedules, project cost, and other details. Having a copy of the mortgage broker's submission is important if there are any future questions about the loan.

The old maxim, *If you want something done, do it yourself,* applies in the business of trust deed investing. If you don't review all the documentation and have concerns satisfied, don't expect the mortgage broker to do this for you. When there are errors, have them corrected before funding. After funding, you have lost your leverage.

There are details that if not corrected initially, can cause problems later. There is nothing more frustrating when a problem comes up that could have been avoided by correcting a detail at the beginning of a transaction.

Checking documents will require careful thought to every detail. There are details that on the surface may not be important. However, don't be deceived by an apparent innocent detail. For example, if a Trust Deed Note has a clause in a separate document, the borrower must formally acknowledge the clause by initialing or signing the attachment. If the attachment is not formally acknowledged, even if the borrower has agreed to the clause, at a later date he could deny that he accepted the clause. When there are unusual clauses buried in the Trust Deed Note, it would be prudent to have the borrower initial the clause even if he signs the document. This is especially true if there has been legislation or case law requiring borrower's acknowledgment of a clause. Usually the clause requires bold printing with a specified font size.

THIRTEEN COMMANDMENTS OF TRUST DEED LENDING

1. *Always* take possession of the Trust Deed Note. (There are special exceptions. In the case of a self-directed IRA, the IRA holder takes possession of the Trust Deed Note. In the case where there are several lenders, such as with a fractionalized loan, the mortgage broker usually takes possession of the Trust Deed Note. However in these cases, a copy of the Trust Deed Note and Trust Deed with your name listed as the beneficiary must be obtained. A signed agreement with the mortgage broker, listing his duties and limitations when he holds the documents.)

2. *Always* make sure that the Trust Deed is recorded.

3. *Always* make sure that you have title insurance showing your Trust Deed in the proper priority.

4. *Always* make sure that you record a request for notice with respect to all senior Trust Deeds at the time you make the loan and again promptly when your address is changed.

5. *Always* personally inspect the property that is the security for your Trust Deed. You have to ask yourself, "Could I sell the property in this locality?"

6. *Never* lend money on a Trust Deed where you can't afford to keep senior lien payments current while you foreclose on your own Trust Deed.

7. *Always* insist that the Trust Deed Note and Trust Deed show you as the beneficiary on a new loan, not the mortgage broker that arranged the loan. (This is not always possible, if the mortgage broker initially funds the loan.) However the assignments must show you as the beneficiary.

8. *Always* make sure that the Trust Deed Note and Trust Deed are assigned by separate assignment. The Assignment of Trust Deed must be recorded when you are buying a loan. This must be done even if the Trust Deed Note and Trust Deed is *seasoned*, that is, it has been in existence for a while with payments being kept current.

9. *Always* keep your original Trust Deed Notes and Trust Deeds in a safety deposit box, fire resistant filing cabinet, or in a similar secure environment. A copy can be kept in your office file as a working reference.

10. *Always* make sure the property taxes are not delinquent, that any senior trust deed payments are kept current, and that the fire insurance is adequate and in force, with the premiums paid.

11. *Always* fund using an escrow company, title company, or mortgage broker trust account when you fund a loan or receive a payoff.

12. *Always* have an *exit plan*. An *exit plan* is defined as a viable method of deposing of the Trust Deed. This translates to the loan not costing you money and having a return of and on your investment. The property should have enough equity for a refinance by another investor or can be taken over by foreclosure or a deed-in-lieu of foreclosure with no loss after disposition due to a bankruptcy or borrower's waste.

13. The special rule. If you have an annoying itch about the loan, take particular care when you check all the details and don't be afraid *not* to take the loan.

TRUST DEED PURCHASE CHECK LIST

1. Property address: _____

2. Property Info (SFR, Condo, Sq. Ft., Br.) _____

3. Appraisal value: _____ Date of appraisal: _____

4. Your appraisal value: _____

5. Loan-to-value: _____

6. Loan amount: _____ Period of loan: _____ Interest rate: _____
   Impound amount: _____ Held by: _____
   Position: _____ Collection of rents document (y-n): _____
   Jump rate clause on advances (y-n): _____ Late payment clause (%, days): _____, _____
   Voluntary-involuntary foreclosure clause (y-n): _____
   Prepay penalty clause (amt., period): _____ _____
   Jump rate for nonpayoff of loan when due (amt., period): _____

7. Points to lender: _____ Points to broker: _____

8. Senior lien, amount of first: _____ Interest rate: _____ Prepay (y-n): _____
   Lender: _____
   Senior lien, amount of second: _____ Interest rate: _____ Prepay (y-n): _____
   Lender: _____
   Mechanic's lien(s) released (y-n): _____

9. Insurance by: _____
   Period insurance for: _____
   Amount of insurance: _____
   Type of insurance (fire, homeowner's): _____
   Have claims been filed for any loss (y-n): _____ (If yes, downward adjustment of
   market value equal to approximately five years of increase in insurance cost.)

10. Rented or owner-occupied: _____

11. Names of all property occupants: _____

_____

12. Title insurance company: _____

Homestead (y-n): _____

Assessments: _____

Other liens: _____

Title insurance type: _____

13. Credit rating of borrowers (FICO score): _____ (date): _____

Participated in a prebankruptcy credit, financial, or educational course (y-n):_____

Previous bankruptcies with dates: _____

Previous foreclosures: _____

Judgments, liens: _____

14a. Borrower's name: _____

_____

Borrower's profession: _____

Borrower's income: _____

Coborrowers' names: _____

Coborrowers' professions: _____

Coborrowers' incomes: _____

Spouse or Domestic Partner Quitclaim Deed (y-n): _____

14b. Internet results on borrowers: _____ (None or questionable writeup)

15. Reason for loan: _____

_____

16. Salesperson's name: _____ Broker of record's name: _____

Broker's company name: _____

Address: _____

Salesperson's license #: _____ Broker's license #: _____

Address: _____ Address: _____

Salesperson's phone #: _____ Broker of record's phone #: _____

Section 15

FORECLOSURE PROCESS

Figure 15. *You've had your fun, but you forgot to pay.*

Trust Deeds provide for a trustee, a third party, to hold legal title of the encumbered property. In reality, property owners don't fully own the real estate when Trust Deed documents are used. They only have the use and the future right to own the property. Only after all of the conditions of the Trust Deed Note and Trust Deed are fulfilled will they legally hold title to the property.

The trustee can foreclose on the property in the event the terms of the note are not observed or the note is in default because of nonpayment. In effect, the trustee tells the borrower to observe the terms of the Trust Deed Note or give up his limited rights to the property. These rights can include collection of rents and the use of the property as provided by the provisions of the Trust Deed Note and Trust Deed.

A Trust Deed Note with the companion Trust Deed provides for a fast method of recovering the security (property). This process is called a foreclosure. There are times when reference is made to a mortgage in California. This is most often loosely used to mean a Trust Deed Note secured by a Trust Deed. Unfortunately the word mortgage has more than one meaning. One of the meanings is to obtain financing. This would be stated as, "I will have to mortgage my house." The other meaning refers to the documentation, and you would state this meaning as, "I have a mortgage on my house." The latter meaning is ambiguous in that it can mean a mortgage or a Trust Deed.

There are virtually no mortgages used in California. This is due primarily to the long time period required to process a judicial foreclosure that is required by a mortgage. Foreclosing when property is secured by this type of documentation is complicated. In fact it would be a challenge to find a lawyer that is experienced in setting up a mortgage in California.

A Trust Deed generated when there is a hard-money loan can also have a judicial foreclosure (with restrictions[1] if the property is one to four residential units). Judicial foreclosure is a legal procedure using the court system. The judicial foreclosure takes a longer time, and is not normally practical in that the borrower most likely doesn't have sufficient money to cover the loan and your legal cost. The California statutes provide for a shorter time, but in practice, the time cannot be significantly shortened because of court time availability, depositions, lawyers' schedules, and statutory time periods. The additional potential problem in a judicial foreclosure is that the old owner can reclaim the property up to one year after the completion of the action. The only time a judicial foreclosure

---

[1] It should be noted that judicial foreclosure cannot be used on purchase-money loans for residential property with four or less residential property because of California statutes. The purchase-money loan definition occurs when four or less residential property is purchased. This type of loan is called a nonrecourse loan.

might be justified is if the property security isn't adequate and the borrower or a coborrower has other financial resources. If a judgment is awarded, it is effective for ten years. This judgment can be extended for another ten years. (This long-term judgment can have a detrimental effect on borrowers that may want to obtain credit in the future. This threat often is enough to induce a borrower to ante up.)

Foreclosure on real estate property can be accomplished using a statutory procedure where the court system is not required. In a statutory foreclosure, when the terms of the Trust Deed and Trust Deed Note are breached, the lender can notify the trustee to proceed with a foreclosure. If the trustee is unavailable, not knowledgeable, or unwilling to perform, this will require you to use a foreclosure company. You can do your own foreclosure by substituting yourself as the trustee. This is highly discouraged due to the complexity and lack of a disinterested party appearance.

Usually in a foreclosure, a foreclosure company is employed. The foreclosure company or an employee of the foreclosure company is the substituted trustee. The substitution is oftentimes required because the named trustee in the Trust Deed document is not associated with the selected foreclosure company. By substituting the foreclosure company as the trustee, the foreclosure can proceed in a direct and timely manner without going back to the original trustee to authorize the process.

The use of a foreclosure company is recommended. This is their business. Most have dealt with practically every conceivable problem in foreclosure that the initial trustee probably has not dealt with or seen. The foreclosure company, because of its experience and the availability of a retained attorney on call, will be able to provide advice on the various pitfalls, and alternatives in the decisions that may be required.

In California, a judicial foreclosure can be initiated to recover the full amount of the hard-money loan. This can be done on Trust Deeds (non-purchase-money type of loan) or mortgages. The judicial foreclosure also can be used on commercial property and apartments of more than four units that are acquired with purchase money. This judicial foreclosure might be used if the equity in the property disappears because the property valuation has been reduced or the property has been wasted by the owner or tenant. If there is a foreclosure where the hard-money junior loans are wiped out, there is still hope. A lawsuit can be filed to recover the loss.

Both the statutory and judicial foreclosure can be started at the same time. At some point, depending on the situation, one of the actions would have to be abandoned. Don't expect to recover your cost on the abandoned foreclosure action.

HOMEOWNER COUNSELING

Borrowers that are delinquent on their payments due to involuntary loss of the homeowner's income or any person who contributes to the homeowner's income are entitled to notification of counseling services no later than forty-five days after a mortgage payment is due but has not been paid. This requirement is specified in the Federal Housing and Community Development Act of 1987, Section 169. The U.S. Department of Housing and Urban development (HUD) makes the How to Avoid Foreclosure pamphlet (HUD-PA-426-H) available, which provides discussions on the avoidance of foreclosure. The pamphlet provides office addresses and telephone numbers of HUD offices for counseling services. A pamphlet can be obtained by contacting the U.S. Government Printing Office or a HUD office. A Web site pamphlet version is available at: http://www.hudclips.org/sub_nonhud/cgi/pdfforms/pa426h.pdf.

The problem with carrying out this requirement is knowing when the borrower has involuntarily lost his income. He may not volunteer this information or he may not disclose that this is the reason payments have not been made. If you have knowledge of the above condition, the borrower should be advised of the available help.

FORECLOSURE BLUNDER

Partial Payment

Once it has been determined that there is no alternative but to foreclose on the property, it is imperative not to accept any partial payments from the borrower. Only the full amount to reinstate the loan should be accepted. Accepting a partial payment could complicate and delay the foreclosure procedure. If a loan payoff is received that does not cover all of the amount due, such as back interest, late fees, insurance costs, foreclosure costs, accepting the partial amount could be interpreted as a de facto acceptable payment of the loan amount by a court. Additionally, you could put yourself into a situation where you might be liable for the borrower's legal fees and damages.

Accepting late payments on a regular basis might prevent a foreclosure based on the late payments, because the courts may view this as a de facto waiver of the late payment clause.

Junior Trust Deed Holder

If the senior lender impairs a junior lender's security, this could create a superior equity of the junior lender. Court action would be required to create such a superior equity.

When a foreclosure is conducted, if a junior lender files a bankruptcy, this will also stay your foreclosure. Completing the foreclosure might require litigation.

COLLECTION OF RENT CLAUSE

If the rent is significant, it may be advisable during the foreclosure to obtain a court order to receive the rent from the tenant. If the borrower agrees to have you collect the rent, a separate agreement to do this should be signed and notarized. This usually will only occur if the Trust Deed Note or Trust Deed contained a collection of rent's clause. The rent should be placed into a trust account so as not to have it interpreted as monthly interest payments. In this manner, the property is at least performing. The credit bid would have to be adjusted to reflect the amount received. It should be noted that after a foreclosure sale, any rent agreement or lease ceases to exist providing that:

- it has not been recorded prior to your loan,
- you did not have knowledge of the lease prior to funding of your loan,
- you do not accept the lease (rent) agreement. (Court action requirements apply to pre-1997 collection of rent clauses. Notes with post-1997 collection of rent clause do not usually require court action.)

REINSTATING AMOUNT

The amount that is quoted to the foreclosure company should be an accurate and true amount. If there is an overstatement of the cost, the borrower can dispute the amount and obtain a court-adjoining order to stop the foreclosure. The adjoining order is not easily obtained and usually requires posting a bond.

SELF-DIRECTED IRA

When the Trust Deed is in a self-directed IRA, it is important to notify the holder of the IRA not to accept any payments from the borrower unless it is for the full reinstatement amount. The IRA holder should also be instructed to send any received payments to the foreclosure company.

SELLING THE TRUST DEED

Before initiating a foreclosure, it may be to your advantage to sell the Trust Deed. Prior to a foreclosure, the market value can be higher. If the property is unique, where a contractor might be interested in the property, calls to contractors might have advantages. If the property can be used for a driving range or a service station, calls to these types of investors may allow the disposition of the Trust Deed without the potential problems of a foreclosure. However, it is advisable to disclose the payment history. To do otherwise could subject you to legal action.

PROPERTY INTEREST TRANSFER

When an interest in property is transferred, a Quitclaim Deed and not a Grant Deed should be used. Every so often a buyer of a property or an escrow company will request a Grant Deed. The implications are enormous as to your responsibility. With a Grant Deed you are agreeing to defend the title in the event there are challenges. A *novation* might also be requested. *Novation* is a substitution of the terms of a contract with new obligations by mutual agreement. Your attorney should review any novation agreement. In the case of ownership transfer, the commitment should not exceed the obligation in a standard Quitclaim Deed.

OTHER FORECLOSURE COSTS

Although money can be made in owning foreclosed property, there are precautions that should be taken to avoid problems. Cost containment and fast action is required.

The example below will show the cost of property ownership. The return from any real estate investment should not only reflect the risk, but also the expense and effort.

Consider an investment of $100,000. At an interest of 15 percent, the return from a hard-money loan for a one-year period would be $15,000. Taking the same $100,000 and purchasing or acquiring in foreclosure, a real estate *good deal* at below the market value might provide the same potential return. The good deal usually has deferred maintenance at best. In reality, there probably is a lot of major work such as carpet replacement, new roof, landscaping, dry wall repair, door replacement, trim molding replacement, and total painting of the improvements inside and outside. This can run $15,000 to $20,000. The cost to sell usually is about 8 percent of the sales price. (The cost for a real estate broker hard-money lender investor that lists the property himself would be only 3 percent instead of the typical 6 percent. The 3 percent difference is really earned as sweat equity.) If the property can be sold for $150,000, this would provide an apparent profit of $23,000 ($150,000 less $12,000, (8 percent average selling cost), less $15,000 fix-up cost, less $100,000 initial purchasing price). The real additional return is $8,000 ($23,000 apparent profit minus the $15,000 one-year interest charge from a hard-money loan). For a one-year period, this type of investment might be worth the effort.

This amount of return does not provide for the time, sweat equity, and trouble as well as the potential downside if the market is slow. This would be caused by high interest rates or poor economic conditions where there are few buyers.

If the property can be cycled in a shorter time period, the savings in the time and the associated cost will increase the spendable money. A three-month ownership for the above example would provide additional spend-able money. The reason not to have equity in property for a long period is due to the time value of money. Equity in property reflects an investment that is not producing revenue unless there is a high property appreciation or paid rent. An investment that is not producing revenue can be decaying money due to inflation and loss of potential income from other invest-ments. If the property is rented residential property, there is an additional problem. The property will usually take longer to sell or the sales price will be less. Tenants are notorious about not allowing property to be viewed by prospective buyers. This difficulty reduces the number of potential buyers. Even offering a reduced rent or a dollar amount after the property sells to obtain cooperation usually doesn't help that much.

Although it can be argued that the $100,000 could be used to purchase several properties, money would have to be borrowed at a cost, so the total profit would be uncertain. If the property is owned longer than one year, the taxes might be less because of the return being a capital gain. However, the carrying cost might negate the savings in income taxes.

There is a method that some property owners use to avoid the tax on the gain realized on the sale of residence. This can also be done on homes that have been acquired in foreclosure or purchased for rehab. (The rehab cost might be added to the cost base and therefore reduce the apparent gain if expended within a time period of the sale as defined by the tax code.) This tax avoidance technique is accomplished by making the property a primary residence. When this is the case, the gain on the sale is tax free on the first $250,000 for a single person and $500,000 for a married couple when certain time periods are met. The property must be lived in for 2 of the last 5 years. After 2 years, the tax-free status on $250,000 (single) and $500,000 (married) can be repeated. There is the downside of the inconvenience of dirt, dust, and living out of boxes while refurbishment is being done. There are some special rules and exceptions that need to be followed—so contacting your tax accountant would be wise.

REFINANCE OF LOAN

When a trust deed foreclosure is being considered, alternative solutions must be considered to avoid the possible revenue loss due to ownership of the property.

If there is equity in the property for a refinance of your Trust Deed, referring the refinance to a mortgage broker can earn you some finder's fee points. There will be times the mortgage broker cannot refinance the property due to the borrower not being realistic. After filing the foreclosure, the borrower's head usually clears and the refinance will in all likelihood occur. If there isn't enough equity to refinance, you may not receive all of your investment, interest, and cost.

PARTIAL OWNERSHIP OF A TRUST DEED

When there is partial ownership of a Trust Deed Note, the ownership is considered tenancy-in-common. (*Perkins v. Chad Development Corp. (1979) 95 CA3d 645*). This allows any of the tenancy-in-common owners to file a singular foreclosure. (*Los Angeles Lighting Co. v. City of Los Angeles (1895) 106 C 156*).

Each of the tenancy-in-common owners are entitled to an accounting of all profits or proceeds, including the partial ownership of the property, if acquired by one of the other tenancy-in-common owners.

PRE-FORECLOSURE NOTICE

Before initiating a foreclosure, it is advisable to send a ten-day notification of your intent to foreclose. This should be sent to the borrowers (property owners) individually. Hopefully one of those notified will step in and cure the default. Typical notifications are shown in Chapter 19.

NON-DISCLOSURE

In the trust deed business it is important to keep the business to oneself. The volunteering of any information to junior lenders, senior lenders, mortgage brokers, and other apparent disinterested parties could potentially jeopardize an investment. Consider a trust deed lender that is junior to your trust deed loan or a lender that does not have a secured loan. He might initiate a legal action claiming a prior position. This probably would be unsuccessful, but could create some discomfort and cost. If praise is needed, consider patting yourself on the back in the privacy of your own room while looking into a mirror.

WHAT SHALL I DO?

If a foreclosure has been initiated and it is determined that the equity has evaporated or is significantly less then the amount that has been invested due to waste of the property, deferred maintenance, carrying cost, sales cost, or reduction in property value—a determination will have to be made on whether to continue or cancel the foreclosure sale.

Part of the determination is the Trust Deed's position on the property. If the Trust Deed is in first position, the options essentially are as follows:

A. Proceed with a judicial foreclosure. (Note: Not allowed on purchase-money loans on properties with four or less units.) This would only be practical if the borrower has other assets or will be coming into assets and the value of the real property will not cover all of your cost plus the investment and interest. With a judicial foreclosure, the amount that is not covered by the property can result in a judgment against the borrowers for the shortfall.

B. Proceed with a statutory foreclosure. This would be the usual direction. It will allow acquiring the property in a relatively short time. However if the amount recovered after considering the foreclosure cost and sale cost is near zero or less than zero, an abandonment of the foreclosure might be considered. You should contact your tax accountant to determine the best way to establish a loss for tax purposes.

If there is equity remaining after evaluation of all the cost, the foreclosure probably should be completed. This would at least save some of your investment and establish a loss for tax purposes.

The foreclosure auction will have a minimum bid, called a *credit bid*. The *credit bid* represents the amount owed to you and would consist of principal, interest, and other costs. You, the note holder, would establish the credit bid, prior to the auction. In the case where there is no overbid of the credit bid, you, the lender, would end up as the property owner as consideration for the Trust Deed Note. If there is an overbid of the credit bid, you would receive cash equal to your credit bid but not more. The credit bid can be set at an amount less than the amount the borrower owes, but not larger. The over-bidder of your credit bid, would pay the bid amount to the auctioneer in cash, check, or a certified check, and become the property owner. The form of this payment is left to the discretion of the trustee (Civil Code, 2924h). The auctioneer, a representative of the foreclosure company or trustee, would then pay you the amount of your credit bid in this overbid situation.

A downward adjustment to the credit bid may be desired. A lower bid would allow or entice an investor to easily bid at the foreclosure sale. This would provide recovery of some of the investment without the cost of selling the property after the foreclosure.

The auction credit bid amount is very important. If the credit bid includes all of your costs (investment, interest, foreclosure costs, legal fees), there is the acknowledgment that the bid satisfies the debt. This could prevent claiming a tax loss until the property is sold. Consultation with a tax accountant to decide the best approach on the credit bid amount is recommended. Most tax accountants are not current in this area and extensive probing and investigation may be required to obtain a satisfactory answer.

C. Proceed with a judicial and statutory foreclosure. This approach might be used if the best approach cannot be determined initially. At some point either the judicial or statutory foreclosure will have to be selected. Both cannot be finalized together. A determination will have to be made prior to critical events, such as court appearances or the final statutory foreclosure auction. The critical event may be when the cost to proceed with both actions becomes prohibitive due to legal fees in a judicial foreclosure. Remember, the statutory foreclosure, once completed, precludes the judicial foreclosure approach. The additional cost of using both types of foreclosure cannot be recovered. This means that if a judicial foreclosure is finally used, the statutory foreclosure cost cannot be collected. The reverse is also true.

D. Do nothing and hope a junior lender will foreclose and change the Trust Deed into a performing loan by making the interest payments. You may have to initiate a foreclosure to encourage the junior trust deed holder to act.

There is also the possibility that the property will appreciate, so that in the future your investment can be recovered.

The junior lender may want to buy your Trust Deed. Your first position would most likely allow for the sale at face value plus any late payments and cost. If the junior trust deed holder knows that you are concerned, he may ask for a discount. What you do at this point will depend on the amount of potential loss you can tolerate.

If you are a junior lender, the options are similar to those listed above. The significant difference occurs if the senior lender initiates a judicial or a statutory foreclosure. In the case of the judicial foreclosure, a real estate attorney should be contacted to determine the correct course of action. If the foreclosure is statutory, and the ownership is undesirable, by doing nothing the ownership is avoided and a tax loss will be generated. The foreclosure by the senior lender will establish the tax loss. There is also the outside chance that a bidder will exceed the senior lender's credit bid. This overage, after payment of the senior Trust Deed and foreclosure costs, would belong to the next junior trust deed lender or lien holder. If there is a junior lender that is senior to another loan, they will, of course have first claim. It may be possible to purchase the senior loan at a discount if you want to own the property. If this is the case, a foreclosure will still be required to obtain possession.

When there is adequate equity in the property, you will want to bring the senior Trust Deeds current and initiate your own foreclosure.

If the property is one that you don't want to own, the foreclosure company should be notified to provide all information on the property and liens to callers on the foreclosure to help potential bidders.

Information fliers on the property could be distributed to real estate offices and refurbishment companies. Advertisements could be placed in local newspapers. The intent here is to generate interest on the foreclosure sale in order to enhance the probability of increasing bids on the property. Great care must be taken in any information that is passed out. If there is an error, a bidder could come back at you for any loss he had experienced.

There may be a time when your junior trust deed foreclosure has been initiated and you later determine that it is not economical to proceed.

Here a cancellation of the sale and not the foreclosure may be desired. There also may be situations where only a delay of the sale is needed. This would be the case to allow the property owner to sell the property or locate funds to bring you current. More times than not, the property owner is just asking for time to file a bankruptcy. Fortunately the borrower in a Chapter 7 or Chapter 13 *may have to* take part in a credit counseling session in the prior six months, before filing a bankruptcy application.

If the senior lender completes the foreclosure, a copy of the trustee deed of sale will help establish the loss for tax purposes.

If the loan is a hard-money loan, a suit can still be initiated, within the statutes of limitations, to obtain a judgment against the borrower. This would usually be a futile effort, because the borrower probably does not have any money now or will not in the near term.

Foreclosures can be initiated when there is a violation of the terms of the Trust Deed Note. Typically these would be:

- the senior or junior trust deed loans, or both, have not been paid after the interest payment grace period,
- the property taxes are delinquent. (Deferred taxes would not be considered delinquent.),
- the condo association fees are delinquent,
- any assessments are delinquent,
- the fire insurance payment is delinquent,
- any mechanic's lien payments are delinquent,
- There has been waste of the property. This might include allowing water damage through improper drainage, a roof not being repaired, or any condition that can cause additional damage to the property.

However, it may not be advisable to foreclose if an alternative approach with the borrower can be reached, such as advancing additional money in an impounded account to correct the problem. If the infraction is small, it would be difficult to find a foreclosure company that would proceed with a foreclosure.

Some senior loans have an impounded account that is used to pay the taxes and insurance. If this is the case and the senior loan is delinquent, there is a likelihood that the taxes and insurance are not current. The senior lender will use their own institutional lender's insurance coverage to protect their loan. This insurance will not cover the junior owner's Trust Deed.

In the case of a construction loan, there may be funds in an escrow account (controlled funds). These funds would belong to the lender of the construction loan. After the foreclosure, the lender could claim the funds.

It would be wise to verify the status of payments of all Trust Deed Notes against the property. One payment delinquency that may not be obvious is where the Trust Deed is held in your IRA account. Even though you request that payments be sent to your address for forwarding to the IRA account, some borrowers may send the payments directly to the IRA custodian for a while and then stop. This would mask the borrower's nonpayment.

DEED-IN-LIEU OF FORECLOSURE

This on the surface is a cheap way of gaining control of the property without going through the foreclosure cost and time delay. This approach however has potential problems.

When a property is obtained with a deed-in-lieu of foreclosure, all liens are assumed. This not only includes the senior loans, the junior loans, and known liens against the property but any hidden liens. These liens might be mechanic's liens, judgment liens, income tax liens, or liens that are recorded just before you record your property Trust Deed. If the owner signed a Quitclaim Deed to the property and had it recorded, your deed-in-lieu of foreclosure would be impacted and a protracted legal battle would be in your future. When a property owner starts to get into money problems, almost everything around him goes bad. You don't want to inherit his problems.

One of the situations that should raise your antennas is when there has been or is going to be a divorce. There can be court ordered liens (not recorded) that have been generated and not disclosed. This may not be due to the borrower being deceptive but due to the borrower being unaware of what is going on.

If there is adequate equity in the property, a deed-in-lieu of foreclosure, may be acceptable even though you could be purchasing additional debt. If the remaining equity after considering all liens is a small negative, it may still be desirable to obtain control of the property. This will stop the potential waste of the property and cost to evict the owner. Many property owners often don't believe that they are about to lose their property and won't sell with a deed-in-lieu of foreclosure. Only after you file a foreclosure will they start to see the reality.

A signed, notarized statement from the property owner should be obtained stating all of the loans, liens, and judgments that are known or recorded against the property. If this statement is untrue, this will give you a good case to file a suit for their false statement.

The second problem is that the existing loans may not be assumable. After obtaining the property, a foreclosure procedure could still be started by any of the lien holders, senior and junior. If this is the case, a refinance or a payoff of the loan(s) to stop the foreclosure might be required. A refinance of loans will have the potential problems of a judicial foreclosure due to the removal of the purchase-money status on residential property with four or fewer units.

Even if a deed-in-lieu of foreclosure is a possibility, it may still be better to foreclose to wipe out all junior liens and assume any senior loan. Hopefully the senior lender will allow an assumption or the market interest rate will be low, allowing a reasonable refinance.

Accepting the property in lieu of foreclosure or buying the property by paying the owner for his remaining equity, after considering all expenses, will have an advantage for the borrower. This would save his credit. He also would receive part of his equity in the property that he would not necessarily receive in a foreclosure. The amount of his equity would be after all liens and cost as shown below are considered. He will need to be reminded that if he tries to sell the property, there is a cost of owning the property until it is sold, sales commissions, and escrow closing cost.

The other result in using a deed-in-lieu of foreclosure is to establish a more opportune time to market the property, rather than waiting for the foreclosure to go through its cycle.

The potential expenditures with a deed-in-lieu of foreclosure purchase of the property are:

- unpaid senior and junior trust deed loan payments,
- senior and junior trust deed attorney fees,
- senior and junior inspection fees (drive-bys),
- interest payments until the property is sold,
- late payment fees,
- loan assumption and processing fees,
- unpaid property and supplement taxes,
- unpaid condo assessments,
- unpaid condo fees,
- condo ownership change fee,
- Mello-Roos assessment,
- yours' and other lenders' foreclosure costs against the property,
- unpaid insurance,
- mechanic's liens,
- title insurance,
- environmental rules and regulations cost,
- presale fix-up cost,

- prepayment penalty,
- sales commission and escrow fees,
- hidden liens.

A title search should be done to determine the property lien status prior to firming up the deal. If a foreclosure was started, there should be information available from the foreclosure company's Trustee Sale Guarantee Policy (TSG).

With a deed-in-lieu of foreclosure, the existing senior and junior loans would still be in effect and may have to be paid off because of a due on sale clause. Most Trust Deed Notes have a due on sale clause also known as an acceleration clause. The clause requires that the loan cannot be assumed and that the entire loan must be paid. This clause can also be found in most junior Trust Deed Notes. The early payoff on a loan *may* require a prepayment penalty of up to 80 percent of six months interest. A review of the loan's Trust Deed and Trust Deed Note must be made to avoid surprises.

A Beneficiary Demand, when the preliminary indicators are positive, should be requested from all lenders and lien holders. There will be a small fee but the money is well spent. The Beneficiary Demand, sometimes called a bene or demand, will show all of the back interest due, principal due, interest rate accrual, prepayment penalty, and any other obligations that may not have been paid such as late payment fees and insurance advances.

It is advisable to use an escrow and obtain title insurance to verify that all the liens are known. The title insurance will also indemnify you for a loss if there are liens recorded that are not reported by the title insurance company. The title insurance will also insure that the recording is done without other new liens being recorded just prior to your obtaining a deed-in-lieu of foreclosure.

If there is a Trust Deed that is junior to your Trust Deed, it may be desirable to notify the holder of your intention to foreclose prior to accepting a deed-in-lieu of foreclosure. The junior trust deed holder might be willing to pay you a fee to delay your foreclosure so he can file his own foreclosure. He may be willing to sell his Trust Deed to you at a discount. However many junior lenders in this situation, don't believe that the equity isn't there. Not until you file a foreclosure will their heads clear. Hopefully they will decide they are going to take a hit and conclude something is better than nothing.

If the junior lender elects to foreclose, he will be a guardian angel by keeping your trust deed loan current. Your option to foreclose would still be available if the junior lender does not make the required payments after his foreclosure.

WHEN A FORECLOSURE IS STOPPED

In the event the borrower brings all delinquent payments up to date, there is no legal or moral justification to proceed with a foreclosure. However, verification should be made that there are no unpaid required payments such as taxes, insurance, assessment, and condo fees, along with the late fees and legal fees that may have been incurred. A legal fee could have been imposed by a condo association due to nonpayment of condo fees. If these items are not included as the reason for the foreclosure, the trustee will not require these payments to be brought current when the foreclosure is removed. This is why when a foreclosure is filed, a general statement should be made that the borrower brings *all* arrears current prior to terminating the foreclosure. The trustee will only reinstate the Trust Deed when the stated foreclosure reasons are rectified or you allow some of the arrears to be unpaid. This might be acceptable to allow the property to be taken out of foreclosure in order to gain better terms for the borrower to refinance. The amount of money received by the foreclosure company to reinstate the loan should be *reviewed by you prior* to the foreclosure company removing the foreclosure. The only recourse, if agreed upon unpaid arrears are not subsequently paid and new substantial defaults occur, is to initiate a new foreclosure procedure.

If the foreclosure is terminated because the borrower has brought current all late payments and paid the foreclosure cost, a notice of recession must be filed with the County Recorder's Office. This will normally be done by the foreclosure company.

Borrowers are in a state of denial when a foreclosure is taking place. They very often are positive that something like this couldn't happen to them. They believe that by some strange magic, the foreclosure will go away. It isn't until near the end that reality occurs. They may put the property on the market, but all too often, at an unrealistically high price without adequate marketing time. They don't take into account that it will take time to sell a property, even at a reasonable price, and the escrow period after a sale can take up to 120 days. The exception to marketing time is when there is a shortage of properties for sale. When this is the case, properties are appreciating and a refinance is usually possible negating the need for a foreclosure.

FORECLOSURE COMPANY SELECTION

The selection of a foreclosure company is critical. It is not advisable to do your own foreclosure although you could legally do so. Don't select someone you like, or an acquaintance that wants to get into the business. A professional company with an adequate number of years of experience should only be used. A visit to the company's office should provide information about their professionalism. They should have their forms on a computer, a retained lawyer, adequate staff, and use a title company that has their own title plant. They should have their foreclosures organized and filed. If the office has piles of files lying around on desks and on the floor, this is an indication of a poor operation.

SEQUENCE OF THE FORECLOSURE

The sequence of filing a foreclosure in most cases is straightforward. The process requires gathering all the details on late payments, late fees, and advances paid. This information with copies of the Trust Deed, and the Trust Deed Note can be faxed or e-mailed to the foreclosure company. When you arrive at the foreclosure office with the original Trust Deed and Trust Deed Note—all that will be required is to verify that the generated documents are correct, sign the appropriate documents, and pay their fee (if required at this time). The amount of the up-front fee varies between foreclosure offices. The amount can be between nothing and $1,200. The full foreclosure amount will have to be paid at some point. The original Trust Deed and Trust Deed Note usually will be retained by the foreclosure company. The sequence followed by most foreclosure companies is as follows:

1. Generate Substitution of Trustee.
2. Generate Declaration of Default and Demand for Sale.
3. Generate the Notice of Default.

A *Notice of Default* provides the borrower with a legal notice that the terms of the loan are in default. The Declaration of Default and Demand for Sale and Notice of Default will require that the jump rate (if applicable), advances, daily interest amount, and prepayment penalties be determined. The prepayment penalty can be charged if the note contains a voluntary or involuntary prepayment in the due on sale clause, and not prohibited by other statutes and case law. (See other discussions on prepayment.) Any other obligations that need correction will also be added to the documentation before the foreclosure will be terminated. The various forms generated by the foreclosure company will require the Trust Deed Note holders' signature. It is extremely important to verify all the details generated such as the address of the property, borrowers' names, the addresses of the borrowers, advances, payments that are delinquent, and the spelling of all names. Any error can cause the foreclosure to be restarted if an error is challenged in a legal action.

4. The foreclosure company should generate a status report, as of the report printing, on the amount that must be paid to terminate the foreclosure. An updated report should be periodically submitted to you. You should review this report in detail and request corrections of any errors or omissions. The corrections would include any new advances that you make such as payments on senior loans and property insurance.

This report is almost like a check. If you do not verify that it is correct, you could lose some of your money if the loan is brought current. If the foreclosure goes to auction, the amount of your credit bid will be established using this information. The credit bid will also include the foreclosure company's cost. Hopefully an overbid will occur at the auction. This overbid will be received by the foreclosure company. They will then pay your portion of the credit bid. Hopefully there will be another trust deed investment available.

5. The foreclosure company will order the Trustee Sale Guarantee Policy.

The foreclosure will then proceed with the filing of the Notice of Default with the County Recorder's Office and notification of the borrower(s). The notification will be sent to the borrowers by the foreclosure company. When there is more than one owner of the property, separate notices should be sent to each of the property owners. This is very important in the case of a divorce and one of the owners resides in a separate location. In the case of several owners where one of the owners resides in the foreclosed property, if only one notice is sent to the property, the resident owner may not notify the other owners. With separate notifications, if one of the owners has moved or his address is unknown, hopefully by addressing the owners separately, the post office will have a forwarding address.

With luck the borrower's head will clear and the required payments will be received by the foreclosure company. If the borrower doesn't make the necessary payments, the foreclosure could go to sale. The borrower may contact another lender and refinance the loan for a payoff. This isn't too bad a deal if there is a prepayment penalty. This is usually six months interest on 80 percent of the loan. This payment will significantly increase the yield on your investment. The only problem with a payoff is the money will now have to be reinvested to continue a reasonable return. Hopefully a better performing loan will be found.

Every so often the borrower does not have enough money to remove the property from foreclosure or will have funds arriving from some magical place. You will have to decide if this is true or how much of a payment is acceptable. If the borrower has the property in escrow and can show you signed, verifiable documents, a delay might be warranted. In most cases these statements about magical funds are just a ploy to delay the foreclosure so a bankruptcy can be filed.

Remember, do not accept any payments from the borrowers or other persons that would credit the payments to the Trust Deed Note. This would also include rent unless there is some other agreement where the money will be held in a trust account. Any and all payments must be sent to the foreclosure company for their administration.

A foreclosure cycle will take about four months if there isn't a bankruptcy or other complications.

The cycle will consist of the following:

1. Notification period—three (3) months. (The loan can be reinstated during this period by the payment of deficiencies and foreclosure cost by the trustor.) If other payments such as taxes or senior loan payments have not been made, these can be required to be paid if included in the notification of foreclosure.

2. Publication period—twenty-one days. (Usually takes longer due to weekends, holidays, and the available publication date.) Borrowers still

have redemption rights during this period. The acceptable publication newspapers are shown in the TSG.

3. Posting on the foreclosed property of the Notice of Trustee Sale. This must be done twenty days prior to the sale (auction).

The loan can be reinstated within five days of the established auction date only with the approval of the beneficiary. The trustor, if the lender refuses to accept payments and the reinstatement of the loan, can only stop the foreclosure within the five-day period by paying all of the trust deed principal, interest, prepayment penalties, advances, and foreclosure costs. The trustor still has the right to reinstate the loan prior to the five-day period preceding the auction. To do this, the trustor must bring current all back payments and other required payments. The required payments would be as stated in the foreclosure documents.

There is a special problem that can occur to the trust deed investor that becomes an *equity buyer*. An *equity buyer* is one that purchases the property and pays the owner the value of the remaining equity in the property. This is caused by Civil Code 1695. This problem can happen with the sale of the property in foreclosure to an equity buyer. If the equity buyer takes unfair advantage of the seller, the seller can reclaim the property for up to two years. There are special exclusions in the civil code that will prevent this from happening. Extreme care should be taken by the equity buyer to conform to the requirements of the civil code. The danger occurs where there is litigation. If this happens, payments can stop until it is straightened out by the buyer and seller or court action. If there is a buyer that is interested in the property, it may be advisable to sell the equity buyer the Trust Deed. If this is done, the equity buyer's legal status will have changed. This will allow the equity buyer to complete the foreclosure or purchase the property with a deed-in-lieu of foreclosure. This approach will not only provide a fast and safe return of the investment, but will avoid the civil code rules.

254 • *Avoid Market Loss with Trust Deed Investing*

PROPERTY SALE BY AUCTION...AT A LOCATION ADVERTISED

There will be variations in the time period for the foreclosure process. This will be due to the actual filing day of the week of the Notice of Default, the day of the week the advertising period starts, a bankruptcy filing, and any income tax lien's resolution. The trust deed holder may also request a delay of sale to help the borrower complete a sale, obtain a new loan, or obtain funds for a payoff. Care should be taken that there is a valid source for funds and that this is not just a delay tactic by the borrower. A verification, whenever possible, should be made for the reason provided. Most times if you grant a delay, you will regret it. This is because the borrower files a bankruptcy.

After the notification and publication period, the sale can take place. A delay of the sale can take place by instructing the foreclosure company not to have the sale on the scheduled auction date. A new auction date must be set at this time if there is a delay. The delay might be made to facilitate the payoff of the loan. The property may be one that the trust deed holder doesn't want to own and the borrower only needs a few days to complete a sale escrow. The delay also could be granted to allow the borrower to obtain a new loan through a loan broker that is taking more time than anticipated. This delay normally will only cost a few days, often a good investment. There is the danger the borrower is just gaining time to file a bankruptcy, an action that can create significant delay and cost. An auction delay can be done three times. If there are other delays caused by bankruptcy filings, actions by a taxing agency, a mutual agreement, or judicial action—these delays do not count against the three times. When there is an auction delay that exceeds three times, under civil code restriction, a new Notice of Trustee Sale is required (Civil Code 2924g).

If the property has significant equity, there are several things that may occur. The auction will have an overbid of your credit bid or the property will be refinanced. With significant equity, there is a small probability that you will acquire the property in foreclosure.

When there is significant equity, your favorite mortgage broker can be contacted to try to refinance the loan for the borrower. This will provide the opportunity of obtaining a referral fee from the mortgage broker. Refurbishing companies can be contacted to inform them of the auction of the property. The refurbishment company would only have to provide funds for the auction for a short period. You can, after the auction and recording of the trustee's deed, lend the refurbishment purchaser funds to replace the auction funds. The eviction of any tenants and refurbishment of the property would in this manner, not be your immediate or hopefully your eventual headache. The refurbishment company may provide a place for your funds at a reasonable interest rate as well as the possibility of obtaining points for funding the loan. Remember to use a mortgage broker for this new loan.

If the property is auctioned and no other person has bid on the property, you as the holder of the Trust Deed Note and Trust Deed now own the property. The foreclosure company will have made a credit bid on your behalf for the property at your stated amount to satisfy the loan. The amount could be set at a lower number than the normal credit bid. This amount will have been determined by you and submitted to the foreclosure company prior to the auction. Although you can bid at the auction, you would have to provide any overbid amount as prescribed by the foreclosure company.

After the auction, the foreclosure company will request funds from you to pay for any balance owed. The amount to be paid is usually only unpaid foreclosure cost to complete the foreclosure and transfer title. The total amount that will have to be paid should have been included in the credit bid. Before the foreclosure company will record the sale, they will request that the balance due be paid.

A copy of the recorded trustee's deed should be obtained as quickly as possible, in the event immediate proof is needed of the title transfer. This can be done by getting the original trustee's deed from the foreclosure company and hand carrying it to the County Recorder's Office for recording and paying the recording fee. A copy of the County Recorder's stamped document can be obtained from the County Recorder's Office for a small fee. Typically the document might be needed to show tenants, ex-owners, or an eviction company.

If an eviction is required, the trustee's deed must be recorded (perfected) prior to a three-day eviction notice being served. An eviction company will only start an eviction with proof of your ownership of the property. If the trustee's deed recording is done by the foreclosure company or a title company, it may take several weeks before a copy can be obtained. Your address for this mailing by the County Recorder's Office should be on the trustee's deed.

There are special actions that must be taken after the trust deed auction. Fire insurance including a clause to cover vandalism must be on the property, if not previously obtained. Your name must be listed as the person who will be paid if there is a loss to the property. If there is a fire loss, the payoff funds could go to the old owner if the necessary changes are not made. If the property will be vacant more than thirty days, a special insurance policy will be required.

If there is a property tax owed on the property, this should be paid. However, if the property tax late fee has been imposed, the payment may be delayed up to the date that additional delinquency fees will be imposed. These delinquency fees are high and accumulate very fast. There could be a supplemental tax imposed. This is calculated from the date that you owned the property. This supplemental tax reflects any increase in property value. Often this amount can be contested if there are comparable sales that show a lower value or the condition of the property is extremely poor.

If there are senior loans that have impound accounts, these impound accounts may pay the taxes and insurance. It is important to check with any senior lender to learn the impound status. If the property is to be sold immediately, an ownership change on the senior Trust Deed and Trust Deed Note would not be necessary. This immediate sale would avoid a trust deed assumption fee. If the property is to be retained and the loans assumed, any existing senior lenders should be notified and changes made to their documentation. This is to insure that impound funds are properly credited and do not go to the previous owner. The ownership change would also allow the interest payments to be credited to you. This would appear on the IRS 1099-INT form that would be submitted by lenders at the end of the year.

Condo association fees should be paid. This will avoid any additional late fees. If the property is to be sold immediately, the condo association ownership change may not be desired. This is to avoid the change in ownership fee. If the condo association fees were delinquent, it would be wise to bring them current to avoid a possible foreclosure by the condo association.

One of the tax aspects that should be considered is the time of year the sale takes place. If the foreclosure sale is in one year and the disposition of the property is in another year, there can be taxes due on the amount of interest in the credit bid. The total amount owed by the borrower, normally the credit bid, usually contains interest that has not been received. This uncollected interest might be imputed by the IRS and taxed for that tax year after you obtain ownership of the property. This is because when the property is received, the interest is effectively received and is therefore taxable.

There is a potential problem in avoiding the interest tax. When the credit bid is set low to negate the interest, if there is an overbid by another buyer, there will be a loss of your interest. If there is an overbid, the additional bid money goes to the junior lien holder or, if none, to the old owner, not you. If you plan on bidding to win the auction and avoid the taxable interest, you will need cash or a cashier's check to overbid. (There are foreclosure companies that will accept a personal check.) The only practical approach is to wait until the day of the sale to detect if there are any potential bidders. If not, the lower credit bid number can be given to the auctioneer. The lower credit bid can be given to the auctioneer up to the time the price is announced three times.

There is still the danger that an unknown bidder can turn the corner or jump over a bush, make an overbid and cause the loss of your unstated interest. The only recourse now is to call for a delay. This delay can be made up to the time that the auctioneer says sold, if the auctioneer will allow this. A credit bid for the entire amount that is due to you can then be made at the new auction. An alternate approach, if the trustee agrees, is to set the credit bid at a low value and reserve the right to increase the bid during the auction. This alternate approach is very often done by banks and lending institutions.

There is also the consideration, depending upon the tax laws at the time (they are always changing), that the property can be sold as a capital gain. The capital gain tax rate may be lower than your normal tax bracket. In the case where the property is to be kept long term, a lower bid, not including the non-paid interest, will allow for the purchase of the property at a discount price. This will convert the short-term ordinary interest income to a capital gain income when the property is sold long term. With a lower credit bid, the county's assessed value of the property and resulting property tax might be lower. The Tax Assessor's Office unfortunately does not always use the credit bid as part of their appraisal. They believe the sale is a distress sale and the auction price is lower than the market price. Even though they are very often wrong, it will be hard to convince them otherwise.

As the auction day approaches, the actual auction sale could be delayed due to an income tax lien (federal or state) on the property or the borrower filing a bankruptcy. In both cases the auction will not happen until the problem is resolved.

One of the annoying problems when the borrower files a bankruptcy just before the foreclosure auction is the consequence if the auction is held. This eleventh hour filing is commonplace. If the auction is held and the filing of the bankruptcy is legal, the notification period with advertising must be redone. The notification and advertising cannot be done until a Relief from Stay is filed and hopefully granted, or the bankruptcy is *dismissed* or discharged. Even with a discharge there can be a period where the court has not released the property, preventing the filing of a new foreclosure. *Dismissed* is the disapproval of the filing without a resolution. Your foreclosure company can give guidance on the time delay requirements.

INCOME TAX LIEN

In the event there is an income tax lien on the property, this will be announced by the title insurance company. Usually, this will require a delay in the auction and possibly posting a bond to allow the foreclosure to proceed. The foreclosure company should be able to provide guidance on the latest position of the taxing agencies. When it can be shown that there isn't any equity left, the taxing agency usually is inclined to release the property.

BANKRUPTCY ACTION

In the event there is a bankruptcy filing, this action will be announced by the borrower's bankruptcy attorney, the borrower, or your title insurance company. The bankruptcy filing will impose an automatic stay on the foreclosure procedure. This means that the foreclosure auction cannot go forward. This will stop some aspects of the foreclosure until a Relief from Stay is obtained from the bankruptcy court. A bankruptcy can also stop you from filing a foreclosure against other property that the bankruptcy filer owns jointly or separately. If the borrower announces this action, a bankruptcy file number and date of filing should be obtained to insure that a bankruptcy has been filed. Every so often a borrower will call your foreclosure company and state that the property is in bankruptcy. This may not be true.

The filing of a bankruptcy petition in the bankruptcy court by a junior lender can also stop a senior lender's foreclosure from moving forward.

A bankruptcy attorney or the foreclosure company can help you in determining the number of days to specify for a foreclosure postponement. This typically is thirty days. The actual time will be determined by the district where the filing has taken place, the foreclosure company, and the bankruptcy chapter that is being used.

Often the debtors are hurting themselves by filing the bankruptcy. If there is reasonable equity, potential bidders will be discouraged with repeated delays in a foreclosure auction. This will in all likelihood eliminate bidders and a potential overbid of the credit bid. The overbid amount would go to any junior lenders and then to the debtor. The debtor by filing the bankruptcy has lost most if not all of his equity.

As part of your business, a copy of the bankruptcy filing and other bankruptcy actions should be obtained. Copies can be obtained from the Bankruptcy Court Record's Office. This cost will usually be between $0.10 and $1.00 per page. The Bankruptcy Court Records will provide information on bankruptcy filings, dates, details about the filing, and if there is a request for a Relief from Stay filed by other lien holders. If a senior lien holder has filed a Relief from Stay, you will have to cure that default to protect your interest and proceed with your own request for Relief from Stay. You cannot use someone else's trust deed Relief from Stay (junior or senior) to proceed with your foreclosure.

Any contact with the bankruptcy personnel or bankruptcy trustee should be courteous. They can help you tremendously in finding files or processing documents. In a bankruptcy action, a bankruptcy trustee is appointed by the Bankruptcy Court to handle funds and be a neutral representative of the Bankruptcy Court, creditors, and bankruptcy filer. This trustee does not receive a large amount of money to handle the case. They by necessity will have many cases and will usually be overloaded.

If the bankruptcy is filed in a different county than where the property is located, there could be other properties belonging to the borrower. A search should be conducted to learn if the borrower owns additional properties in other counties. If the borrower has equity in other properties, opposition to the bankruptcy can be strengthened. This unfortunately would require going to each County Recorder's Office to check their files.

It is not always required that a release (Relief from Stay) from an automatic stay be filed. It will depend on the type of bankruptcy filing, the details of the bankruptcy, and the time requirements to obtain a release from automatic stay. A good attorney should be able to give you guidance on your options. Filing a Relief from Stay requires time to obtain a court hearing and could exceed the time for the bankruptcy court to complete its discharge or dismissal cycle. If the amount of time between filing and waiting for a discharge or dismissal of the bankruptcy is about the same, in all probability no action will be required. You should however, obtain legal counsel and monitor the progress of the bankruptcy. A "good" attorney is defined as one who does not take your case and file a Relief from Stay when a filing is not required.

Your foreclosure company should be able to provide names of several bankruptcy attorneys. In the event the bankruptcy is filed in a different county than where the property is located, a referral from foreclosure companies in the county where the bankruptcy is filed would provide a starting point to evaluate bankruptcy attorneys. It would be prudent to check with the State Bar Association and the Better Business Bureau to evaluate the credibility of the recommendations. By checking with the Better Business Bureau and the Bar Association, a determination can be made if there have been any complaints against the subject attorney.

It is recommended to hire an aggressive bankruptcy attorney that is familiar with the local bankruptcy judges. If the attorney isn't familiar with the bankruptcy judges, you will put yourself at a disadvantage.

The attorney will probably require a retainer fee. This can run between $250 and $1,000 depending on his policy and his hourly rate. It doesn't pay to be penny wise. After several attorneys are targeted, an interview of the attorneys should be done. This not only will aid in your attorney selection but will also give you insight on the type of problem you are dealing with. You can also observe an attorney in action by finding out where and when he will be presenting an argument. The local U.S. District Bankruptcy Court is open to anyone and observing the attorney in action can help you make a decision.

An attorney that has been recommended by a nonlawyer who has had experience with the recommended lawyer should be considered. An attorney who can be trusted may have some suggestions. However, there is a tendency among attorneys to recommend another attorney in the hope of receiving a referral in return.

The attorney must be responsive to the client's needs. The number of articles that a lawyer has written is no indication of how well he will perform. It should be remembered that an attorney, like any specialist, cannot advise you about your business dealings. Attorneys do not know your business. You will still have to orchestrate the action of your attorney to get him to perform to your wishes. This can at times be difficult due to an attitude problem of some lawyers, that only they have the smarts.

A check on the attorney's status can be done by contacting the State Bar of California membership directory on the Internet. The Web site address is www.calsb.org/mm/sbmbrshp.htm.

Employing an attorney, (when required), can be done after the borrower files a bankruptcy schedule, plan, or statement.

Due to the complexity of filing a Relief from Stay, hiring a bankruptcy attorney will often be necessary. When an attorney is hired to obtain the Relief from Stay, it should be made clear to the attorney that you must review all documents prior to filing or submission. This is to insure there are no major or minor errors. An error such as not stating the Trust Deed is in your trust, the amount owed, or an incorrect date can cost you time and money because you will have to refile to correct errors. Time is your enemy, so any delay could cost you money.

There probably will have to be an appraisal on the property to show the present value. Sometimes the debtor will have placed the property on the market. If the property's listed price is lower than that the market value, an appraisal may not be needed. The debtor has acknowledged the property value. The debtor might still argue that the price is set very low to obtain a fast sale. It is important that the property have some remaining equity but not too much after including your costs incurred to date. This will help show that the loan was a secured loan and not an unsecured loan or business loan. If your loan used a standard Trust Deed Note, this should not be a problem to you. If the equity is very large, the bankruptcy court probably will allow the borrower to market the property or refinance the loan.

The amount of remaining equity will need to be proven with a bona fide appraisal. Some bankruptcy attorneys will suggest a market value analysis from a real estate broker. My suggestion is to use an appraiser with an MAI designation.

In the case where there is a large amount of equity, your loan is in effect performing. The only downside is that the interest you will receive on advances, such as insurance or payments on senior liens, could be set by the bankruptcy judge at an interest rate lower than the Trust Deed Note's stated interest rate.

In the event there is substantial equity in the property, the borrower will in all likelihood have hired a good bankruptcy attorney and a fight will have begun. If there isn't too much equity, the borrower may file *pro se*. *Pro se* is when the borrower is acting as his own attorney. In the case of a Chapter 11 or 13 without an attorney, the required bankruptcy plan will probably not be filed, due to the complexity.

If there is little or no equity left, the judge, who has enormous power, can do a cram down. Fortunately this rarely would happen when your security is protected with a Trust Deed. A judge would in all probability be reversed in a higher court if a cram down were done. The time and cost however can be a significant problem.

The bankruptcy attorney will prepare various court required documents and obtain a court hearing date. The court required documents would require your signature. This would be the time to do a detailed review of the attorney's prepared documents. It is important to be very assertive in your review of all bankruptcy documents to avoid bad things from happening.

If you have filed a foreclosure prior to a bankruptcy filing, the required statutory time period can run with the bankruptcy time cycle. You can repeatedly delay the final auction date until the bankruptcy cycle has been completed. During a bankruptcy, auction delays for the foreclosure sale do not count against the statutory limit. Small time increments of a couple of weeks delay in the foreclosure sale should be used due to the unpredictability of events.

The dispositions of the filing of a Relief from Stay by the bankruptcy court can be a dismissal, discharge, or removal of a property from the bankruptcy proceedings. The dismissal is done when a plan is not approved or the creditor did not complete the required filings. The discharge is given when the creditor is forgiven his unsecured debts. (Recent bankruptcy law will still obligate debtors under certain conditions to make payments on unsecured debts.) Secured debts fortunately in almost every case are not forgiven and remain an obligation to the debtor. The removal of the property from the bankruptcy court jurisdiction can happen when there isn't significant equity in the property. When any of the three court actions are issued, you are closer to a foreclosure auction.

With every bankruptcy, there is a meeting of creditors held by the court appointed trustee prior to the bankruptcy court hearing. A call should be made to the trustee's office one business day prior to the meeting to verify that the meeting is still scheduled. This meeting will allow you or your attorney to question the debtor about his assets and other pertinent items. It is not a free-for-all session, and questions must deal with assets.

The presentation by your attorney during the bankruptcy court hearing to the judge should be short and to the point. The judge has several cases to hear in a short time period and will not tolerate too much presentation or will tune out if the presentation is lengthy. There is always a dilemma on which lawyer should present his arguments first. The concept that the "first presenter loses" can be countered by "the second presenter loses" due to the first being able to have another round of arguments. There are no good guidelines. It depends on your lawyer's method of presenting his arguments. In either case, debtor's points or anticipated points should be countered and your own points made. Arguments such as funds needed for you to live, the debtor's frivolous filing, debtor's continuous nonpayment, or small or no remaining equity in the property are the ones most likely to be listened to by the judge.

Your attendance at the hearing is important so you will be recognized as a person and not a case number by the bankruptcy judge. Your attorney may suggest that you not attend. However, it is my belief that it is important not only for the judge to see you, but for you to monitor your attorney and let the attorney know you are evaluating his performance. It is advisable to generate the arguments that the attorney can use in his opposition to the bankruptcy. You as the creditor would be more knowledgeable about the loan, the debtor, and the property. The points to be made by your attorney should be reviewed prior to the hearing, so they are fresh in your attorney's mind. Attorneys unfortunately do not spend an adequate amount of time preparing for a case. This will require you to make sure that your attorney has the salient information so he can do a proper presentation. This information review is usually done only minutes before the hearing and should be presented in writing to your attorney. This will allow your attorney to refer to your notes and add his thoughts to the presentation.

The bankruptcy attorney should be monitored closely. There is a tendency for the attorney to attend to other business. One of the ways to do the monitoring is to find out each of the steps in the bankruptcy that will be accomplished and when. A diligent follow-up should be done to determine that the tasks have been accomplished.

In the event the attorney does not respond in a reasonable period of one to three days or a meeting cannot be arranged, changing your attorney may be necessary (but expensive). Some attorneys think of themselves as supreme beings. Questioning them can create a hostile relationship that can be counterproductive. If an acceptable answer cannot be obtained by phone, a face-to-face meeting with your attorney may have to be conducted to have your case worked properly.

If a bankruptcy plan for the borrower to recover from his debt is required and submitted, your attorney should file an objection to this plan. This filing would be in addition to the objection to the bankruptcy filing. Hopefully a rejection to the plan and a relief from the automatic stay can be obtained. The objections could include normal scheduled Trust Deed Note payments have not been received, the plan did not include all of the debts, there is no evidence that the debtor has income to make the payments including the balloon payment, and the big one, there is no equity left in the property. When there is significant equity, even if the plan is not approved, the bankruptcy court will usually allow ample time for the property to be sold. This shouldn't be a problem for you due to your loan actually performing, even if payments are not received. You will eventually receive the arrears when your demand is submitted to the escrow company handling the sale.

One of the dangers of the plan being approved and when the debtor does not fulfill his obligation is that the foreclosure may have to start over again. A stipulation in the plan *that the foreclosure can continue in the event the plan requirements are not fulfilled* should be requested to be added to the plan.

There are waiting periods that the statutes require before a foreclosure sale can be conducted, when you obtain a bankruptcy dismissal, discharge, or a Relief from Stay. These periods would be seven days for the state of California and ten days for the federal government. The actual delay will be specified by the title company and foreclosure trustee. A copy of the bankruptcy court's discharge, dismissal, or Relief from Stay should be obtained from the court's record room. This document can then be shown to your foreclosure company so they will proceed with the remaining foreclosure statutory requirements in a timely fashion.

After a bankruptcy has been dismissed or a Relief from Stay granted, there is no protection against a debtor filing an illegal new bankruptcy. This will cause another delay. During the bankruptcy, it is important to delay the foreclosure auction in small increments so the debtor does not have too much time to refile a new bankruptcy.

The borrower may come up with all kinds of devious ways to avoid the foreclosure auction. Only by monitoring the bankruptcy progress closely can these tricks be detected. There are rules that prohibit some of the tricks, but there are too many legitimate ones that can be used, even if unfair. This might be a fraudulent or legal sale of the property, serial bankruptcy filings if several people are on title, or a change in the bankruptcy chapter type used in a new bankruptcy filing. Even after a release from automatic stay has been obtained, the borrower might refile the same bankruptcy chapter. Although this is generally not permitted by the bankruptcy rules, the borrower will do rash things. This will require additional action on your attorney's part to obtain a bankruptcy court order to allow the foreclosure sale. As an alternate, the debtor might be asked to sign a voluntary abandonment of the legal or illegal bankruptcy. If the debtor has an attorney, any contacts should be through this attorney.

If money is to be offered to the debtor to move out of the property, this should be done as soon as possible after the bankruptcy dismissal, discharge, or Relief from Stay is received. An agreement should be generated that states that the tenant agrees to move out of the property. This agreement should be signed by you and the tenants. The money should not be paid until the property is totally vacated. Keys to the property should be exchanged for the money *at the street sidewalk*.

When dealing with a bankruptcy, do not discuss your business with anyone except your attorney. You should avoid talking directly to the debtor or making any attempt to collect a debt that is in bankruptcy without the bankruptcy court's sanction. If contact does occur, an independent competent witness should be present to avoid any frivolous charges by the borrower. Do not try to record the meeting without the written or the recorded voice approval of all recorded parties due to various laws that prohibit such actions.

The four bankruptcy filing types are:

- Chapter 7,
- Chapter 9,
- Chapter 11,
- Chapter 12,
- Chapter 13.

Recent federal bankruptcy law requires that most debtors take part in a credit counseling session six months prior to filing an application for bankruptcy. This implementing "means test" is to determine whether a debtor is eligible for Chapter 7 (liquidation) or must file under Chapter 13 (wage-earner repayment plan). The law is in its infancy and the impact on trust deed holders is not fully settled.

Additional details about bankruptcy can be found at Web sites http://www4.law.cornell.edu/uscode/11/and http://www.usdoj.gov/ust/.

Chapter 7

Chapter 7 is called asset liquidation. An appointed trustee sells non-exempt property of the debtor. The generated funds are then divided and given to the creditors. There is no attempt to salvage the business, but rather to dissolve all the debts associated with the business. There is some danger of cram down. The borrower may try to keep his residence out of the bankruptcy, but there is no guarantee. In a Chapter 7, the trustee of the bankruptcy has the power, with the court's approval, to remove the debtor's residence from the proceedings. When a residence is pulled into this type of bankruptcy and a foreclosure is required, an attorney should be employed to obtain a Relief from Stay or have the property removed from the bankruptcy procedure. This would only be necessary if the borrower does not elect to remove the property from the bankruptcy.

Cram down in this case is the reduction of the trust deed loan amount by the court. This reduction amount would be shared by the other creditors. There could be another situation where the interest payments for the Trust Deed are reduced. The face value will remain the same, but the market value of the Trust Deed will have been reduced. This would be reflected in the trust deed's market value if sold. The discounting of the Trust Deed would be required to find a willing buyer at the reduced interest rate.

When a bankruptcy is filed, all assets come under the jurisdiction of the bankruptcy court.

A Chapter 7 filing can only be filed every six years.

Chapter 9

Chapter 9 bankruptcies are rare. Municipalities can file under this bankruptcy code for protection.

Chapter 11

Chapter 11 is used when the borrower wants to restructure a business. There is also the danger of cram down of your Trust Deed.

The debtor's obligations are restructured in a plan of reorganization. The plan ranks creditors into categories. Secured obligations generally are separated. When there are wage claims, these are classified as priority claims. Unsecured claims are generally separately classified.

Creditors have the right to vote to accept or reject the proposed plan. Some types of creditors must accept the plan. The bankruptcy court must also approve the proposed plan.

Approval of the plan effectively discharges the Chapter 11 debtors from their prebankruptcy obligations. The Chapter 11 plan of reorganization is a contract between the debtors and creditors. The new contract payment obligations are substituted for the discharged prebankruptcy obligations.

Chapter 12

Chapter 12 is an adjustment of debts of a family farmer with regular annual income. The debtor shall file a plan not later than ninety days after the order for relief under this chapter, except that the court may extend such period if the need for an extension is attributable to circumstances for which the debtor should not justly be held accountable.

Chapter 13

Chapter 13 is a personal bankruptcy. The amount of trust deed indebtedness on the property usually is immune to this type of bankruptcy. The interest rate could be affected. Payments are controlled by the bankruptcy trustee after approval by the bankruptcy judge. If the borrower or other creditors try to get some of the equity, there could be cram down.

This chapter cannot be used if the creditor has an unsecured debt larger than $290,000 or secured debts of roughly larger than $870,000.

When a Chapter 13 bankruptcy is filed, there are several special requirements:

- This type of filing requires a payment plan. Part of the Chapter 13 bankruptcy requirements is that preexisting payments must be made, as required by the Trust Deed Note, prior to the approval of the payment plan. If these payments are not made, the court in response to a petition would in all likelihood dismiss the bankruptcy.

- There is a requirement for the Chapter 13 debtor to make all the scheduled payments per the bankruptcy plan and also the secured debt payments after the plan is approved. If these payments are not made, it is a noncompliance to the Chapter 13 requirements. If there is any noncompliance to the plan, a petition to the court could result in a dismissal. One of the other downsides to a Chapter 13 bankruptcy is the interest payments can be set at the legal limit of 10 percent.

- The borrower must submit a bankruptcy plan within fifteen days, a list of all debts, and a schedule for payments of the debts. The fifteen-day period is somewhat misleading. Depending upon the bankruptcy court, the debtor may request an extension and may be given an additional thirty days, prolonging your agony. If an extension is given, the bankruptcy could still be dismissed by the judge, for noncompliance. The debtor could even cancel the bankruptcy and refile.

- If the Chapter 13 payment plan is approved by the court, and the requirements of the plan are not met by the borrower, a new foreclosure must be started. The bankruptcy court approval would be required to start the new foreclosure. It is important therefore, that every effort be made to have the payment plan disapproved by the bankruptcy court.

- If the bankruptcy is dismissed, the borrower will not be able to file a new bankruptcy for 180 days. The bankruptcy court will generate an order of dismissal five to seven days after it is determined that there are no subsequent filings. The need for an attorney will not be necessary in this situation. However, signed copies of the order of dismissal from the bankruptcy court should be obtained so the foreclosure company can continue with the foreclosure sale. These signed copies can be obtained from the Bankruptcy Court Record's Office. Some debtors will immediately file another (illegal) bankruptcy, requiring more negotiation or litigation.

The filing of a bankruptcy action does not stop the clock during the three-month statutory foreclosure period. This will continue to run. The bankruptcy action does however impact the advertising and posting sequence. The advertising and posting of the property should be delayed until the court provides relief to avoid repeating this sequence and expense.

After your foreclosure auction, the borrower could still file an action to have any foreclosure set aside. This in all probability would not be successful, but will require a good attorney to argue your case.

Other Bankruptcy Cost

If the borrower is having trouble making payments on your Trust Deed, he will in all likelihood be having trouble with other loans. It is important to learn immediately the status of all senior loans on the property. If a senior lender is about to foreclose, it will be necessary to immediately bring these payments to a point where the senior lender will not file foreclosure. This will prevent additional charges by the senior lenders because of the foreclosure costs and ensure that your junior trust deed foreclosure can occur first.

Some senior lender's fees can contain attorney charges and cost of property inspections if allowed in the Trust Deed Note. If the senior lender's fees seem excessive, demand that the lender submit a detailed list of charges. If you cannot get satisfactory information, you will probably have to file a small claims suit to recover your payments. This probably would not be successful. To go to a full legal court filing would be too expensive for this small amount. The property inspection fee is always excessive and there is little that you can do about it.

If the property is a condo or PUD, there can be delinquent association assessments and fees that could be senior to your loan. This could put your loan in jeopardy if a foreclosure and Relief from Stay are obtained by senior lien holders. Payments would be required to avoid this costly outcome. When there is an assessment, this translates to a significant amount of money that you would have to pay to avoid being wiped out by a foreclosure.

It is important to service your loans aggressively by not delaying the filing of a foreclosure when the terms of the Trust Deed Note are breached. This will help avoid other lien holders adding to your cost and pain. Borrowers often ask for time to cure their default. Reasons such as stocks are being sold, a property is closing, or the property is being refinanced are the common ones used. Usually they just need time to file a bankruptcy.

When a borrower is selling or refinancing his property, an attempt may occur to avoid the prepayment fee or ask for an early payoff discount. If there is adequate equity in the property, there is no need to give a discount. A procedure used to avoid the prepayment fee by the borrower is to initiate a note default. The borrower may instigate the foreclosure by not making his monthly payments. If the lender does not know the property is being sold or refinanced, the subsequent filing of a foreclosure by the lender would call for the full payoff of the loan without a prepayment fee, if the Trust Deed Note has only an involuntary payoff clause. This is why it is important to have an involuntary and voluntary payoff clause included in the Trust Deed Note. California law for loans after July 1, 2002, prohibits a prepayment fee for *covered loans* if a foreclosure is invoked.

After the foreclosure there are other potential and real costs as follows:

- unpaid senior trust deed loan payments,
- senior trust deed attorney fees,
- senior trust deed inspection fees (drive-bys),
- senior loan interest payments until the property is sold,
- late payment fees,
- loan assumption and processing fees,
- unpaid property and supplement tax,
- unpaid condo assessments,
- unpaid condo fees,
- condo ownership change fee,
- Mello-Roos assessment,
- foreclosure cost from other senior lenders on the property,
- unpaid insurance,
- mechanic's liens,

- title insurance,
- environmental rules and regulations costs,
- presale fix-up costs,
- prepayment penalty,
- sales commission and selling costs.

LOAN ASSUMPTION

After the foreclosure sale, the senior lenders might be sent a notification stating your intention. This could include the assumption of the loan or the pay off of the loan. If you plan on selling the property, keeping the loan payment current may allow you to just pay off the loan from the escrow funds. This will avoid loan transfer fees and allow you to work on your timetable. Your monthly payments can include principal, interest, insurance, and taxes. Any excess that impounds after the close of your sale is usually sent to the sales escrow holder and then to the original owner, unless you include in the escrow instructions that you are to receive your fair share.

If you send in a request for assumption of the loan, the lender will send the necessary application forms. If the loan is to be paid off with cash or refinanced using a different lender a Beneficiary Demand will have to be obtained. This would normally be done by your escrow officer. If it is your intention not to assume the loan, refinance the loan, or pay the loan off, you should do everything in your power to dispose of the property before the lender starts a foreclosure action and creates additional cost. Lenders may still do this even if they have accepted your monthly payments.

Section 16

MAINTENANCE
AND COST TO SELL

DRIVING TIME TO PROPERTY

The property should ideally be a short driving distance to your residence. This allows for easy inspection of the property prior to funding and periodic drive-bys after funding to verify the condition of the property. In the event you own the property through foreclosure, it will be easier to monitor and repair or refurbish the property. Your time can then be spent doing real work, rather than driving back and forth.

In most cases, some refurbishment and maintenance will be required after a foreclosure.

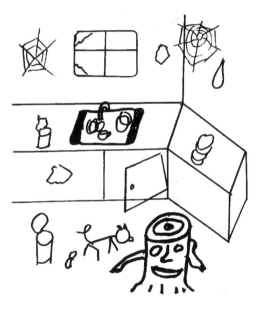

Figure 16. *I didn't know people could be this bad.*

Owners that need to borrow money and can't make their payments won't use their money to maintain the house or make improvements toward the end of their ownership. There is also the danger that any recent improvements on the property will be destroyed by the past owner after the foreclosure sale. Their thinking usually is, if they can't have the improvements, no one will.

The exception to having a Trust Deed on property within reasonable driving distance to your residence would be when properties have a low LTV. Here, there is a very low probability of owning the property and having to do repairs. If a foreclosure is required, there will be enough equity for the owner to refinance or there would be overbids at a foreclosure auction. Also, with adequate equity, the owner will be able to set a lower sales price for a fast sale and still end up with some money.

INSURANCE

The insurance policy payments on the property should be kept current prior to foreclosure. The policy should cover fire and vandalism with full replacement. Your name should appear on the policy as a lien holder. After a foreclosure, the past owner should not be on the policy. Even if there is still time left on the insurance, a new policy should immediately be obtained. The old policy rebate dollar value would most likely be small compared with the potential problems if a claim must be filed. The old owner in all likelihood will probably cancel the insurance to receive any rebate on the policy, leaving the property uninsured if you do not act.

Oftentimes senior trust deed monthly payments include funds for an impound account that is used to pay not only the taxes, but in many cases the insurance. It may be difficult to change the ownership on this insurance policy or obtain another insurance policy from the same insurance company because of their policies. This is the reason that a new insurance policy should be obtained from a different insurance company. Senior lenders should be informed about the insurance company change.

The insurance must cover the full amount of your loan and any other senior loans. If the property is occupied by a tenant, the insurance should not be for an owner-occupied property. In the case of a foreclosure, the owners' occupancy status has been changed to a tenant-occupied status. If a policy has not been obtained before the foreclosure auction, a change to the insurance should be immediately done to reflect the non-owner occupied status. The good news is that the non-owner occupied status insurance usually will cost less. Even if it is believed that there will be an overbid at the foreclosure sale, a new policy should be in place. The cost of this is small compared to your total investment. The policy probably will be issued for a full year but quarterly payment usually can be made. When the property is sold, the unused payment can be prorated and returned.

Usually insurance for condos is paid by the association. Part of the association's monthly fees pays for this cost. If the property is a PUD or a townhouse, in most cases the association's insurance will not cover the structure associated with the units. Here, additional insurance should be obtained. By contacting the association, a determination can be made on the portion that is not covered.

TENANT/EX-OWNER EVICTION PROCEDURE

The removal of a tenant or ex-owner can at times be difficult. Due to the foreclosure, the tenant probably will have lost his security deposit. Unfortunately for you, the old owner most likely will have retained or spent the security deposit. This will require giving the tenant a time equivalent to the security deposit or dig deep into your pocket to pay the amount of the deposit at some time in the future. The tenant is in a powerful position because of what he might do to the property. If you don't compensate the tenant, you will still be obligated to refund the security deposit and give an accounting (Civil Code 1950.5).

It may be desirable to retain the tenant, if he is acceptable. It is important to have him fill out an application form and sign a new rental agreement. This should be done immediately after the foreclosure sale. Although a screening fee might be desired to check his credit, a tenant that has lived in the property would probably be reluctant to come up with the fee. The fee is limited to $30.00 (AB 2263, the limit will be adjusted to the Consumer Price Index starting in 1998.) From your standpoint, avoiding the vacancy and eviction cost will more than compensate you if you do decide to obtain a credit report. If the tenant is willing to pay the economic rent in a timely manner and maintains the property, it would be foolish to change the occupancy.

Part of the new rental agreement generation process would include a walk through inspection to establish the condition of the property. Pictures should be taken of any damage. The new rental agreement should define the owner's and tenant's responsibility for maintenance. The amount of security deposit, if any, should be defined.

Before the tenant leaves the property, a move-out inspection should be preformed (*AB 2330*). Normal wear and tear cannot be charged against the security deposit. Pictures should be taken as evidence in the event of a small claims suit. Unfortunately, furniture and other items can hide damage so an additional move-out inspection should be preformed after the tenant leaves. At the first move-out inspection, the tenant should be handed notification of the second inspection and the time that it will be preformed so he will have an opportunity to witness the inspection. Picture documentation should again be recorded. Any unused deposit must be returned to the ex-tenant within twenty-one days after he moves out.

It is also possible that the tenant will want to purchase the property. If this looks workable and the property is not a keeper, have the tenant go to a lender and obtain a prequalification letter for a loan. It is important to verify that the tenant has the necessary down payment, income, and credit rating before tying the property up for several months. All too often, a tenant wishes he owned the property. Most of the time, it is just a dream.

If you keep the tenants and the tenants pay the rent with a check, it is advisable to go to the tenant's bank immediately and cash the check. Alternately, but not as effective, is to call the issuing bank and verify that there are sufficient funds to cover the check amount, prior to depositing it into your bank. Not all banks have this convenience, so going to the issuing bank or one of their branches may be required. If there are adequate funds in their checking account, a hold can be placed on the funds for a small fee. This is to prevent the tenant from placing a stop payment on the check or withdrawing the funds to create an insufficient funds situation if they plan on moving out of the property.

If it is determined that any tenants require eviction—a discussion with the tenants should be done to find out their attitude about leaving the property. When a discussion is held with the tenant or ex-owner, it is highly recommended to have a witness present. This witness should be a disinterested party, no mates or relatives, so there is no question about their neutrality. At this time every attempt should be made to record the names of all occupants of the property. If there doesn't appear to be a potential problem for the tenant to move out, it is still important to provide the tenant with a thirty- or sixty-day notice (as appropriate) to vacate the property. If you don't have the notice in hand, let the tenant know that you will be issuing a thirty- or sixty-day notice, so they don't become too upset when they receive the document. If the tenant is delinquent with the rent payment, a three-day notice can be issued. If the tenants are unavailable after three attempts to serve, the three-day notice can be posted on the door or in a conspicuous place on the property. To be valid, the posting must be done by a neutral party. In the case where the tenants' names are unknown, they should be identified as John Dos 1 thru 10 with their description in the notification document. The notice must also be mailed to each of the tenants. The mailed notice to the tenant must have a proof of mailing using a Post Office's certification of mailing. This can be obtained from the post office clerk who will issue certifications of mailing and take the letters from you for mailing. If the tenant appears to be a problem, the eviction is best done with an eviction company. Eviction attorneys are very familiar with all of the arguments and ploys that are used to avoid eviction. The slightest error in the documents and procedures can invalidate the unlawful detainer action when presented to the Small Claims Court. The unlawful detainer action, can be started three, thirty, or sixty days after serving the notice plus five days mailing time, if mailed.

For each of the types of service, three, thirty[1], or sixty day, a declaration of notice of service to tenants should be completed with the type of service used for presentation to the Small Claims Court. This declaration should contain the names of all tenants in the property, be dated and signed.

The laws on eviction can change. An eviction attorney should be up to date on any changes to the statutory law, case law, and how to handle the assigned small claims' judges. Residential, commercial, and income property have different procedures that must be followed. The presentation in the Small Claims Court to obtain an unlawful detainer decree should not be attempted yourself. The exception to this is if you have the experience to handle any counterclaims or adverse claims the tenant might make. Judges will often lean toward the tenants and give them additional time, unless the tenants' actions are outrageous.

Evicting a tenant when the rent has been received and the payment is current will require the service of a thirty- or sixty-day notice as stated above, unless for cause. Remember that rents are usually paid in advance. It is best not to take any rent payments beyond the notice period. If the

---

[1] There is an exception to the use of the thirty-day notice. When a tenant that has a month-to-month contract and has occupied the property for over one year, the thirty-day notice must be changed to sixty days (*Senate Bill 1403*). The bill also states that a tenant must be given a sixty-day notice if eviction is not for cause. The bill does not address the condition of a foreclosure and therefore, it might be assumed that previous law and case law would prevail. However, it would appear that a foreclosure could not take away the rights of a tenant because of an involuntary condition imposed on the tenant. There are several potential problems, such as if the tenant signs a new month-to-month contract with a new owner. This issue could cause litigation if a thirty-day notice is invoked. When a tenant has been evicted by a new owner for refurbishing or reconstruction, there are detailed notifications that need to be followed to rerent the property.

property was damaged beyond normal wear and tear, a small claims suit will have to be filed to recover the damages in excess of the security deposit. This would probably be a fruitless exercise because you would not be able to conclusively prove who did the damage. If the tenants move out early, there is no reason not to return the prorated portion of their rent, even if you never received the last month's rent and security deposit from the old owner. You don't want to antagonize the tenants and provoke them into getting even.

In general, tenants and ex-owners will say anything you want to hear. It is important to be gentle but firm. A reasonable time should be granted for the occupants to move. If the tenants or ex-owners plan to move soon, establish a date. If there is a problem and no time can be established, a money inducement may be required. The amount can be $500 to $1,000. It would cost that amount to hire an eviction attorney. The ex-owners or tenants should understand that the amount will be reduced by $50 or $100 per day that the ex-owners or tenants overstay on the property. It should also be established that the amount would be reduced if there is cost to repair any damage in excess of normal wear and tear. The final amount of money must only be paid after all the tenants have left with their possessions and the keys to the property given to you at curbside. Don't be too tough on the payment reduction. You don't want to antagonize the tenants or ex-owners. A gentle letter of agreement should be generated to document the understanding. The letter should also state, in gentle terms, that the tenants or ex-owners should maintain the property because of the legal requirements of health, safety, and liability. The agreement might also contain a statement that any personal property not removed will be considered abandoned and is of no value. Even if the occupants agree to move out with or without the payment of money, the three-day, thirty-day, or sixty-day notice should be served. Tenants and ex-owners will change their minds due to not finding suitable housing and may need a nudge. Tenants and ex-owners can be a problem later if they perceive that there is some money that can be extracted from you. You don't want to be too generous and put ideas into their heads.

At no time should full or partial rent money be accepted from the ex-owners. To do so would be an implied acceptance of them as a tenant. In reality the ex-owners are tenants and can be a greater problem than a normal tenant. Often further discussions with these tenants-in-suffrage (you are the one suffering, due to the rents not being received) will be required to keep track of their thinking and plans. This will provide you with information on how to proceed in the future.

In no event should the property be rented to the ex-owners. There is a great danger that the ex-owners will start to grieve their loss and waste the property. If no agreement can be reached, an eviction attorney should be hired.

If after the eviction process (unlawful detainer action filed in Small Claims Court), has been completed and the tenants or ex-owners have not moved out, a marshal will physically remove them from the property. This should be done without any announcement. A restraining order may be appropriate to prohibit the tenants or ex-owners from coming within 500 feet (or what the court deems appropriate), especially if there is evidence that they will damage the property. After the marshal has removed the tenants or ex-owners and their possessions, the property should be secured immediately as indicated below. The need to make the property secure is obvious. There may be times when someone may attempt to move into the property without permission. If someone forcibly enters and moves into the property, the police must be called and the trespasser removed.

There is a special caution on entering the property after a foreclosure. The tenants or former owners (even without your permission) are still in possession. They have the right to prohibit you from entering the property. Even after a 24-hour notice (a period deemed reasonable), unless you have the tenants' permission to enter, you are on thin ice. There is the danger of a legal suit (most likely unsuccessful), a formal complaint to the police for forced entry, battery, and danger of injury to you if the property is entered without permission. A 24-hour notice is required to show the property for sale, but only during business hours, unless other periods are agreed upon (Civil Code 1945). Every effort, however, should be made to have the occupants of the property grant permission for entry. The only exception to entering the property without a 24-hour notice is if there are circumstances that the property could be damaged without immediate action on your part. In this case, entry can be made to do emergency repairs.

The 24-hour written notice can be left at the property with a responsible person or at the normal entry so it can easily be seen. If the notice is by mail, six days would be required prior to entry. The notice of entry should state the date, time, and purpose. A 24-hour oral notice can be given providing a previous 120-day notice was given for entry to show the property to prospective buyers. At the time of entry, written evidence of your entry must be deposited inside the unit.

In any event, an impartial witness should monitor the entry while the tenant is in possession. Possession can mean that although the tenants are not present, they by virtue of not abandoning the property can claim possession. Even after the ex-owner has vacated the property, care should be taken in entering. Although rare, there could be a booby trap.

Verify that the old owner has removed all items so there is no reason for them to return to the house. There have been cases where the old owner has taken a chain saw to the front door to gain access.

If the tenants or ex-owners have left in the middle of the night and left personal property, this can create a problem. There are notifications necessary and covered in Civil Code 1951.3, 1983, and 1991. A note stating where the personal property is stored should be left in an obvious location on the property. A witness to this action can be valuable in the event the old owner starts making claims against you.

The personal property must be stored and then disposed of. The statutory requirements are complex. Details are specified in the California Civil Code 1980 to 1991. In general if it is believed that the personal property has a value less than $300, it can be kept or destroyed after the statutory requirements have been met. If the personal property is sold, the money less selling cost must be sent to the old owner.

In the case of commercial property, the right of entry is generally governed by the terms of the lease. There may be an implied right of entry depending on the terms of any lease and an implied covenant of good faith and fair dealings (*Sachs v. Exxon Co., U.S.A., supra, 9, CA 4th at 1498, 12CR2d at 242*). Entry would be by mutual agreement and most likely not during business hours so as not to cause disruption.

If there is any resistance, the police should be called to help induce the occupants to allow entry. Their presence, however, may not help in the entry, because the issue is a civil matter.

SECURITY OF PROPERTY

In the event that you own the property after the foreclosure auction, *all* locks should be changed, including the code on the garage door opener. The windows and slider doors should have a stick or bolts inserted to prevent easy opening. Bolts should be placed inside the garage door or a good lock installed on the outside. Door locks are easily picked, so a good quality dead bolt should be installed on the garage side door. This type of securing of the property usually will work only for "honest" people.

When there is a close-by neighbor, it is suggested that you ask him to give you a telephone call if anyone is at the property. He usually will be helpful, because the former owners probably did not take care of the property at the end of their tenancy, and were a scourge on the neighborhood. Additionally, they would not want transients moving into the property.

If the property is isolated and there is no neighbor available to watch the property, a caretaker should be employed to occupy and protect the property from ex-owners or vandals as soon as it's vacant. The caretaker should be watched, to verify that he is watching the property as agreed. There is a reason for the caretaker monitoring. Someone that accepts a caretaker job may have problems and may not be the most reliable person. You are only establishing a presence in the property to discourage any illegal actions.

The power and water should be turned on and put under your name. This will provide these services during the repair, refurbishment, or sale period.

A radio or TV should be left on at all times with the window coverings closed so no one can look into the house. A light on a timer also should be used to present the illusion that the property is occupied.

REPAIR OR REPLACEMENT OF SINKS, CABINETS, TOILETS

The sinks, cabinets, and toilets should only be replaced if the replacement effects a fast sale or produces a significant increase in the sale price. Very often a little cleaning and touch up paint can do wonders to reduce the sale time and increase the sales price.

VANDALISM

The danger of vandalism and theft is always present. Security measures as indicated above should be implemented. The house should be monitored at irregular times to verify that no one enters the house. If there is a real estate lock box, remove it if it can be easily removed by unscrewing a few bolts. You also can call the real estate board or old listing office to have the lock box removed. If they do not appear to want to respond in a reasonable time, an indication that the box will be cut off should get their attention.

PAINT AND CARPETS

After possession is taken, an evaluation of the property must be made. If paint is required, off-white inside and earth tones on the outside are suggested. It is possible that only the outside trim will require painting to present a sharp curbside appearance. As part of the evaluation, the time anticipated to market the property should be made. The time for you to paint the house as compared with a professional must be determined. Saving $1,000 when the carrying cost of the house is $3,000 per month doesn't make sense if it takes you a month to paint the house.

If the carpets are only dirty or heavily stained, a professional carpet cleaning company is recommended. They have cleaning solutions and knowledge that can do wonders. If the carpets are worn, ripped up, or animal damaged with urine, installing new carpets with new padding is recommended. The cost of new padding is minimal. Animal odors usually cannot be removed if the padding is not replaced. It is recommended that neutral color carpets at a cost comparable to the house value be installed. Carpet allowance is sometimes offered when carpeting is not installed. Many buyers cannot envision how the house will look when carpets are not installed so the allowance approach is not always successful.

TERMITES

In the event the property has termites, there are two ways to go. The easiest way is to use a lender the does not require a clear report if a termite-clearance certification is not specified in the contract of sale and escrow instructions. Lenders that retain the trust deed loan for their own portfolio very often fall into this category.

The second and usually the only way to deal with the problem is to obtain a termite clearance certification. The cheapest methods are to use electric discharge, freezing, or chemical *treatment* to destroy the termites. This usually can be done at a lower cost than tenting. By getting several estimates, a final cost might be found that is significantly lower. Termite companies often will give you an estimate as long as you do not request a report. These alternate approaches to termite treatment instead of tenting are usually your best option, especially if the property is attached to other units. When the property is tented, people in attached property will have to move out for several days. This would be at your expense unless you can convince them that they also need their property tented and will share the cost. There may be times that adjacent owners will not move out for the termite treatment. A money inducement may be required.

ROOF

An evaluation of the roof condition must be made. If possession of the property is during the rainy season and the roof leaks, immediate steps must be taken to cover the leaking area on the roof with plastic. The condition of the roof will dictate if repairs can be done or the roof must be replaced. The cost of a new roof may not be recovered in the sale of the house. However, the repair or replacement of the roof is often necessary to make the property salable and essential to prevent any additional damage to the interior of the house. When the property is sold using government funding (such as VA or FHA), the remaining life of the roof becomes important.

PROPERTY PREPARATION FOR SALE

A small investment to clean up the property and improve the landscaping will hasten the recovery of your investment by expediting the sale. In most cases it will also produce a profit on the fix-up cost.

A gardener might be hired to trim shrubs and trees and do some dress up of the landscape to better show off the property. Often only the removal of weeds and cultivating of plants will be required. All debris and garbage should be removed. If there is a significant amount of cleanup required, a dumpster should be ordered to speed the process. Cheap local labor can be used to do the bull work. The lawns should be resodded or reseeded, if required. Lawn and plants should be fertilized and watered on a regular basis to bring the property back to life. Ground cover and trees should be trimmed. A few shrubs and flowers might be added. Lawn edging should be replaced if missing or rotten. Blacktop driveways should be patched as necessary and covered with a black top dressing. Care must be taken that the new black top dressing isn't tracked into the house.

If there is a good view that is blocked by trees or shrubbery, the obstruction should be removed. If the blockage is caused by a neighbor's shrubbery, the neighbor, when politely asked will usually allow you to trim the problem, providing the cuttings are promptly removed. If there is an unsightly view, a high fence might solve the problem.

With vacant property, any good color coordinated furniture that can be placed in the house will help in the sale. Some buyers need to be shown how their furniture will fit into the house. If the house is small, furniture can hinder the sale. Placing artificial flowers in strategic locations also will help.

TIME

Time can be your worst enemy. The longer the property is kept, the greater will be your potential loss. It is very important to put the property on the market as fast as possible, but not too fast. The exception would be when property is appreciating at a fast pace. The property must have good curb appeal when placed on the market. Otherwise, potential buyers will be turned off and will not return even after the property is sanitized. The listing price must be realistic. Don't get caught with your hand in the cookie jar. If the sale won't produce a breakeven point, a decision will have to be made to own the property until it appreciates or take the hit by reducing the price and only recovering part of your investment.

MARKET VALUE

Determination of post-foreclosure market value is similar to determining the market value when a Trust Deed is being purchased. The value determined when you funded the loan, will probably be different from the one that exists after a foreclosure. This would be due to a change in the condition of the property and a different economic environment. The new economic condition would be the result of the time of year, interest rates, military base closings (openings), inflation, deflation, or unemployment rates. Buyers are looking for a good deal. You have to adjust your offering price to give good value. Some brokers offer a property at a price range. This doesn't make much sense in my mind. Buyers consider the lower offered price as the start of a negotiation.

The better method is to look at properties on the market in the general area and in the same general price range. The sale price that you establish should be slightly lower than the competition if a reasonably fast sale is to be achieved. If the property is priced the same as the competition, you are taking a chance that one of the other properties will sell first. This will add market time to the sale or, in other words, loss of money due to lost interest that can be obtained from investing in another Trust Deed. Buyers that have been looking at properties can detect a better deal by as little as $500.

Looking at expired listings is also useful in determining market value. If a house similar to yours has not sold, do not expect that yours will sell at the same listed price unless the economic conditions have changed.

Don't expect to obtain the same price as similar new property. New has always sold better than resale property. Many buyers want to move into brand new property.

Your property in all likelihood will be vacant, with no furniture. The vacancy is better than having tenants in the property. Tenants very often will hinder the sale of the property. They don't want to move or suffer the inconvenience of having buyers view the property. Even if the property is offered to them at a lower rent or an offer of cash after the close of escrow, they very often will not be absolutely cooperative. What they say and do very often are two different things. Unfortunately, tenant-occupied property often sells at a price lower than similar vacant property.

The actual sales contract price is very important. If a contract of sale is obtained, there is usually no sale until the bank appraises the property, provides a loan, and closes escrow. There are solutions to a low appraisal by the bank. This is for you to carry back a small second Trust Deed to provide the bank with their needed cushion. If the cash is needed, this second can later be sold uncomfortably at a discount to provide you with the return of some of your investment. The buyer can often come up with a larger down payment using a gift from a parent. Unfortunately the only solution sometimes is for you to reduce your price.

If the property cannot be sold in a reasonable time due to the market conditions, it may be prudent to rent or lease the property until market conditions improve. A lease option also may be an alternate approach. The option should not be too long. The future market value with prices going up or down is hard to predict. There is nothing worse than the property having a significantly higher value when the option is exercised. If the property value goes down, the buyer in all likelihood will not exercise his option. The only good thing about an option is you will have the option money to keep. There have been cases where the buyer wants the money back thinking that the option shouldn't have cost him any money. They might even take you to court. If the option contract was properly written, he would in all likelihood lose.

TAXES

Taxes (federal, state, county, and city) are a cost of ownership. They are affected by:

- scheduled depreciation of property occurs as a result of it being income property. This depreciation will reduce the taxable base of the property that will be recaptured at the time of sale or disposition. This is not the real depreciation of property caused by the ravages of time, economic conditions, and use,

- rent received if not offset by operating costs and depreciation,

- property taxes (county), including a supplemental tax,

- gain due to purchasing a junior or senior loan at a discount,

- property market value gain or loss,

- length of time property is held, long or short-term gain.

These factors and how they interrelate can be complex. They will affect the amount of taxes you will have to pay. Consulting a tax accountant is highly recommended before taking actions such as:

- setting a credit bid below actual cost,
- acquisition or disposition of property. The method of acquisition and disposition can also create or avoid taxes (i.e., tax-free exchange. Note that there isn't anything like a tax-free exchange. There is only a delay of paying taxes.),
- depreciation schedule.

Section 17

PROPERTY SALE

Figure 17. *I thought I would be receiving money.*

ESCROW

An escrow company should be used after a buyer has agreed to the terms of the sale. This is to insure that the documents and disclosures are prepared and delivered properly. Escrow will order the title insurance, collect funds, and disburse them, most of the time through the title company.

The escrow will prepare the escrow instructions, Trust Deed, Trust Deed Note, and should know the other requirements that must be completed. These requirements are constantly changing. Unless you are in the business of keeping track of the legal and disclosure requirements, these technicalities might become a problem. The escrow company will also be your interface with your buyer and the title company.

A separate sales contract is not required when an escrow is opened. However, one is recommended so all the terms that have been agreed upon are in a hard copy. There is nothing more frustrating than going into escrow and finding out that there is no sale because of a misunderstanding. There also will be the buyer who will try to squeeze a little more concession before the sale is closed. A detailed written agreement can help prevent this attempt.

A standard real estate purchase agreement form can be used. These forms can be obtained from some stationery stores. A visit to your local real estate board is another approach. They should have the latest forms. Some real estate boards have a packet with all of the forms you might need for a sale. Alternately, a kind real estate agent might provide a copy of a real estate purchase form. The agent probably believes that you won't be able to complete the sale and will use the form as a vehicle to list the property or complete the sale for a commission. If you don't have experience in the marketing and sale of property, it is recommended that a real estate agent be employed. In the long run, this can work out to be cheaper.

If you elect to sell the property yourself, a fee of several hundred dollars might be enough for a real estate agent to help you complete the sales contract. It may be difficult to find a knowledgeable real estate agent who will be willing to just do the paper work. The real estate agent however, if he helps you, is vulnerable to a suit by the buyer.

The standard sales contract purchase form will provide a checklist of the sale contract items that should be agreed upon. It may not list all of the disclosures that are required by law. In the event the property is listed and sold, the buyer's agent will complete the sales contract purchase form and other disclosure documents. The selection of the title and escrow company should be for the seller's and the buyer's advantage. The escrow company should be close to the seller and the buyer if possible. If you are experienced in the sale of real estate, the escrow should be close to you. This would allow easier monitoring of the escrow process with periodic calls and visits to the escrow officer.

The selection of the title company is only important if there is a problem with obtaining a reduced *short rate*. A *short rate* is the title insurance fee offered when a property is resold within a short period. Some title insurance companies will reciprocate with a short rate. A title policy binder might be appropriate if the property is to be kept for a longer time than the short rate defined period. This binder will provide a lower title insurance cost when the property is later sold. The time period of the binder often may be too short if the property is to be kept more than one year. The binder would usually only be honored by the original issuing title company.

The typical fight between agents on the selection of escrow and title companies is usually a control issue. Most of the agents want to direct the title insurance to the title company that has been providing them with property profiles or has provided other services such as coffee cups for their office. In some cases agents will insist on using their real estate office's owned escrow or title company. For the seller, the selection should be directed to the title company that provided the foreclosure Trustee Sale Guarantee Policy. This in all likelihood would be the title company that you would be using to request property profiles in the evaluation of your other trust deed investments.

The selection of the escrow should be based on an agent having a good working relationship with the escrow officer. There are however, escrow officers that should be avoided. These are the ones that don't pay attention to details. They don't back check the work their secretary was to have done or don't follow up on the work that must be completed. These poor escrow officers wait for things to happen rather than making them happen. Too many escrow officers fall into this category, especially if they are busy. This is why when an escrow is in progress, checking with the escrow officer when an event is to happen and then following up to see that it has happened is so important. Hand-carrying papers or using the escrow company's courier may at times be necessary to expedite the escrow.

There are some real estate offices that own an escrow company. Real estate agents very often will direct the escrow to these companies. Although the escrow company must be a neutral agent, they may not provide the best available service, charge the lowest price, or work in your best interest. As stated above, the selection of the escrow and title should be the decision of the buyer and seller, not the real estate agent. There may be times that you will want to go along with the agent's selection. If the agent has an escrow officer that does an excellent job, and you are only guessing about an escrow company and escrow officer, you should probably defer to the real estate agent's selection.

ESCROW COST

Although in theory the escrow cost is negotiable, not too much reduction can be achieved. Typically it is paid by the buyer and seller in somewhat of a standard fashion. This will however vary depending on the real estate area's practice. The type of financing—conventional, Federal Housing Administration (FHA), or Veterans Administration (VA)—that the buyer selects will impact both the buyer and seller. In general the charges shown in the table below will be charged to the respective participant.

	Buyer	Seller
Standard escrow	one half	one half
		(Seller can pay full
		amount for VA&FHA loan*)
Title Insurance	loan title	seller's title
Transfer tax		usually
Sales commission		usually
Loan points	usually	could be seller
		With a VA, FHA
		or conventional Loan
Documents prep.	usually	could also be seller
Transfer tax		usually
Reconveyance fee		usually
Notary fees	usually	could also be seller
Pest control		usually
Appraisal	usually	
Recording fees	usually	
Tax service fees	usually	could also be seller
Credit report	usually	
Processing fee	usually	
Prepaid taxes	usually	
Prepaid insurance	usually	
Prepaid interest	usually	
Sub escrow	usually	could also be seller

* VA and FHA have different requirements where the seller must pay certain fees. The cost of fees the seller will pay should be limited. One of the largest cost items are the points for the loan that the seller must pay. The points therefore should be limited. This is to prevent an interest rate Buy Down. With a Buy Down, points are charged to obtain a lower interest rate and can become very high. Prior to signing any sales contract, the exact cost of the fees should be established by contacting the loan broker. These amounts or a limit to the amounts the seller will pay, should be written into the sales contract.

Chart 1, *Escrow cost*

REAL ESTATE LISTING

Listing of the acquired property after foreclosure and paying a commission will oftentimes be required. Putting the property on the real estate MLS and the Internet can be money well spent. This exposure not only can result in a faster sale but a higher sales price.

In selecting a real estate office and agent, it is important to do a survey of the real estate offices in the area. Determine those that are advertising and have produced the most sales, not listings. Remember that you are interested in selling the property not just listing the property.

An evaluation of the agent that will be handling the listing must be done. Do not accept the first agent that greets you when entering the selected real estate office. This agent probably will be "on the floor" and have first choice of customers that walk in or call in. There is no guarantee that this agent will have adequate experience in handling all aspects of real estate. A discussion with the office manager or broker will provide some direction. Don't accept the statement that the floor agent will have the office manager's guidance. Ask for an agent that has been in the real estate business for several years, is knowledgeable, has done successful transactions, and doesn't need guidance. The agent must be familiar with the area where your property is located, know the available financing terms, and be flexible in his thinking to complete a sale. A beginner, although you would like to help him, won't advance your cause. Don't be swayed by a pretty face. The generation of a real estate contract, subsequent negotiation, and sale of a property cannot be done remotely by an office manager effectively. To do an adequate job the performing agent must be in the trenches so he can get a proper feel of the sale and subsequent negotiations. If the office manager won't put you in contact with one of his better agents, be prepared to go to a different real estate office.

It is important to have a written commitment on actions the agent and the agent's office will do. This should include advertising in local newspapers and how often. There will be properties that will have to be advertised in specialized newspapers and magazines. If this is the case, determine if the real estate office is willing to pay for the cost. Advertising in throw away papers or office generated newsletters does not typically sell property. They may help to expose your property but primarily are used to obtain listings. The listing must be placed immediately on the MLS. Placing the availability of the property on the Internet with companies that use Realtor.com *with* pictures is mandatory to obtain top dollar for your property. Putting the listing on the real estate office's Internet site may help sell the property, but won't do the total job. Buyers want to look at all of the properties available and would be limited in their search if they only looked at the listings from one real estate office. There would also be the problem of buyers finding your property if it is only on one real estate office's Web site.

The real estate office or real estate agent must carry errors and omissions insurance. The insurance should cover unintentional misrepresentation and mistakes. The insurance should also pay for the agent's legal defense even for groundless lawsuits by the buyer or seller. If the buyer or seller is harmed due to negligence, the real estate agent should have the financial pockets to pay for the deductible portion of damages. The insurance carrier will only pick up the tab above the deductions.

Holding an open house will produce buyers. This is however more of an advantage to the agent to pick up buyers for the sale of other properties. It is important to have the agent agree to hold the house open for the full advertised time period and not close the house and take a walk-in buyer to sell a different house. This is a practice that is sometimes done by unreliable agents and frowned upon by most brokers. The agent also should agree to make high quality fliers, with pictures, to be placed in the local real estate offices, in front of and inside the house that is for sale. When there are several real estate boards, the flyers should be put into the other board members' real estate message boxes. A real estate board's pitch session with a subsequent caravan should be included in a marketing plan. Each property is unique and the marketing plan specifics can be different.

If the real estate agent does not respond in a reasonable period to your phone messages and provide a detailed status report either in writing or verbally, contact the agent's broker and state the problem. Hopefully this should correct the situation. If the problem is not corrected, terminate the listing and find a new real estate office. There shouldn't be a problem in having the listing canceled due to the unresponsive agent's lack of due diligence. The real estate office manager may suggest a different agent. This may be acceptable. A detailed interview must be conducted with the suggested agent to determine if he is acceptable. If you elect to cancel the listing and the real estate office does not comply, a call to their local real estate board may be required. If this doesn't work a call to the Department of Real Estate reporting their behavior should work. This however should be used as a last recourse because of the time-consuming potential Department of Real Estate hearings.

It is important to obtain a written cancellation of the listing and the release of all fee obligations. If this cannot be obtained, you may have to suffer until the listing period expires. To avoid this potential problem, a short listing such as a thirty- or sixty-day period is recommended. During the negotiation of the listing period, arguments are usually advanced that proper marketing cannot be done. The response to this would be if the real estate agent is doing a good marketing job, an extension will be given.

During the time between obtaining the property from foreclosure and putting the property on the market (listing it on the MLS), a *pocket listing* could be given to a few real estate agents. A *pocket listing* is a verbal agreement (sometimes written) given to an agent, agreeing that you will sell the property for a given price and set of terms. This would give some exposure of the property before all the rehab work is done. Putting the property on the MLS before the intended work is completed can have a chilling effect. Buyers and even real estate agents can be turned off by poor-looking property. They may not become interested in the property later due to their first impression.

LEASE OPTION

When property is offered as a lease option—terms, price and the kind of option are all interrelated—there usually is option money paid by the lessee/optionee for the option. This option price is usually paid up front. There will be times that the buyer doesn't have the full amount for the option. In this case, installment payments might be appropriate. The amount of the option is usually fixed and not returnable. The buyer is purchasing the first right to buy the property.

There will be times when a portion of the rent will be used as the option money. This is similar to an installment purchase of an option. Again, the portion that applies to the option will not be returned, but could apply toward the purchase price. The option money is not always applied toward the purchase price. If the option to purchase is not exercised, the option money usually is never returned to the lessee/optionee. It is important that the lessee/optionee understands this condition, and that these terms are written into the option contract.

In a rising market, the option period should be short or the price set higher. The higher price is to provide for the sale at a potentially appreciated price when the option is exercised. However, the price should not be too high, otherwise the lessee/optionee won't be interested. There usually is a considerable amount of delicate negotiation before the price and terms are finalized. The buyer will want to get the property at the lowest price, and the seller will want to receive the greatest price. Don't be too greedy. If you are, you may continue to own the property and debt service. As a trust deed investor, the object is to have performing loans. This is effected by having a performing Trust Deed and not owning property.

The option contract, lease contract[1], and the sales contract should be signed at the same time. In a lease/option, the credit of the buyer is important. A credit report should be obtained and the buyer's income should be verified. The procedure is similar to renting property. In fact you are renting property in addition to selling the property with special terms. With a lease/option the final phase of selling the property will require the buyer to qualify for a new loan when the buyer exercises his option. If there is a seller carryback, it is important that the buyer has a track record of meeting his commitments.

---

[1] Not all options contain a lease contract. Often a lease is not involved when land, apartment, and commercial property is being optioned.

The optionee's past performance in renting property should be checked. This isn't as important as with a standard renter. If the buyer puts up a significant amount of option money, he would have the option money to lose if he doesn't exercise the option. He also will have a degree of pride-of-ownership in the property and should take better care of the property. A standard renter would not be inclined to take as much care of the property.

During the option period, it is recommended that the optionee not do any major work on the property. There is the danger that he will not complete the work and abandon his option, leaving you with a large project. Worse, he could file a lawsuit claiming that you owe him money for the work performed.

There is one type of option buyer that is out there. He will approach you and ask to lease the property with an option. The amount of rent with option installment payments offered is lower than the economic rent. He really has no intention of buying the property but is only looking for a rental that is priced lower than the economic rent. He can walk away at any time. Even with a lease, because these types of buyers have nothing, a suit will produce little. Additionally, because of the option, you most likely, would not prevail in a lawsuit. Due to his experience, he will also generate situations to claim the property is uninhabitable. This will be done by removing garbage cans and plugging toilets, thereby claiming that you have not performed as a landlord.

ALL-INCLUSIVE TRUST DEED/WRAP LOAN

All-inclusive Trust Deed (AITD) or wrap loans are infrequently used, if done within the letter and terms of most present Trust Deed Notes. Newly configured AITDs, therefore are usually convoluted to avoid the restrictions that can result in downside dangers.

The AITD is used in order to assume any existing loans. The AITD loan would be configured so that a new Trust Deed Note would be wrapped around the existing loans. This wrap is usually done with various types of contracts.

AITDs are used primarily on properties that are difficult to sell when the prevailing interest rates are very high, the buyer has no down payment or a small down payment, or the buyer has poor credit. Predominately they are used to take advantage of a low interest rate on an existing loan.

An AITD is configured using the low interest rate of the existing Trust Deed Note and generating a Trust Deed Note that covers the equity plus the existing Trust Deed Note. The portion of the AITD Trust Deed Note that covers the equity will usually have a higher interest rate. The wrapped loan could then have an overall interest rate, after combining the two interest rates, that would be closer to the prevailing market rate.

The configurations vary. Some of the AITDs would charge an overall interest rate for the sales contract. This would allow a seller to make money on the interest spread between the market rate and the assumed loan. Other sellers will only charge for the interest on the equity being sold. In either case, the payments would cover the existing loan's interest and the seller's equity interest.

A problem occurs when the existing lender forecloses on the property due to the violation of their Trust Deed Note terms. This would leave the buyer, if he made a down payment in the purchase of the property, out on the street with empty pockets. The seller of the property could lose their property equity because of the foreclosure. The only way the foreclosure could be stopped is to have cash available to pay off the foreclosing lender and refinance the property. With this type of transaction, usually the buyer doesn't have the cash to pay off the foreclosing lender, lacks adequate income, or has poor credit to obtain a normal loan.

It should be noted that there are Trust Deed Notes that are assumable, where an AITD can be legitimately used. These are usually only found in private party Trust Deed Notes. Old institutional Trust Deed Notes may appear to be assumable but due to legislation and case law are not assumable.

Various methods have been devised to keep lenders in the dark. These include a contract of sale, a long-term lease, an option contract, or long-term open escrow. To facilitate the transaction, an escrow would collect the payments and disperse the funds.

Most Trust Deed Notes have provisions that prohibit an AITD or a loan assumption. Unless you have carefully reviewed the Trust Deed and Trust Deed Notes to verify that this financing is not prohibited, it would be best to avoid making loans on properties with this type of financing.

TIME TO SELL

The time to sell a property could be long when the interest rates are high or the property is too near a busy or noisy street, a store, or a noisy school. Strangely, there are buyers that don't mind these factors that others would find objectionable. The sales price oftentimes must be adjusted to reduce the time to sell. Usually something (money or terms) must be offered so a buyer can't refuse.

SALES CONTRACT TERMS

In granting of terms to buyers, it should be remembered that buyers' and sellers' values usually are different. This will allow for negotiations to satisfy both parties. Care should be taken not to give the store away just to get into escrow. Remember a sales contract is just that, a contract that is binding by law. It must be written accurately, without ambiguity, and taken seriously.

Items that will have the most important consequence in a sales contract are as follows:

A. *Time (of Escrow).* The inclusion of the clause, "time is of the essence" should be included. This is to insure that the sales contract is completed by the contracted time. A contract without this clause, would allow a buyer to drag out the closing, with the resulting additional cost to you. With the clause, you can terminate the contract if the sale is not concluded by the end of the time-to-perform period.

B. *Repairs to Property.*

1. *Roof.* This can be very expensive if the buyer insists that corrections be made. Some lenders such as FHA and VA can require that roofing be replaced or repaired if its remaining life is too short. Typically FHA is more stringent. A limit should be set in the sales contract on the cost that you are willing to pay.

2. *Section 1.* This part of the purchase agreement sales contract, covers termite inspection. The clause deals with possible dry rot or termite infestation. This would require the removal of any dry rot and extermination of any termite infestation. The dollar amount can be limited to a set dollar value but usually isn't limited due to the necessity of a clear termite report to complete a sale. There would be some cost problems if extensive repairs were required. In rare cases the lender may allow the repair money to be left in escrow and the work done after the close of escrow.

If the lender does not require a clear termite report, any repair cost should be limited or the property sold as is. The sales contract most likely would not include a clear termite report requirement.

3. *Section 2.* This part of the purchase agreement sales contract for the pest control and correction are in most cases not required by lenders if excluded. The section deals with potential future damage due to existing conditions and can cost a bundle to correct. This cost should be avoided if possible. If this cannot be avoided, an initial estimate should be done and adjustment made to the sales price.

4. *Plumbing and heating systems.* This can be very expensive if the buyer insists that corrections or replacement be done. Some lenders such as FHA and VA can insist that plumbing and heating systems

be replaced or repaired. A limit should be set in the sales contract as to the cost that you are willing to pay.

5. *Asbestos and lead paint.* The existence of toxic material will have to be corrected prior to close of escrow.

6. *Septic system certification.* When a certification is being obtained, there may be a requirement to have the septic system drained, repaired, or replaced prior to the close of escrow. The best scenario is that the septic system only needs to be drained for certification. There will be a major cost if the drainage field needs to be repaired or replaced.

C. *Sales Contract Cost.*

There are some basic costs in the sale of the property that usually cannot be avoided. These would include seller's title insurance, seller's escrow, and other associated escrow costs. The escrow company charge might be reduced if negotiated prior to opening escrow. Also some of the cost can be negotiated with the buyer as to who will be charged the expense. There is another method of avoiding the seller's cost. This is using a net sale. Using this method, the seller wants a fixed amount from the sale. This type of sale however is frowned upon by the Department of Real Estate.

The expenses to be careful about are the costs associated with VA and FHA sales. Although the major costs and points of this type of sale can be paid by the buyer, the sales contract must say they will be paid by the buyer. There are costs that must be paid by the seller. Additionally, the buyer cannot pay more than a fixed amount on specific charges. In the negotiation of the sales price, allowance must be made for these unavoidable costs. If the property is offered as a VA or FHA sale, the initial listing price should take this expense into consideration. It should be remembered that if the listing price and resulting sales price is too high, the property will not *appraise* (appraised value is less than the sales price) by the VA or FHA appraiser. This will prevent the approval and funding of the loan and close of escrow. Additionally if the sales price is too high, no one will make an offer.

D. *As Is.*

The California statutes on foreclosure allows an as is condition sale. This will provide some protection to a foreclosure property seller. It does not totally defend the seller if there are known problems and he attempts to hide the defects.

Omitting the term as is can become one of the most costly items in a sale if not included and noted correctly. Litigation can be initiated by the buyer if defects are found in the property after closing, and an as is clause is not included.

When a property is acquired in foreclosure, there is an assumption that you as a lender would not be aware of any defective structure or systems in the property. This allows you as the seller to make a general statement that, as an owner through foreclosure, you are not aware of any deficiencies (if this is the case) and the property is being sold as is. This statement should be part of the sales contract and part of the escrow instructions.

Due to the recent California disclosure law requirements, the buyer of the property has the right to negotiate the cost to inspect the property (*AB 452*, Correa). As a seller of the property obtained in foreclosure, you would not want to pay for the inspection. To do so might be interpreted as all defects in the property are being disclosed. This would place the responsibility of the adequacy of the inspection on you, the seller.

E. *Other Terms.*

There are other expenses that will be unique to each type of property being sold. They have a monetary value and must be evaluated.

In general, at no time should the buyer be allowed to live in the property prior to closing escrow. The only exception of course is when the present tenant is buying the property. During the escrow period, the tenant should pay rent. If this does not occur, there would be no incentive to speed the close of escrow. This can happen because in many cases the rent will be less than the payments on a new Trust Deed Note, taxes, and insurance. There is also a loss of interest on your equity for the duration of the escrow. A sales contract clause might be added so that if the escrow does not close by a specific date, the rent would increase to equal the monthly carrying cost plus maintenance of the property.

The buyer should not be allowed to modify the property or do maintenance of any kind on the property before the close of escrow. If the escrow doesn't close, the ex-buyer probably would demand compensation for the work. The other peril associated with the work is if the repairs or changes are not finished in a workmanlike fashion. This work will have to be completed or the property restored. There is also the liability if someone is injured on your property.

TRACKING PROGRESS OF YOUR ESCROW

Escrow can be opened over the phone or going directly to the escrow office. Going to the escrow office is generally the best method. You will become a real person to the escrow officer and hopefully receive better service. The escrow officer will want a copy of the sales contract and ask many questions about the transaction.

You will also be able to get additional information about the latest disclosure requirements and the companies that provide the service. At this time you can ask and usually receive a discount for the escrow charges.

The escrow instructions should be prepared for signatures in a day or so depending on the number of transactions that are going on in the office. When you receive the escrow instruction, check every detail before signing the document. If there are any questions or an area of the instructions you don't understand, question the escrow officer about them. If the answer does not make sense, ask the questions again until you are satisfied with the answer.

You can feel a little better after opening escrow on the foreclosure property. However, don't count your money yet. There are many impediments to the closing of an escrow. The only way to partially guard against them is by tightly monitoring the escrow process. When working with the escrow officer, it is important to learn from the escrow officer what will happen next and when it will happen. There will be times when close checking may have to be done on a daily bases. As part of the monitoring of the escrow, *every detail* in the escrow instructions must be verified. There are some not so good escrow officers and escrow secretaries. To speed the escrow, problems should be anticipated to avoid them. Don't rely on the mail for items that are critical. Hand-carry critical items or have the title insurance company representative do some of the delivery to insure the job gets done.

The finance company that will be funding the loan very often is the stumbling block in the closing of an escrow. It is advisable to track the finance company in a similar fashion as the escrow. In the case of the finance company, it is more difficult to get detailed information. This is because of the paper mill that exists. Usually when questions are asked, the answer will come back that the documents are in a different office, in committee, or they are waiting for some other documents. It will require diplomatic action on your part to obtain a solid answer.

When dealing with an escrow officer, if he does not respond properly, the threat can be made that the Corporation Commission will be contacted. However, do not expect the Corporation Commission to act very fast or at all in your behalf. If there is a loss caused by the escrow, a small claims action probably will be the best approach. If the escrow is a broker operated and controlled by the Department of Real Estate, the Department of Real Estate is the monitoring agency and this would be the agency where a complaint would be filed. This should only be done, however, as a last resort, unless you like filling out forms, going to court, and testifying.

After the escrow is closed, check the escrow cost against the estimated closing costs to verify that they are correct.

IMPOUND ACCOUNT

There is a portion of the sale of the property that should be tracked carefully. That is the original lender's impound (trust) account. This account could be sent to the original owner. This can happen even though all the impounded amounts are paid by your advances to senior lenders. This can be avoided usually by notifying the lender, escrow holder, and title insurance company that these funds have been accumulated due to your payments and must be returned. This danger will occur when the property is sold or the loan is assumed. Even when the loan is assumed, it is important to advise the lender that the impounded account is yours by virtue of its being generated by your payments on the Trust Deed Note and must not be sent to the original borrower. Often the impounded account will be sent to the title company for distribution. The title company and escrow company should be reminded that the funds must be returned or credited to your account. If your foreclosure credit bid included your monthly mortgage payments, this amount has been paid in effect by the acquisition of the property and you cannot claim the money. Only if the final amount that you receive was less than the credit bid would you have some claim to the impound account refund. This however can be disputed.

INSURANCE REFUND

In the case where you have made the property insurance payments, any refund after cancellation of the policy may be returned to the original owner. The payment to the original owner happens because the insurance policy will list the ex-owner as the owner of the insurance policy. The insurance company's information on their computer doesn't make a clear distinction of who paid the insurance. It must be made clear to the insurance company and insurance underwriter that the refund should be returned to you. Often when there is a sale or foreclosure any refund is sent to the title company for distribution.

If you foreclose on the property, the foreclosure credit bid should include the amount of your insurance payment. This amount has been paid to you in effect by the acquisition of the property. It by rights does not belong to you. Only if the final amount that you receive is less than your credit bid would you have some claim to the insurance refund.

In the case where the original owner paid the insurance, the unused funds belong to the original owner. You don't have a direct claim on them. Any claim made by you therefore would be inappropriate. The only time that a refund would clearly belong to you is if you acquired the property with a deed-in-lieu of foreclosure and the terms of the purchase stated that any refunds belong to you.

DISCLAIMER DISCLOSURE

When a property is obtained in a foreclosure, the condition of the property is very often unknown. As stated above, the California statutes provide for this, by allowing a disclaimer as to the condition of the property by the owner of property acquired in foreclosure. This is not the case when a property is acquired in a transaction such as a deed-in-lieu of foreclosure.

The lead-based paint status of pre-1987 residential property however must be disclosed at the resale of property acquired in a foreclosure. See Section 5, under *LEAD-BASED PAINT HAZARD DISCLOSURE REQUIREMENTS.*

Section 18

TRUST DEED SERVICING

Figure 18. *This paper work is so messy!*

Servicing of Trust Deeds can at times be frustrating because of nonpayment by borrowers. However, when payments are made, this is the best part of the deal.

NOTIFICATIONS TO BORROWER

After a loan is funded, it is important to send out a letter to the borrower stating the terms of the loan such as when the first payment is due, the amount of the payment, and to where the payments are to be sent. Some mortgage companies send out a letter, but the information is not always clear or some of the information may be missing.

In the case where the loan is funded from an IRA account, it is important to be explicit how the payment check should be written and where the check is to be sent. The check must be made out to the bank that is holding the IRA account. Typically the check must be made out to "the bank" FBO (for the benefit of) "your name" IRA.

PAYMENT RECORDS

A payment record form should also be sent out to the borrower. This is to aid the borrower in keeping track of his loan payments. Sending a payment book back and forth is not necessary or at times desirable. This would only complicate the servicing of the loan. Borrowers that need a hard-money loan often do not behave in a consistent fashion. Often they will not send the payment book with their payment. If the payment book is lost, a new copy would have to be sent out. When a payment book is used, a master copy must be retained so the payment record is not lost. An alternate approach is to make up payment slips for each payment and send them to the borrower. Here again there is a high probability that the borrower will not send the slip with his payments or lose the slips.

There is a special situation where the borrower makes partial payments. If you accept the payment, it might be interpreted as a de facto payment for the full amount. In general any partial payment should be sent back to the borrower. If a partial payment is to be accepted, the borrower should be notified by mail that the payment is only a partial payment. Ideally there should be a signed acknowledgment by the borrower that the payment was only a partial payment.

When talking to parties involved with your loans, notes should be taken on the individuals contacted, phone numbers with extensions, company names (e.g., insurance company, bank or mortgage company), and the results of the conversation. This information should be kept in your personal log or with a notation on your calendar.

BORROWER INQUIRES

There is a federal provision that requires that any borrower who makes an inquiry about a loan must have a response within twenty days. In addition, any discrepancy must be resolved in sixty days. Obviously, if there is a disagreement, and you have made every effort to answer questions, there shouldn't be too much of a problem. Usually the problem is an unrecorded payment or error in arithmetic. A diligent response on your part will help dispose of any questions and not eat up your time with borrower's additional inquiry. A good working relationship with your borrower is always desirable. Inquiries by the borrower or others will cost you time and therefore money. A service fee can be charged to the person making the inquiry. Unless a loan is being paid off or refinanced, don't hold your breath while you are waiting to receive the service fee.

YOUR ADDRESS AND PHONE NUMBER

The address used for all trust deed business contacts should be a PO box number. This is important for several reasons. The mailing of all recordings and notification of insurance should be to one location to avoid any confusion that could occur if you moved. Second, borrowers could become unstable and try to inflict harm on you or your family if they know your address. You might be tempted to give out your address to a seemingly harmless borrower. There is no guarantee that this individual will remain this way and could become a dangerous borrower. Their friends may tell them they have been had, they may have a mental breakdown, or they are crooks that need money. Even though it may be convenient to give out your address for the borrower to make a payment, it is best not to make this mistake. As a last resort, you could meet the borrower in a public location to receive the payment.

Your phone number(s) should be unlisted. An alternate method is when you get your phone service to have your name listed using a pseudonym. Your address should not be listed in the telephone directory. If it is listed, anyone could look up your address using the reverse directory available at the library, Internet, or most real estate offices. There will be times when it will be convenient to give a borrower your phone number, or the mortgage broker could give your phone number to the borrower. The pseudonym telephone listing with no address will help reduce the potential danger of a borrower coming to your home.

It is still difficult to keep your address private. If you own property, make any purchases, receive any magazines or newsletters, or enter a contest, your address will be on several lists. Anyone can, for a small fee, obtain your address.

NOTIFYING SENIOR LENDERS

When a Trust Deed is obtained, it *may not* be prudent to notify senior lenders that you hold a junior loan. This notification would only be considered when your loan has prepaid interest for several months. Borrowers, when they start to get into financial trouble, will not make payments on all of their loans. If there were prepaid interest on your loan for several months, there wouldn't be an indicator of nonpayment on senior Trust Deeds.

The dilemma is due to many senior lender Trust Deed Notes containing provisions that prohibit the borrower from further encumbering the property. Your notification could trigger the start of a foreclosure. Some lenders believe in their mysterious thinking that their security has been placed in jeopardy with additional encumbering of the property with a junior loan. The reverse is actually the case. The holder of a junior loan would make payments on senior loans to avoid the senior lender's foreclosure, making the senior loan more secure.

The reason to notify the senior lender is to have him notify you if loan payments are delinquent, allowing you to make the payments and start your own foreclosure. Some lenders will notify junior trust deed holders as part of their policy.

As a prudent action on your part in servicing Trust Deeds, a call to the senior lender should be made to learn if it is his policy to notify junior lenders when the borrower is delinquent. If he does not have a notification policy, a call to the loan department every few months is recommended if you have a flaky borrower.

KEEPING TRACK OF PAYMENTS

There are several methods that can be used to track loan payments. This could be a payment schedule form or a payment book. I have found that a payment schedule form is the easiest. Shown below in Section 19 is a sample of a payment schedule form that could be used. The information would include due date, late fee amount, check number, and the amount of payment. In the case where there are a large number of loans, a spreadsheet showing the general information of all of your loans should also be used. A check off when payments are received along with the date can then be noted. A quick glance will show the payments for the month that have been made.

When the loan is first funded, payment should be prorated to the same payment date. This is very helpful in tracking payments. In this fashion, there will be no need to constantly keep checking if a payment has been made during the month. The spreadsheet or a database also could be put into a computer. However, a computer back up file is very important to avoid the loss of information, especially if your hard drive crashes. Although reconstruction of the data is possible, it can be laborious. It is a good idea when the checks are deposited to keep a copy of your deposit slips. When several payments are received and deposited at the same time, you should make a duplicate deposit slip showing each payment. A cooperative bank might provide a photocopy of your deposit slip on request. The copy is very helpful if there is any confusion on the date and the amount of your deposit.

Some banks will service your loan by collecting the payments on your Trust Deeds. Depending on the bank and the amount in your account, there may not be a charge for the service. One of the problems with a bank servicing the loan is the bank's reporting policy. You might not know in a timely manner when a payment is late or not made.

The payment to an IRA account can be made directly to the holder of the IRA account or sent to you for deposit into the IRA account. The latter has the advantage of knowing the payment has been made and on time. If the check had NSF (not sufficient funds), it would in all likelihood be returned directly to you. The disadvantage of having the payment sent directly to you is that the check will have to be forwarded to the IRA holder. If the payments are sent directly to the bank by the borrower, it may be some time before you become aware that a check is NSF in that it most likely would be returned to the borrower. Deposit information often will not be available until the next bank statement is received. This could be as long as three months and would delay the filing of a foreclosure in a prompt fashion.

When the payments from a fractionalized loan are sent to the mortgage broker, your portion can be sent directly to your IRA account. The mortgage broker, however, should send you a copy of the check so you can be aware that the payment was made.

LATE PAYMENT PENALTY

When a payment is received that is later than the grace period, usually ten days or as stated in the Trust Deed Note, a late payment demand notice should be sent to the borrower. The small late fee amount doesn't justify filing a foreclosure. In fact it would be difficult to find a foreclosure company that would file a foreclosure for only one late fee. Very often the borrower will not send the late payment fee. This isn't too great a problem. If the late fee isn't paid, just notify the borrower with a demand for the payment each time there is a late payment and the amount due. Also keep track of the monthly payment check numbers, the payment due dates, and the dates the monthly payments are made. If notification isn't sent out for each late payment, it cannot be legally collected.

When the loan is past due and not paid off, if late payments are received without a late fee, the late fees might not be legally collected even with a demand letter, depending on the situation.

When the loan is to be paid off, include the late fees along with any other fees in your Beneficiary Demand. In the event there is a foreclosure for other causes, include all these late payment fees along with any other advances that are made. It is a good idea to keep the borrower's envelope, showing when the late payment was mailed, as evidence.

A payment that is returned by your bank for insufficient funds and not cured within the grace period becomes a late payment. This will require a written notice to the borrower, requesting the late payment fee and the not sufficient funds fee charged by the bank. Even if a replacement check is received, the bank's fee is collectable. Some hard-money lenders will charge an amount over the bank's fee for the NSF due to the additional handling required. Unless the Trust Deed Note allows for this in some fashion, I don't believe the additional charge is appropriate.

Every so often, a borrower will try to become clever and predate a payment check to make it appear that the payment is on time. The important date is the postmark on the envelope. One of the other devious methods used is to change the date on a postage machine. This normally doesn't work for the borrower. The post office customarily processes, all envelops through a canceling and dating machine.

When the borrower starts to get into monthly payment problems, your antenna should go up. Extra precautions should be taken in this event, in cashing any checks that are received. A check received without your name on it should be treated with suspicion. This check payment without your name is like sending cash. However, if there is no money in the bank, this is not cash and the borrower knows it, therefore the carelessness. To avoid a bad check charge, which your bank will charge for insufficient funds, you can contact the borrower's bank that the check is written on or one of their branches. Some bank checks have the bank's phone number listed on the check to aid in fund verification. A branch bank may not in some instances cash the check, but will let you know if there are sufficient funds to cover the check. If possible, by going to the issuing bank or one of their branches, the check can be cashed and a bank check issued for a small fee. Carrying around a large amount of money from a cashed check isn't recommended these days. Alternately when there are sufficient funds in the borrower's bank, a *hold-funds request* for a small fee can be placed on the check to allow the check to clear through your bank. A *hold-funds request* places a hold on the exact amount of the check and is implemented by the borrower's bank.

If a payment is due on the 1st, the postmark should be no later than the 10th, when the grace period is ten days. Some hard-money lenders charge the late fee if the payment isn't in their hands by the tenth day.

When a check is returned for insufficient funds, there should be some concern on the status of senior loans. If there are other indications, such as nonpayment of insurance, you can almost be certain that payments to senior lenders are not being made. A check of the senior loan payment's status should be made by calling the senior lender. A few will provide the information over the phone, but most will require a copy of your Trust Deed and Trust Deed Note. Faxing the documents should be adequate in most cases.

An alternate approach to collect on bad check payments is to use the bad check law. This law, *ABN 522* (Katz), effective January 1, 1996, allows for recovering bad checks in a civil action. This law provides for collecting of up to three times the amount of the bad check limited to $1,500 in addition to the face value of the check. The maximum amount that can be collected is $5,000. Another option would be to pursue collection against the bad check writer criminally. This procedure provides for recovery up to the face value of the check. To accomplish this, a call can be made to the district attorney's office. You will be mailed a bad check complaint form and a merchant guide packet on how the criminal recovery program works. You must return the original check along with the complaint form, within sixty days of the check issuance, to the district attorney's office. There is no fee involved for the merchant. The complaint is reviewed and entered into the system. Notice will be sent to the writer of the check, notifying him that a complaint has been filed. The check writer has thirty days to respond. In exchange for the district attorney not proceeding with a criminal prosecution, there are three steps the check writer must complete. They must pay the face value of the check, pay the diversion program fee and attend a life management skill course. If the check writer fails to respond within thirty days of receiving notice of the complaint, they may be prosecuted criminally.

TRACKING OF INSURANCE COVERAGE

You should verify that the property has adequate fire insurance when the loan is first being generated. If the coverage is inadequate, the mortgage broker should include in the escrow instructions the requirement for a new fire insurance policy or additional fire insurance coverage. Part of the loan processing would include notifying the fire insurance company that you are a lender in the specific loan position on the property. Part of your due diligence in reviewing the escrow instructions is to verify the correctness of the fire insurance directive. The fire insurance company will later send a statement on the date of coverage and the amount of coverage on the property. You should verify that the amount and type of coverage are correct. The statement should also show you as a lien holder and show the position of your Trust Deed. In the event the insurance policy is terminated, a notice will be sent to the trust deed holders of this event, if properly entered into the insurance company's database. A thirty-day prior notice is required of the insurance company in order to cancel the policy.

If the policy is going to be canceled, a written notice to the borrower or a phone call is appropriate to have this problem corrected. If the borrower does not correct the problem, an insurance payment should be made or a new insurance policy obtained to protect your investment. The existing fire insurance company may extend the coverage by accepting the delinquent payment. In the event the present insurance company will not accept payment, a different insurance company will have to be found. If the borrower doesn't reimburse you for this advance, a foreclosure could be started but usually isn't, due to the situation not being enough of an infraction of the Trust Deed Note. However when the situation comes to this, any senior loan payments probably will not have been made. This is usually because the borrower is running short of funds and is unable to make payments on his obligations. If this is the case and your security is put into jeopardy, a foreclosure must be started before things get more out of hand.

To ease the monitoring of insurance coverage, it is recommended that a spreadsheet, a yearly calendar, or an appointment book be used to note the anniversary of all your trust deed insurance policies. The insurance status can then be easily monitored when you have several Trust Deeds.

CHANGE OF OWNER-OCCUPIED STATUS

There will be times where the property changes from an owner-occupied status to a tenant-occupied property. The property condition with tenant-occupied status in all likelihood will change due to the lack of pride-of-ownership. There would not be too much difference in this condition and an owner-occupied condition that the property would revert to during a foreclosure. The issue with a new tenant-occupied status is the payment of rents and the security deposit. Because of this possibility, the collection of rent's clause should always be included in the Trust Deed documents even if the property has an original owner-occupied status. This allows action on your part if there is a change in occupancy and rents need to be collected.

The easiest way to learn if the property is tenant occupied is to knock on the property door and ask. Also, by talking with neighbors, a lot of information can be obtained. Tenants usually don't take very good care of property. If the lawn is unkempt, you should become suspicious that the property is tenant occupied. If the borrower starts using a post office box, you should become suspicious that the borrower doesn't live at the property.

If the property is sold at a foreclosure auction, any lease or month-to-month contract is terminated. This would be the case unless a lease was recorded or you had knowledge of its existence prior to your trust deed recording or after the recording by virtue of a de facto acceptance. In a foreclosure, a lease, like a junior Trust Deed is wiped out. This action of the foreclosure will allow for an easier eviction of the tenants, if desired. There is always the problem of knowing the number and names of the tenants. The best way of handling this problem is to contact the tenants before the foreclosure sale to obtain their names. They usually are cooperative because they want to know the status of the property. At the same time it should be possible to find out the details of the rental agreement and if there is a security deposit. Some tenants will stop paying their rent after a foreclosure is started to compensate for the loss of their security deposit. However, if they do not pay the rent, they could be evicted by the borrower before the completion of a foreclosure through the use of a three-day notice.

TITLE INSURANCE VERIFICATION

Sometime after the loan escrow closes, you should receive your title insurance policy. You should read this document and verify that your lien position is correct. Other liens that were to have been removed should not appear on the document. The information is found in the title insurance policy, Schedule A.

TRACKING SENIOR LOAN PAYMENTS

When a Trust Deed is generated and the loan processed, a Notice of Default document should be recorded. This will provide a notification by mail if there is a foreclosure being processed by other lenders on the property. The notice will be sent to the recorded Notice of Default specified address. If your address changes, a notarized address change should be filed with the County Recorder's Office.

Although this is a period where you can correct the senior loan default(s) by paying the delinquent back payments, late payment fees, and foreclosure costs, it is better to cure the default prior to their filing of a foreclosure. This will save equity in the property because of the cost of foreclosure. These advance funds, if you have to pay the senior loan payments, can provide a return of anywhere from 7 percent (approximate allowable statutory rate) to the jump rate that could be as much as 20 percent depending on the status of the property and the terms in your Trust Deed Note.

There is a foreclosure that can be troublesome. This is the one where the senior lender is filing a foreclosure because the property has been sold and a senior loan was assumed without the lender's approval. You as a junior lender usually, per the terms of your note, have the right to foreclose on your loan. However, if the senior lender has already started the clock and it has exceeded three months plus the statutory twenty-one days, the full amount of the senior loan may have to be paid. The actual period the loan can be reinstated is five days prior to the scheduled trustee's sale auction. The lender might stop his foreclosure upon request and allow you to proceed with your foreclosure. However, you may still have to pay off the senior loan.

In the case where the senior lender is foreclosing because of delinquent payments, the senior lender must, by statute, accept the payments. After you have foreclosed on the property there is no guarantee that the senior lender will allow the assumption of the loan, especially if it is a low fixed interest rate. If the loan is at a rate higher than the current interest rate, the lender may allow an assumption, providing you can qualify for the loan. In the case of most variable loans, the lender must allow the assumption of the loan in accordance with the Trust Deed Note terms, providing you can qualify for the assumption.

TRACKING PAYMENT OF PROPERTY TAXES

When a loan is processed and a Trust Deed generated, a contract can be obtained for the notification of nonpayment of the county taxes.

If the taxes have not been paid and the term of the loan is short, less than five years, no action on your part will be required. This would only apply if there were adequate equity. Using unpaid taxes as a cash source is not an economical method of obtaining a loan. If the loan is long, where the property could be sold for taxes, you should pay the taxes and, if appropriate for your situation, file foreclosure for nonpayment of taxes. When you pay the taxes, these advanced funds (effectively loaned to the borrower) would receive interest at the trust deed's prescribed rate in the Trust Deed Note or at the statutory rate if unstated in the Trust Deed Note.

BURNING MONEY

When a Trust Deed has to be put into foreclosure and then removed, it's like burning money. This is due to the accumulating costs that didn't have to happen. If the borrower was diligent in his payments or contacted the lender and presented a compelling case, often the foreclosure would not have had to take place.

INHERITANCE TAX ON TRUST DEEDS

When Trust Deeds are inherited, there are tax consequences. The Trust Deed bequest is not taxable provided the estate value is below the federal statutory limit (see amount exempt below). Subsequent interest payments on the Trust Deed, however, are taxable to the beneficiary. Payments could include principal and interest. The estate is responsible for any taxes on the principal and the beneficiary is responsible for taxes on the interest income. In the case of a discounted trust deed purchase, the taxes on the gain can be either the estate or the beneficiary depending on the nature of the discount. The discount could be prepaid interest or a true discount (reduced purchase price) that increases the yield or compensates for some risk. A tax consultant should be contacted to find out the tax obligations.

The amount of an estate that is taxable and the inheritance tax due is forever changing. Your tax advisor can give you the latest numbers. Listed below are the latest scheduled numbers. Hopefully, there will be cash on hand or a life insurance policy to pay for these taxes. If not, property or Trust Deeds will have to be sold to generate the cash.

YEAR	AMOUNT EXEMPT FROM ESTATE TAX	HIGHEST TAX BRACKET
2001	$ 675,000	55%
2002	$1,000,000	50%
2003	$1,000,000	49%
2004	$1,500,000	48%
2005	$1,500,000	47%
2006	$2,000,000	46%
2007	$2,000,000	45%
2008	$2,000,000	45%
2009	$3,500,000	45%
2010	Unlimited	N/A
2011	Possibly $675,000 (If present law is allowed to sunset.)	Possibly 55%

The exempt amount is per person. With proper planning, married couples can double the amounts.

FUND CONTROL/PERMIT SIGN-OFF

When a loan is made with controlled funds that are to be used in the construction or completion of a building project, the various phases must be completed prior to supplying additional funds for the next stage. These phases can include site preparation, foundation preparation including underground plumbing, power, septic system, heating system, parking, design, or site layout, framing, plumbing system, electric system, insulation, drywall, roofing, stucco, driveways, cabinetry, landscaping, and final inspection. Each of the inspections must be done in an approved sequence. If the electric and plumbing are not inspected prior to dry walling the interior, the inspector can require that the dry wall be removed so an inspection can be done. The inspection is necessary because some contractors will do a shoddy job and hide electrical splices behind the dry wall. Some shoddy contractors will not obtain and pay for the required work permits. Part of your evaluation of the contractor or rehab borrower's estimate is to verify that the cost for the permits is included in the work to be performed. The inspection tag that is attached to the building must show the inspection approval for each phase. When you are dealing with a contractor who doesn't have a good track record, you should contact the city (or county) inspector's office to verify that the inspection was actually done.

TAX ON INDIVIDUAL RETIREMENT FUND (IRA)

If the source of funds for the Trust Deed is from an IRA, there are special conditions that come into play. The beneficiaries can be a trust, spouse, or other heirs. How the beneficiary is designated and the payout method will affect the taxes that will have to be paid. Naming a younger beneficiary can slow down the required withdraw of the fund after your death. This will allow the IRA fund to continually grow using the pre-taxed money.

The minimum required distribution (MRD) begins when the owner of the IRA account reaches seventy and one half years old. The amount that is required to be withdrawn is 6.25 percent of the value at the beginning of the year and is reduced each year thereafter to avoid depleting the IRA account. At this time, the MRD should be taken to avoid a high penalty. The penalty is 50 percent on the amount not withdrawn. The first distribution can take place in the year the owner reaches seventy and one half years old or by April 1 of the following year. The second distribution will have to be taken in the following year. Taking both in the following year would increase the amount of distribution that will be taxed as income for that year and might bump the tax rate.

When a younger beneficiary is named, upon the death of the owner of the IRA, the distribution amount will be based upon the beneficiary's life expectancy. This would reduce the MRD. The MRD would be calculated from a standard life expectancy table. The beneficiary must take the distribution the following year of the original IRA owner's death. The distribution is small (i.e., for a beneficiary that is thirty years old, the distribution is 1.9 percent), leaving the major IRA account available for investment.

Upon death of the IRA owner, if the beneficiary is a spouse, the IRA account can be rolled over into the survivor's IRA. This allows the naming of other children or grandchildren as beneficiaries.

When a trust is named as the IRA beneficiary, there are special rules that apply.

If no beneficiary is named, the IRA account must be distributed in five years to the heirs of the decedent's estate.

If this sounds confusing, there is help. The trustee of the IRA account is required by law to compute the amount of the MRD.

The importance of being aware of these rules is to arrange your investments so there are adequate funds at the end of each year for withdrawal, to avoid penalties, or the necessity of selling a Trust Deed at a discount. There is another approach that is permitted. It would be to reregister the Trust Deed with the required withdrawal amount being a percentage of the Trust Deed but with an IRA account holder fee. This would be similar to fractionalizing the Trust Deed with the required percentage amount being allocated to you. The IRA holder would then send out the necessary 1099-R statement specifying that this amount has been distributed.

The laws are forever changing, so consulting with your tax advisor is advised.

Section 19

TRUST DEED PAYOFF

Figure 19. *Will I be glad to get rid of this slow-pay borrower.*

NOTIFICATION OF BALLOON PAYMENT

When a loan's term is about to expire, or sometimes expressed as maturing, the borrower must be provided with a good faith notification of the balloon payment. When there is a jump rate that can and will be imposed, the borrower must be sent a good faith notification informing him of this fact. If the notification is not sent, the jump rate may be lost if the borrower brings legal action. A sample form letter is shown below. This notification must be in the same language negotiated in the original Trust Deed and Trust Deed Note.

On purchase-money or hard-money loans on residential property one to four units with a balloon payment for a loan over one year, it is important to provide the borrower a notification of the maturity date in writing not later than 90 days prior to the note due date. This notification should also be made no earlier than 150 days of the maturity date to provide proper notification (Civil Code 2966). This can become an issue when the loan payoff is to occur and the borrower has not kept up his payments. If notification is not provided, the loan is effectively extended. Although a foreclosure procedure could be started, it cannot continue until the California statute 90-day period has transpired. The foreclosure and balloon payment period can run together. However to make one's life easier, the 90-day period should start at least one day prior to the foreclosure procedure. The notification should contain the following statement. "This note is subject to Section 2966 of the Civil Code, which provides that the holder of this note shall give written notice to the trustor, or his successor in interest, of prescribed information at least 90 and not more than 150 days before any balloon payment is due." Due to the complexity and potential of other legislation and case law, it is a good idea to always provide written notice on any loan that is becoming due with: the due date, amount due, method of payment, and rights of the borrower that shall apply. The amount of notice for loans less than one year should be reasonable. A notification period of 30 days might be used to satisfy a judge that you have acted reasonably.

Notification must be delivered or mailed by first-class mail with a certificate of mailing obtained from the United States Postal Service to the trustor or his successor in interest at the last known address of such person. If the notification is not given, this does not invalidate the terms of the Trust Deed Note. Interest shall continue to accrue for the extended term at the contract rate. Scheduled payments specified in the note shall be credited to principal or interest under the terms of the note.

It is always a good idea to include in your Trust Deed Note a clause providing for an extension of the loan if mutually agreed upon. The extension might call for several points to you if the extension is granted. Receiving the payoff can be a mixed blessing. If the borrower was a slow payer, the money might be better reinvested with a prompt-paying borrower. If the payoff borrower paid on time, you may want to refinance or extend the loan. It is always a good idea to include in your Trust Deed Note a clause providing for an extension of the loan if mutually agreed upon. The extension might call for several points to you if the extension is granted. A new loan might be rewritten at the present market rate and with different terms, if this is acceptable to both you and the borrower. This could be a good loan where the performance of the borrower is known. A new borrower's performance could bring a new set of problems. When the payoff is going to happen, this is the time to include any unpaid late payment fees in the demand statement. If you don't include them, there isn't much of a chance that they will be sent to you by the borrower after the Full Reconveyance is recorded.

LOAN MATURITY NOTIFICATION (Balloon payment due)

October 24, 2005

To:

Subject: Loan maturity/balloon payment notice,

       Property located at:

Dear Borrower:

Please take notice that the above subject loan will mature on xx/xx/xxxx. In order that you may make proper arrangements for your final payment, the following information is provided:

              Date final payment is due.............

              Amount of principal due...............

              Amount of interest due................

              Amount of other charges...............

              Please make this final payment to:

              James Lender

              PO Box 92018

              Carlsbad, CA 92018

The amount of the final payment noted above is only an estimate and is based on your continuing to make your next regular payments on time as they become due.

(If there is a jump rate stated in the Trust Deed Note and it will be imposed, the following additional statement should be used.) "In the event the final payment of the note is not made, an increase of (increase percentage or if stepped, the step increase) will be imposed until the amount due is received."

(If the loan is purchase money and over one year on one to four residential units, the following statement should be added.) "This note is subject to Section 2966 of the Civil Code, which provides that the holder of this note shall give written notice to the trustor, or his successor in interest, of prescribed information at least 90 and not more than 150 days before any balloon payment is due."

Please contact me for further details or if you have other questions.

Very truly yours,

_____ _____

James Lender   Date

(Either of the following statements may be added to your notification letter.)

(In the event you would like an extension of the loan, I will do this for X years with X points (X percent of the loan). To accomplish this, sign the bottom of this letter and return with your check for $ XXX.XX. Please include a list of any other liens that have been placed against the property with details.)

OR

(In the event you need assistance in refinancing your property, you can contact me.)

Acceptance the XX month/year extension of the loan offer.

_____ _____

Jane C. Borrower   Date

If the loan is to be refinanced or extended, there should be a verification of the equity in the property. This is to verify that the property still has lendability. The loan period should be short, similar to the previous loan period. As a condition of the extension, property taxes should have been paid if due.

Your loan may have to be rewritten or extended if the borrower doesn't have the money for the payoff and the property won't support a new loan from a different lender. Although you are looking for a well-secured, performing loan, there may not be any choice but to extend the loan. If the property were acquired in foreclosure, you would have a difficult time selling it and getting back your investment. If the borrower is willing to make the payments, you still have a performing loan. The property hopefully will go up in value to make your loan secure.

There is the risk, with any loan extension, that there is an encumbrance against the property that can take priority over your loan. It would be wise, when a loan is rewritten or extended, to obtain title insurance. If there is a junior lien to your present loan, a subordination agreement signed by the junior lender should be obtained to allow your loan to remain senior. A junior lender or lien holder may not allow this without some compensation. There is a last resort argument to persuade his acceptance. If the borrower cannot pay off the loan, a foreclosure would wipe out the junior lien. This would remove any practicable hope for the junior lender to recover his investment. In the case of a refinance or modification of the loan, a mortgage broker is recommended. This is mandatory if the interest rate for the new loan or the loan extension exceeds 10 percent. There is the danger that if more than 10 percent is charged and the borrower objects to the loan usury interest rate in the future, a court could force the return of all the interest received. (See previous discussion on usury limits.) Using a mortgage broker avoids this danger. The charge for this can be $100 to $200. Some mortgage brokers will ask more, but by shopping around, a reasonable facilitator can be found.

There will be cases where a borrower has not been making trust deed payments, a foreclosure is contemplated, and a Beneficiary Demand is received. It would be only fair and prudent to help the borrower to complete his transaction. The transaction could be a refinance, a sale, or an exchange. If a foreclosure is filed with the associated costs, you would use up some of the borrower's equity, and possibly prevent the transaction from taking place. If the property is put into foreclosure, the borrower may not be able to qualify for a new loan due to the bad credit created by your foreclosure. This could result into a long drawn out exercise, where you could end up with a loss. By assisting with the transaction, your funds can later be placed into a new performing loan. There is also case law that requires you to perform fairly with borrowers.

There is an exception in delaying the filing of a foreclosure when a demand is received and payments are delinquent. This exception would be when the borrower repeatedly opens an escrow or repeatedly notifies you the property is sold, so you will not file a foreclosure. These actions may be just a ploy by the borrower to delay your filing of a foreclosure.

When the payoff of a Trust Deed Note is completed, a Full Reconveyance must be recorded. Since the trustee has this responsibility, a Request for Full Reconveyance should be sent to the trustee. This request can at times be a problem due to the Trust Deed document specifying a trustee that doesn't presently exist or can't be located. A Substitution of Trustee and Full Reconveyance document would have to be generated to solve this problem. As the creditor, you can substitute yourself as the trustee. The Substitution of Trustee and Full Reconveyance is one document. The County Recorder's Office however will treat it as two documents and charge accordingly for the recording.

When an escrow is used, the escrow company will be doing the recording using a title insurance company. Coordination on the transmittal of documents should be done with the escrow officer to prevent any loss of documents. In some cases you will be coordinating the transmittal of documents with the title company. The title company usually has most of the title responsibility even though the escrow company is the initial interface. A Request for Full Reconveyance or a Substitution of Trustee and Full Reconveyance can be signed by you, the creditor. The document that is chosen will have to be notarized. Unfortunately some title companies will not notarize your document. An independent notary, real estate office's notary, or escrow company's notary will have to be used to perform the task. The recording is a simple matter of taking the completed original document to the County Recorder's Office, giving the document to the recorder, and paying the filing fee. The title company, when they are involved, will take the document and process it for you. They want to be certain the title paper trail is clean. The borrower might be talked into doing the recording. They probably aren't familiar with this process and will have to be walked through the sequence.

LOAN STATUS

There will be times that a loan status request will be received from a lender. The request may be for both the loan balance and the payment performance of the borrower. This can be an indication that a loan may be paid off in the near future. This report should be filled out including any other reasonable inquiry that may be on the request. A fee can be charged for this service. The charging of the fee is reasonable in that you will have to review your file to complete the form. A charge of $15 is not too unreasonable. However, don't expect a payment every time you request the fee. The time to expect the fee is when the requesting lender is paying off your loan.

BENEFICIARY DEMAND

In the case where a loan is being paid off, a Beneficiary Demand form will be sent to you. It very often is not in a suitable format.

The sample form shown below can be used but should be modified for your situation. If you elect to use the escrow company's form, don't be afraid to modify their statements to fit your requirements. You have a large amount of leverage to do this. However, don't go overboard. You must still conduct your business in a fair and reasonable manner.

Every so often a demand will be received that does not have a form enclosed. Using the form below adds an important statement, that the amount to be paid shall be computed to the day *when funds are received.* Most Beneficiary Demand forms don't include this statement. There can be a difference in the amount you should receive and what the escrow company or title company will send. Standard escrow office programs, when they compute the number of days that are to be paid, subtract the start and end of the period. They don't include the last day as an interest day. This can be a significant amount if the loan is large. I recommend that the last day be added to their subtraction result. If a check is mailed, especially on a Friday of a long weekend, the check could be short the interest payments for those days that it sits in a post office. In order to avoid this loss, it is suggested that your make arrangements to pick up your payoff check personally and exchange it for the documents the title company has requested. If the escrow is located some distance, you can receive your funds with a wire transfer to your bank. Wiring instructions for the transfer can be obtained from your bank.

In the event the property is in foreclosure, when a Beneficiary Demand is received, the requesting company, usually an escrow, should be notified that all inquires should be directed to your foreclosure company. A follow-up call should also be made to your foreclosure company to notify them of the Beneficiary Demand and to verify that a demand was made to them. This is to help fulfill your responsibility of providing the Beneficiary Demand within the prescribed period.

When preparing the Beneficiary Demand, it is important to review your note to find the exact payoff terms. Some notes allow for a full pre-payment penalty payment over a specified period of time, only one month prepayment penalty, or even no prepayment penalty. This demand should be returned as soon as possible, but not later than twenty-one days

(California Civil Code 2943(e)(4)). It is just a good business practice to return the completed demand as soon as possible. A transaction could be jeopardized if you are not prompt, or worse if you are sued for damages for not returning the demand on time. Every so often a demand will be received with a request for immediate completion. This might be due to the loan being refinanced by a hard-money lender, the processing of the loan was slow, or the agents involved were not diligent. Although you have twenty-one days to return the completed document, it is an act of courtesy to return the completed demand quickly.

The Beneficiary Demand should show the amount of loan due, the interest rate, the daily interest payment from a specified date, unpaid late fees, fee for NSF checks, other advances and any prepayment penalty. The daily interest payment should be based upon a 360-day year, unless stated differently in the Trust Deed Note. For example, if the pay off amount were $20,000 at a rate of 15 percent per year; the daily payment would be ($20,000 × 0.15)/360. This would work out to $8.33 per day. The 360 days vs. 365 is used to produce an interest payment that is very close to the monthly interest amount.

In the case of a six-month prepayment penalty, only 80 percent of the loan amount is charged the six-month interest. Most notes allow up to a 20 percent payment on the principal in any twelve-month period. Any principal payment in excess of this 20 percent would be subjected to the prepayment penalty. For a $20,000 loan at 15 percent, the prepayment fee would be ($20,000 ×0.15 × 0.8)/2 or $1,200. If part of the principal has been paid in the prior twelve-month period, the additional principal amount that can be paid without a penalty would be reduced. If the loan is amortized, part of the principal is paid each year. When the loan is reaching the end of the loan period, the principal amount paid can be significant. Depending on how the Trust Deed Note is written, you may not be able to include the amortized principal payment amount into the prepayment penalty calculation.

When the principal is paid, the last month's payment is also paid if not previously received from the borrower. In the example of a loan for $20,000 at 15 percent with an escrow close on the 1st of the month, the payment would be (($20,000 × 0.15)/12 + $20,000) or $20,250. The addition $250 interest is due to the payments on loans usually being made after the borrower has had use of the money for the previous month. Very often the borrower doesn't make the last month's payment within the grace period. Any late fee payments should also be added into the demand statement. A notation that there will be a late fee if payment is not made within the grace period should be added to the demand statement. This is required because the escrow very often runs late and the borrower is not making the last payments. In the above example, if escrow closed on the fifteenth of the month, the previous month's payment had not been made, and a late fee of 10 percent imposed—the payoff would be $20,274.95 ($20,000 + $8.33 × 15 + $250 + $250 × 0.10). The $8.33 is the daily interest charge (as calculated above) that is added to the amount due for the last fifteen days. Your demand would include the statement that the escrow officer should contact you to verify the final amount that will be paid. Any additional days required for you to receive your funds should be added to the fifteen days that are in the calculations above.

A charge can be made up to $30 for each Beneficiary Demand, the statutory limit (California Civil Code 2943). Added to this can be other cost such as payoff amount verification, document transfer, and trust stipulation (often required by the title company).

If the Trust Deed Note and Trust Deed are lost, a bond may have to be posted when dealing with a title company. A Substitution of Trustee and Full Reconveyance document will in most cases solve the problem. The potential loss of documents is the reason the Trust Deed Note and Trust Deed are best placed in a safety location such as a safety deposit box to avoid any future problem. A copy should be made for your file, to allow for ease in reviewing the terms of the note.

The original Trust Deed and Trust Deed Note (and original assignments if the Trust Deed was purchased from another lender) must be conveyed to the escrow officer at some time. This would be required when funds are to be wired to your bank account and an exchange is not contemplated. These documents, if mailed, should be sent certified with a return receipt request. If there is any concern about the *escrow company's status,* information can be obtained by calling the California Department of Corporations, Financial Services Division at (213) 576-7690. The California Department of Insurance and California Department of Real Estate databases will also provide information. The Internet links for both can be found at: http://www.corp.ca.gov/fsd/esb.

Escrows are regulated by either the California Department of Corporations or the California Department of Real Estate. The Department of Real Estate is involved when a real estate broker is controlling the escrow. The Department of Real Estate database can be accessed at the locations previously indicated to examine the broker's history.

A physical exchange of the Trust Deed and Trust Deed Note for a certified check is probably the best approach for a loan payoff. To do otherwise can be dangerous if you are dealing with unfamiliar parties. If there is any doubt, the exchange can be done at the certified check issuing bank. When dealing with a title company, which is usually the case, documents can often be signed at the title company office when you pick up your check. You would need to verify that the title company has a notary available. When the title company is known, a title company check can be acceptable.

Sending the Trust Deed Note and Trust Deed to the sale's escrow creates a small problem when there are bad-paying borrowers. These borrowers have been known to open a sales escrow with the full intention of not closing but to delay your filing a foreclosure. With these documents in escrow, opening of a foreclosure could be delayed. Most foreclosure companies will need these original documents to start the foreclosure, requiring you to retrieve the document before the foreclosure can be started. Some foreclosure companies will start a foreclosure with just a copy of these documents.

BENEFICIARY DEMAND

May 14, 2004

To: Century 25, Escrow Department
    4072 Escrow Avenue, San Diego, CA 92116

Property location: 123 Property Street, San Diego, CA 92116

Escrow #: 1313aj

I will exchange for a cashier's check in the amount shown below, a Trust Deed Note dated April 6, 2004, secured by a Trust Deed recorded in the county of San Diego, executed by Bert M. Borrower, payer and Bank of Commerce, Custodian FBO Jeff J. Smith, IRA, beneficiary, together with the Trust Deed noted above with a Request for Full Reconveyance.

The amount due is as follows:

Principal amount	$ 55,000.00
Prepay	$ 3,080.00
Demand fee	$ 30.00
Request for Full Reconveyance	$ 45.00 [1] (*This charge and one for a Substitution of Trustee and Full Reconveyance may not be allowable. The efforts are not fully defined by the civil code. If a Substitution of Trustee and Full Reconveyance is only used, any charge should be reasonable.*)
Notary fee	$ 10.00 ea. (*Typically 2, 4 if there are 2 lenders*)
County Recording	$ 10.00 (*$20 if there is also a substitution of trustee*)
Fund payoff Verification	$ 30.00 (*only if significant effort is required*)
Document(s) transfer	$ 30.00 (*only if significant effort is required*)
Trust stipulation	$ 15.00 (*when required*)
Unpaid late fees	$ (*When applicable*)
Accumulated interest	$ TBD
	—————
Sub total	$ TBD

Interest on the principal amount is also due at a rate of $21.39 per day (14 percent note interest per annum) from xx/xx/xx to the *date funds are received.* (Must also include interest for day that payoff is received.)

Monthly payments that are not paid within ten days of the grace period shall incur a late fee of 10 percent (*or Trust Deed stipulated amount, if different.*) The payment amount shall be added to the payoff amount.

(Note: Monthly payment prior on the loan to the close of escrow will require a minimum two-week delay for verification of funds.)

The exchange can be arranged by calling (619) 555-7238.

_____   _____

Jeff J. Smith   Date

INSUFFICIENT FUNDS FOR PAYOFF BY THE BORROWER

There will be times where the borrower does not have sufficient funds for a loan payoff. This can happen in a refinance of a loan or a loan with a balloon payment.

You have several options. The least desirable is to forgive the shortage. This can be avoided by carrying back a small Trust Deed to bridge the gap. The new trust deed terms can be close to the market interest rate and terms. You probably can set your terms to be a little higher than the market. This will probably be accepted because of the trouble the borrower would have in finding a new lender for a small amount. You should be able to also request and receive points for the loan.

Remember, if the loan amount on residential property, one to four units is less than $20,000 for less than five years, the loan must be amor-

_____

[1] Recent law limits the amount that can be charged for full reconveyance at $45. The amount that can be charged for the Beneficiary Demand may be impacted by the interpretation of Request for Full Reconveyance, Full Reconveyance, and Substitution of Trustee and Full Reconveyance.

tized. Additionally, a loan less than $20,000 having a balloon payment would have to have at least a five-year duration.

On a small loan, a prepayment might not be desired or allowed. A small loan can be an annoyance, so an early payoff should be encouraged. This can be helped by not using a prepayment fee. In these small types of loans it is still important to have title insurance and a mortgage broker to handle the transaction. The title insurance is to insure your trust deed position. The mortgage broker is required to avoid usury interest rates when the interest is above 10 percent.

There will be times when merchandise might be offered as security for the shortfall of the payoff. This may be acceptable. If it is a vehicle, a signed pink slip should be used as the security, with a note or a check for the amount of the unpaid portion of the loan. To insure that the merchandise doesn't disappear during the night, a secured storage might be used. When the security is a vehicle, most borrowers will need to use it, so possession would not be given. The note, when the loan is to be paid off, should show when the collateral is to be returned. It should be determined if there is a lien holder that has a part interest in the collateral. If there is a lien holder, you will have to determine the amount of your equity after a quick sale. This would be the portion after the lien holder is paid. A reasonable fee and your cost could be charged for setting up the agreement.

If a signed agreement for the new loan is not obtained, your loan payoff could be interpreted as a de facto full payment of the loan.

ASSIGNMENT OF A TRUST DEED

There will be times that a Trust Deed Note will not be paid off but sold to an investor. A document similar to a Beneficiary Demand should be prepared for this situation to determine the cash that you will be paid.

When a Trust Deed Note is sold, verification of the trust deed position must be determined by the buyer. This can be done by reviewing the existing title insurance policy and a new Preliminary Title Report. The title insurance policy will show the various liens, encumbrances, recorded judgments, easements, and the tax status at the time the policy was issued. Total reliance on a Preliminary Title Report should be avoided. The Preliminary Title Report may show only part of the encumbrances so a title insurance rider should be obtained to provide protection.

The assignment is accomplished by endorsing the Trust Deed Note or generating and signing an Assignment of Trust Deed Note document. The Trust Deed must also be assigned with an Assignment of Trust Deed document that requires the trust deed's owners' notarized signatures.

One of the critical details for this process is that the Trust Deed Note endorsement has a nonrecourse clause. If there is any loss, this will prevent the new owner of the note from holding the seller responsible for any loss on the loan. An escrow should be used to have all the documents properly prepared and recorded. Although there is a small fee that the escrow will charge, the amount is small compared to the cost that may be created by problems that may occur later. Adding or omitting a word or phrase can have a profound impact if there are future claims on the property. If you elect to not use an escrow, a separate document can be generated or the back of the Trust Deed Note can be endorsed over to the buyer without recourse. The Trust Deed Note should contain the names of the specific buyers before the document is signed. To do otherwise would make the note a bearer note, owned by whoever has possession of it.

These assignment documents can be obtained from your friendly escrow office or title company. The documents can often be found in a business stationery store. The trust deed assignment document must be notarized and recorded at the County Recorder's Office. Without the recording there is no constructive notice of the ownership transfer. Any notices against the property therefore wouldn't be received.

The document has a section that states where the document is to be mailed after recording. This typically would be sent to the new trust deed owner. After the Trust Deed is stamped, a copy can be obtained from the recorder. This is recommended due to the small danger that the document could be lost in the mail. If the document is lost, a copy could still be obtained from the County Recorder's Office.

REQUEST FOR FULL RECONVEYANCE

When the Trust Deed is to be paid off, a Request for Full Reconveyance document must be generated or alternately a Substitution of Trustee and Full Reconveyance document. The Request for Full Reconveyance document will be sent to the trustee of the Trust Deed. The document directs the trustee to generate a Full Reconveyance document and send it to the County Recorder's office for recording. When the trustee receives the request, he will generate a Full Reconveyance and process the request after receiving the necessary fees. This will be a maximum of $45 for the documentation generation and processing. This amount is deemed reasonable (See Civil Code 2941). There will possibly be a $10 notary fee and about $10 for the filing fee that the County Recorder's Office charges. These amounts must be included in the Beneficiary Demand to be collectable. Every so often there is no real trustee due to the use of an old Trust Deed document, the trustee can't be found, or the trustee isn't presently in the business. In this case a Substitution of Trustee and Full Reconveyance document will be required and is usually generated by the title company.

The cost for the generation of the Request for Full Reconveyance document is not defined by civil code. To be on the safe side, a reasonable amount should only be charged. If you generate the document you get the fee, otherwise the fee goes to the escrow company or the entity that generated the document. The work required in the Request for Full Reconveyance is the generation of the document and transfer of the document (mailing to trustee by certified mail). The amount that can be charged in the future may be impacted by case law interpretation and new regulations on the meaning of full reconveyance and request for full reconveyance. The trustee will not act upon the request unless the document is notarized. The usual fee for notarizing a document is $10 per signature. When generating the demand statement for the loan payoff, these charges should be included if you are performing the service. Shown below is a typical Request for Reconveyance. The borrower usually pays these costs.

344 • *Avoid Market Loss with Trust Deed Investing*

REQUEST FOR FULL RECONVEYANCE

TO: _____ (Name and address of trustee)

_____

_____

The undersigned is the legal owner and holder of all indebtedness secured by the within Deed of Trust. All sums secured by said Deed of Trust have been fully paid and satisfied. You are hereby requested and directed, on payment to you of any sums owing to you under the terms of said Deed of Trust, to cancel all evidences of indebtedness, secured by said Deed of Trust, delivered to you herewith, together with the said Deed of Trust, and to reconvey, without warranty, to the parties designated by the terms of said Deed of Trust, all the estate now held by you under the same.

Dated: _____

By: _____   By: _____
     (Beneficiary)   (Beneficiary)

Please mail the recorded Full Reconveyance to:

_____ (Usually the borrower)

(The document must be notarized with *California All-purpose Acknowledgment* attached or identical statements placed on this page.)

(The County Recorder's Office after receiving the original Full Reconveyance will stamp the document with a date, time, and a document identification number. This document will then be returned to the individual identified on the document. At this time, for a small fee the County Recorder's Office will provide a simple copy or a certified copy for an additional fee.)

SUBSTITUTION OF TRUSTEE AND FULL RECONVEYANCE

There is another document configuration that is sometimes used when a loan is paid off. This is the Substitution of Trustee and Full Reconveyance document. If you are aggressive, you might charge $90, however the charge should still be reasonable. The logic of the $90 is that two documents are involved, the Substitution of Trustee and the Full Reconveyance. The assessment that there are two documents, even if there is only one page is the same as the County Recorder's Office and their charging for recording two documents. (Recent law limits the amount that can be charged for a full reconveyance at $45. The amount that can be charged is clouded by the interpretation of full reconveyance when there can be three different documents: a Request for Full reconveyance, Full Reconveyance, and Substitute of Trustee and Full Reconveyance.)

You can substitute yourself as the trustee even when you are the beneficiary of the Trust Deed. If there is more than one beneficiary, only one person needs to be the trustee. However, all beneficiaries must sign the document in the appropriate place. There could be a notary fee of $10 per signature. Some notaries will only charge once for your signature even though you would sign the document twice. (Some documents are setup so there is only one signature required.) A typical Substitution of Trustee and Full Reconveyance is shown below. The document will need to be recorded by the County Recorder's Office. Their charge is about $20. This document can be obtained from some stationery stores, title companies, or escrow companies. There are different form configurations, but most will be acceptable. Shown below is a typical completed form.

Every so often, after all of the necessary reconveyance documents have been submitted, a subsequent request for a demand or notarized reconveyance may be received from a title company. This can be caused by an escrow company or the original title company losing the documents. The cost on your part should be submitted to the title company and upon receiving payment, the notarized documents can be sent. If the documents are sent prior to receiving payment, your odds of receiving money are slim and none. The charges can include notary, document generation, demand, and document transfer fees.

RECORDING REQUESTED BY:

When Recorded Mail document To: |
|
Joe Borrower |
1 Main street |
Home Town, San Diego 92000 |
|
Escrow No. |
Title Order No. |
_____|_____

SUBSTITUTION OF TRUSTEE AND FULL RECONVEYANCE

WHEREAS, Joe Borrower and Mary Borrower   **was the original Trustor,**
County Trustee, Inc., A Calif. Corp.   **the original Trustee,**

and Kevin Lender and Mary Lender   **the Beneficiary,**
under that certain Deed of Trust dated ,and recorded as Instrument NO.1999-0748403,
on January 3, 2000,   **in book, page,   Official Records of the**
County of San Diego, State of California, and
Whereas, the undersigned Beneficiary desires to substitute a new Trustee under said Deed of Trust in place
and stead of County Trust Deed, Inc., A Calif. Corp.
Now therefore, the undersigned hereby substitutes

Kevin Lender   **,as Trustee under said Deed of Trust and**
    ,as the substituted trusteed does hereby reconvey, without
warranty, to the person or persons legally entitled thereto, the Estate now held thereunder.

Dated: _____

(Signature of Kevin lender)

_____
Beneficiary
(Signature of Mary Lender)

_____
Beneficiary
(Signature of Kevin Lender)

_____
Substitute Trustee
(If a standard form is used the Notary statement will appear here.)

(Document must be notarized with CALIFORNIA ALL-PURPOSE ACKNOWLEDGMENT attached or an identical
statements placed on this page.)

Form 1. Substitution of Trustee and Full Reconveyance.

Section 20

TYPICAL LETTERS THAT CAN BE SENT TO BORROWER

Figure 20. *Paperwork, paperwork, paperwork.*

With any mail notification, it is important to be professional and firm in the presentation. If you make it a habit of sending several letters to the borrower to obtain a payment or a response, they will know they have time to wait before you perform an action such as filing a foreclosure. One letter should do the trick. It is very similar to handling a child. The child will respond when he knows you've reached your limits.

The letter forms shown below should be tailored to fit your situation due to the many variations that will exist. In some cases a format letter should be avoided and a simple short note sent to activate the borrower.

If the borrower knows that it is going to cost him a considerable amount of money to take the property out of foreclosure, he should make an appropriate response to your request. If he doesn't, he probably doesn't have any money. The borrower will tell you anything he thinks you will want to hear. This is the reason that only precise written correspondence should be used. If you call, the borrower will work on you with his tale of woe and claim later that there was an agreement (his agreement) on the payments. With a letter, your demand can be very precise. From your standpoint, payment of money is the only thing you should accept unless there are mitigating circumstances that you can live with.

Letter formats that are shown in this section are:

- initial payment notification,
- late payment notification,
- late fee payment notification,
- insurance cancellation action request,
- insufficient payment and property insurance notification.

INITIAL PAYMENT NOTIFICATION

May 17, 2003

To: Kevin Lacy

Lender: James Smith

Property location: 15541 Property Drive, San Diego, CA 92122

Principal balance: $ 20,000.00

Subject: **Payment of interest on loan**

This is to confirm the Trust Deed and Trust Deed Note for a second Trust Deed on your property to James Smith (beneficiary).

I will not be using a payment book. (*Change the statement if you want to have a payment book or payment stubs sent back and forth. This however can be frustrating due to some borrowers not sending the book with their payments.*) You can use the enclosed payment form with your canceled check to track your payments. Please do not mail the payment form to me but retain and update monthly for your records.

Your monthly payment is $250.00 and May 17, 2003, is the date of your first payment. All payments are due on the same date, monthly, thereafter. Any payment not received at the address provided below, within ten (10) calendar days from the due date will incur a late charge of $_____. $25.00 (*Change to $15.00, 6% of the monthly payment, or 10% of the monthly payment as specified in the Trust Deed Note*).

Please remember that, although you have a grace period of ten days, your payment is due on the date shown above. To avoid penalties, **mail early**.

Please make checks payable to: James Smith, PO Box 92018, Carlsbad, CA 92018.

Very truly yours,

_____

James Smith

LATE PAYMENT NOTIFICATION

October 24, 2005

To: Lender:
  Property location:
  Principal balance:

Subject: **Overdue notice**

To date your current payment and late charge has not been received. If your account is not brought current within five days of this notice, I will be forced to initiate **foreclosure proceedings** on your property.

Please take care of this immediately. Notice of Default will be filed on _____ (*date to be filed*) **if total payment is not received,** together with any other payments that may come due prior to the filing. Additional charges can include:

+ Securing property
+ Property inspection
+ Court costs
+ Attorney fees
+ Processing cost

<u>**Failure to cure this breach may result in the sale of your property and loss of your equity.**</u>

Please remit your payment **plus late charge today.** Make payment in the form of a *certified check* to: James Smith, PO Box 92018, Carlsbad, CA 92018.

Label your *certified check* to show your payment month **plus** the late charge.

Payment due: _____
Late charge: _____
Total due: _____

If your payments have been mailed, please disregard this letter.

Very truly yours,

_____

James Smith

LATE FEE PAYMENT NOTIFICATION

May 17, 2004

To: Mr. & Mrs. John T. Borrower
   11111 Borrower Drive
   Carlsbad, CA 92009

Lender: James Smith
Property location: 11111 Borrower Drive, Carlsbad, CA 92009
Principal balance: $_____

Subject: Payment of late fee for the month of _____ on your loan.

   Your $_____ late fee payment was not included with your late monthly payment.

   Please remit your late fee payment check to:

James Smith
PO Box 92018
Carlsbad, CA 92018

Very truly yours,

_____

James Smith

INSURANCE CANCELLATION/REINSTATEMENT ACTION REQUEST

May 17, 2004

To: Ms. Mary Borrower

Lender: James Smith
Property location: 2812 Property Blvd., Oceanside, CA 92054
Principal balance: $ _____

Subject: Insurance Policy cancellation

The cancellation of your insurance policy as of _____ (*date of policy*) has removed the insurance coverage to protect your property against loss per the terms of the Trust Deed Note.

Please contact your insurance agent immediately to reinstate your coverage. If I do not hear from your insurance agent within five days, I will obtain insurance on the property, charge you for this insurance coverage and/or start a foreclosure per the terms of the Trust Deed Note.

If there are any questions, please contact me at:

James Smith
PO Box 92018
Carlsbad, CA 92018

Very truly yours,

_____

James Smith

INSUFFICIENT PAYMENT AND PROPERTY INSURANCE NOTIFICATION

May 17, 2004

Paul Jones
PO Box 55555
Vista, CA 92086

Subject: Property insurance,
       Returned payment check for insufficient funds (NFS).

The property insurance on your property has been cancelled or is inadequate. I have been forced to place insurance on your property to cover my interest.

The cost of this insurance is $_____. This amount must be refunded by return mail.

The interest for the month(s) of _____ is not current, due to your NSF check or nonpayment.

If your account is not brought current, I will initiate foreclosure procedures in ten (10) days.

Foreclosure charges can include:

- Property inspections,
- Court costs,
- Attorney fees,
- Processing cost.

Failure to cure this breach may result in the sale of your property and loss of your equity.

Please remit your payments plus late charge in the form of a **certified check** to: James Smith, PO Box 92018, Carlsbad, CA 92018.

Payment for the

months of: _____ $ _____

Late fee   _____

Returned check fee   _____

Insurance charge   _____

_____

Total amount due: $ _____

Very truly yours,

_____

John Smith, PO Box 92018, Carlsbad, CA 92018

Section 21

SAMPLE COLLECTION FORMS

When payments are received from several loans, they can be difficult to remember. When payment is made, the amount, late fees, and special circumstances of the payments should be noted in some manner.

Figure 21. *Did they pay me last month?*

The forms shown below are offered as a method of tracking your payments. Any form however is of little value unless you are diligent in filling out the form when a payment is received. A payment ledger is mandatory for tracking and to accumulate information for filling out of your income tax return.

When there are several loans it is easy to forget or confuse some of the payments that are made and where they should be credited if not noted promptly. This becomes even more difficult when various payments are for the same amount. The recording is also important in the event there are questions or a dispute about having received a payment or the amount received.

The *LOAN PAYMENT FORM* shown below will provide a permanent record of the amount of payment, the date received and when the payment was due.

The *PAYMENT SCHEDULE REPORT* shown below will note if a payment was late, a not sufficient funds check (NSF) was returned, and if a replacement check was received.

There are a number of other payment forms that can be devised. You will have to determine the best configuration to suit your needs.

355

LOAN PAYMENT FORM

Chk #	Date due M D Y	Date pd M D Y	Amount paid	Interest paid	Principal paid	Paid to M D Y	Loan Balance	Remarks
---	-------	-------	-------	-------	-------	-------	-------	-------
---	-------	-------	-------	-------	-------	-------	-------	-------
---	-------	-------	-------	-------	-------	-------	-------	-------
---	-------	-------	-------	-------	-------	-------	-------	-------
---	-------	-------	-------	-------	-------	-------	-------	-------
---	-------	-------	-------	-------	-------	-------	-------	-------
---	-------	-------	-------	-------	-------	-------	-------	-------
---	-------	-------	-------	-------	-------	-------	-------	-------
---	-------	-------	-------	-------	-------	-------	-------	-------
---	-------	-------	-------	-------	-------	-------	-------	-------
---	-------	-------	-------	-------	-------	-------	-------	-------
---	-------	-------	-------	-------	-------	-------	-------	-------
---	-------	-------	-------	-------	-------	-------	-------	-------
---	-------	-------	-------	-------	-------	-------	-------	-------
---	-------	-------	-------	-------	-------	-------	-------	-------
---	-------	-------	-------	-------	-------	-------	-------	-------
---	-------	-------	-------	-------	-------	-------	-------	-------
---	-------	-------	-------	-------	-------	-------	-------	-------
---	-------	-------	-------	-------	-------	-------	-------	-------
---	-------	-------	-------	-------	-------	-------	-------	-------
---	-------	-------	-------	-------	-------	-------	-------	-------
---	-------	-------	-------	-------	-------	-------	-------	-------
---	-------	-------	-------	-------	-------	-------	-------	-------

Form 2. *Loan Payment report.*

PAYMENT SCHEDULE (Paid to due date)   Payments for the year_____,

Month	Jan.	Feb.	Mar.	Apr	May	June	July	Aug.	Sept.	Oct.	Nov.	Dec.
	----	----	----	----	----	----	----	----	----	----	----	----

EXAMPLE
(*Lake St.*   )
Due *Jan 1* (day of mo.)
Date payment rec'd   (_X_) (_X_) (___) (___) (___) (___) (___) (___) (___) (___) (___) (___)
(*$250.00*) (*1/1/03*)   1/2   2/1

(   )
Due____(day of mo.)
Date payment rec'd   (___) (___) (___) (___) (___) (___) (___) (___) (___) (___) (___) (___)
(   ) (   )

(   )
Due____(day of mo.)
Date payment rec'd   (___) (___) (___) (___) (___) (___) (___) (___) (___) (___) (___) (___)
(   ) (   )

(   )
Due____(date of mo.)
Date payment rec'd   (___) (___) (___) (___) (___) (___) (___) (___) (___) (___) (___) (___)
(   ) (   )

(   )
Due____(date of mo.)
Date payment rec'd   (___) (___) (___) (___) (___) (___) (___) (___) (___) (___) (___) (___)
(   ) (   )

(   )
Due____(date of mo.)
Date payment rec'd   (___) (___) (___) (___) (___) (___) (___) (___) (___) (___) (___) (___)
(   ) (   )

(   )
Due____(date of mo.)
Date payment rec'd   (___) (___) (___) (___) (___) (___) (___) (___) (___) (___) (___) (___)
(   ) (   )

(   )
Due____(date of mo.)
Date payment rec'd   (___) (___) (___) (___) (___) (___) (___) (___) (___) (___) (___) (___)
(   ) (   )

Codes:
X - payment received on time   o - no payment received
L - late payment   lp - late payment received with penalty
B - bad check   br - bad check replaced or resubmitted and good

Form 3. *Payment schedule report.*

AFTERWORD

As with any undertaking, knowledge continues to grow. Knowledge, when gained, should be added to this information. I hope the guidance presented will be helpful and financially rewarding.

Ownership of property is incidental—control is what is important, along with any income and tax benefits that this control can provide. Sale/leaseback, options, exchanging (swapping) property, long-term escrows, with authority to occupy the property, may become the rule. In any event, people will still need to eat, find shelter, be entertained, and clothe themselves. These human needs will always provide opportunities. Trust deed investors should be aware of the potential change in the nature of ownership of housing. This will in part be caused by lower spendable income for many to purchase housing.

In this arena of a dynamic and unpredictable future, it can be guaranteed that houses (shelter) will be around for sometime and have value. People will still want to borrow against their equity (interest). The more things change, the more they remain the same. To be successful, it is important to see and forecast the commonality between the past and the future. This understanding will foretell the trends of the future and foresee potential opportunities.

The recent flat tax proposals will have a profound impact on property value if enacted. It may reduce property value due to the possible loss of deductibility of interest payment. If the interest is not deductible, the value of the property will be reduced. This reduction will have a great effect on property equity and therefore any Trust Deed that you may hold.

ABOUT THE AUTHOR

The author of this book has been an active Real Estate broker for more than twenty-seven years. During this period, he has been involved in the sale of residential and commercial property that covers the full spectrum of real estate. For the last twenty-two years he has invested in Trust Deeds and gained valuable knowledge on the various shenanigans of borrowers that have received loans. This book reflects his experience and the experience of others that have invested in Trust Deeds.

INDEX

CALVET, 187, 189, 191-192
CAP, 57, 123, 187
CAPITALIZATION RATE, 57-58
CARRYBACK, 35, 96, 108-109, 164, 187, 189, 214, 300
CASE LAW, 57-58, 72, 78, 83, 159, 209, 211, 226, 250, 280, 302, 329, 333, 343
CEDARS, 16
CHAPTER, 66, 87, 157, 197, 239, 243, 260, 263, 267-271
CHAPTER, 66, 87, 157, 197, 239, 243, 260, 263, 267-271
CHAPTER, 66, 87, 157, 197, 239, 243, 260, 263, 267-271
CHAPTER, 66, 87, 157, 197, 239, 243, 260, 263, 267-271
CHEMICAL TREATMENT, 286
CHILLING THE SALE, 77-78
CLTA, 204-205
COASTAL COMMISSION, 48, 53
COLLATERALIZING, 83
COLLECTION OF RENTS, 174, 179, 228, 230
COMMERCIAL PROPERTY, 6, 25, 40-41, 103, 121, 134, 217, 232, 284, 300, 361
COMPARABLE SALES, 41-42, 57, 89, 91, 95-96, 256
CONDEMNATION, 43
CONDITIONAL SUBDIVISION PUBLIC REPORT, 54
CONDO, 40, 43-46, 59, 115, 117, 120, 196-197, 225, 228, 243, 246, 248, 257, 272-273
CONSTRUCTION LOAN, 63, 84, 182, 244
CONSTRUCTIVE NOTICE, 186, 194, 217, 342
CONSUMER CAUTION AND HOME-OWNERSHIP COUNSELING NOTICE, 159
CONSUMER PRICE INDEX, 70, 155, 278
CONTRACTOR'S STATE LICENSE STATUS, 61
CONTROLLED FUNDS, 84, 97, 133, 244, 325
CONTROLLED FUNDS/PERMIT SIGN-OFF, 133-134

978-0-595-23802-6
0-595-23802-5

Made in the USA
San Bernardino, CA
17 July 2015